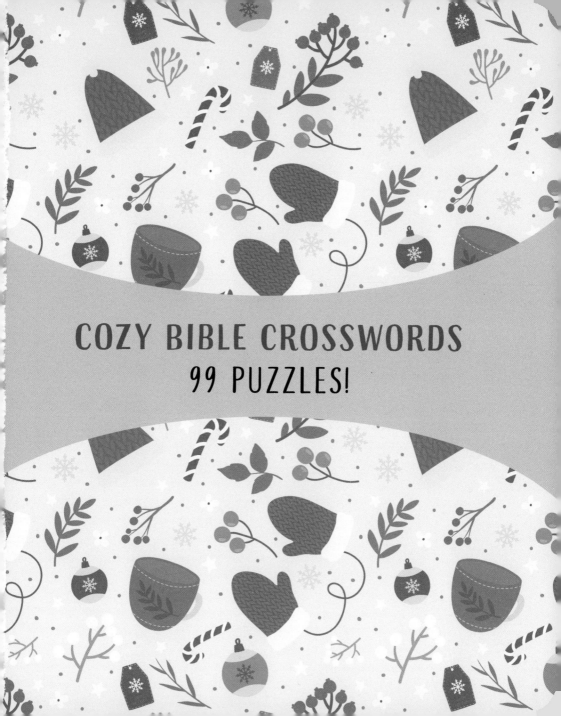

COZY BIBLE CROSSWORDS
99 PUZZLES!

COZY BIBLE CROSSWORDS
99 PUZZLES!

BARBOUR BOOKS
An Imprint of Barbour Publishing, Inc.

Published by Barbour Books, an imprint of Barbour Publishing, Inc., 1810 Barbour Drive, Uhrichsville, Ohio 44683, www.barbourbooks.com

Our mission is to inspire the world with the life-changing message of the Bible.

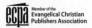

Member of the
Evangelical Christian
Publishers Association

Printed in China.

WELCOME TO
COZY BIBLE CROSSWORDS!

If you like Bible crosswords, you'll love this book. Here are 99 puzzles designed to expand your Bible knowledge and test your ability to properly place thousands of key words—a great many of them drawn from the King James Version of the Bible, with some taken from newer Bible translations as well as other fields of study. You're in for hours of cozy crossword fun!

This collection highlights dozens of key Bible characters—people like Abraham, Adam, and Anna, Daniel, David, and Deborah, Mary, Matthew, and Mordecai. And, of course, you'll find a puzzle highlighting Jesus—along with an even dozen that address the Savior's birth on the first Christmas day. In those nativity-themed puzzles, **bolded text** indicates clues that highlight a particular puzzle's theme.

Of course, answers are provided, beginning after the ninety-ninth puzzle.

Grab a pencil, a warm drink, and a comfortable blanket. . .it's time for *Cozy Bible Crosswords!*

one

AARON'S ERRANDS

by Patricia Mitchell

ACROSS

1 Prejudice
5 Light greenish-blue color
9 Summer stinger
13 "Ye are ___" (Ex. 5:17)
14 Seventh commandment no-no
15 '80s shampoo brand for highlighting hair
16 "Gather a certain ___ every day" (Ex. 16:4)
17 "They shall ___ their swords into plowshares" (Isa. 2:4)
18 Flippered mammal
19 Front of church
21 Harvard's rival
23 Aaron died here (Num. 20:27–28)
24 Anointing element
25 Aaron's sister (Ex. 15:20)
29 U.K. time zone

30 Matron
32 Compass point
33 Dispute
36 Epics
37 Potter's vessel
38 Peter compares the devil to one (1 Peter 5:8)
39 Priestly fabric
40 Nail
41 Tire measurement
42 Bluish-white metals
43 Psalms, e.g.
44 "A ___ gathereth her chickens" (Matt. 23:37)
45 Egyptians would ___ the Israelites to leave (Ex. 12:33)
46 Jacob or Laban, e.g.
47 Very soft fur
49 Energy measurements

50 Wing
53 "He called for Moses and Aaron by night, and said, ___ up" (Ex. 12:31)
55 Navies
57 Jacob's father (Gen. 25:26)
60 "Keep it up until the fourteenth day of the ___ month" (Ex. 12:6)
62 "Hail smote. . .___ man and beast" (Ex. 9:25)
63 Mooring
64 "Whereby we cry, ___, Father" (Rom. 8:15)
65 Canal
66 "No more give the people straw to ___ brick" (Ex. 5:7)
67 Sacred lot carried by Aaron (Ex. 28:30)
68 Eyeglass part

DOWN

1 White-barked tree
2 American state
3 Aaron ministered at one (Ex. 28:43)
4 "I have surely ___ the affliction of my people" (Ex. 3:7)
5 "The LORD saith it; ___ I have not spoken" (Ezek. 13:7)
6 Squelch
7 Uncle Sam's place
8 Lawyer (abbr.)
9 "This is the ___ of Meribah" (Num. 20:13)
10 Something else (abbr.)

11 Nazareth to Jericho (dir.)
12 Golfer's goal
15 Holy of ___
20 "And it shall ___ to pass" (Ex. 4:8)
22 Jordanian capital
26 Accustom
27 Sarai's spouse
28 God does this to broken spirits
29 Weapon
30 One was performed by 25 Across (Ex. 15:20)
31 Genesis 5 data

33 "I am ___ and Omega" (Rev. 1:8)
34 "He is ___" (Matt. 28:6)
35 Moses' "hands were steady until the ___ down of the sun" (Ex. 17:12)
36 "I will ___ unto the LORD" (Ex. 15:1)
39 Italian currency
40 Pharaoh's daughter found one (Ex. 2:5–6)
42 Swiss city
43 Prune beginnings
46 The Jordan, in places

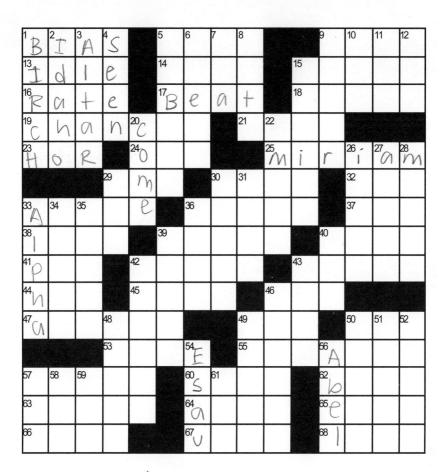

48 Aaron did this better than his brother (Ex. 4:14)
49 Disney deer
50 Worship fervently
51 Language of the Vulgate
52 Burnt offering remains

54 Jacob's twin (Gen. 25:25–26)
56 First murder victim (Gen. 4:8)
57 Computer makers

58 God's people were led through the Red ___ (Ex. 13:18)
59 ___ of the covenant
61 Reduced (abbr.)

2
AMAZING ABIGAIL
by Patricia Mitchell

ACROSS

1 Abigail's husband (1 Sam. 25:3)
6 Measurement replaced by hertz
9 Apt description of Abigail's husband
13 "Horns of ivory and ___" (Ezek. 27:15)
14 According to song, Jesus slept on it
15 "And ye have done ___ than your fathers" (Jer. 16:12)
16 "Thou art God ___" (Ps. 86:10)
17 "The birds of the ___ have nests" (Matt. 8:20)
18 Jesus does this
19 Bag
20 "An angry man stirreth up ___" (Prov. 29:22)
22 His wife was salty (Gen. 19:23–26)
23 Maybe Adam used one in Eden to till the earth

24 Distress call
25 Ark builder
27 Coarse
29 Slain with a sling
33 Spy org.
34 Abigail's servants ___ the way (1 Sam. 25:19)
35 Abigail's husband's party attitude (1 Sam. 25:36)
36 "All we like ___ have gone astray" (Isa. 53:6)
39 Noah, Jacob, Joseph, e.g.
40 What shepherds do
41 Tyre or Sidon, e.g.
42 Kitten's cry
43 "I ___ no pleasant bread" (Dan. 10:3)
44 Some say it was what Eve picked
46 Also known as Myanmar
49 Abigail gave David five measures of it (1 Sam. 25:18)
50 Recede

51 Flightless bird
53 Typing rate
56 "The tongue. . .is. . .full of ___ poison" (James 3:8)
58 Where Abigail and her husband lived (1 Sam. 25:2–3)
59 David, upon hearing Abigail's husband's message (1 Sam. 25:13)
61 Cow sound
62 Doctrine
63 "Noah ___ grace in the eyes of the Lord" (Gen. 6:8)
64 Prophetic gift
65 Excuse
66 Shine
67 "I was blind, now I ___" (John 9:25)
68 Perfect

DOWN

1 Under (poet.)
2 Like Eden
3 Infant's sock
4 Mary's mother, traditionally (var.)
5 Caustic substance
6 Talks with
7 Set of ark animals
8 Medicine deliverers
9 David was one to Abigail's husband (1 Sam. 25:13)
10 Voiced

11 Norwegian capital
12 "Shall bear thee up. . .___ thou dash thy foot" (Ps. 91:12)
15 Wale
20 Member of the legume family
21 Abigail's husband refused this to David's men (1 Sam. 25:11)
24 "My feet did not ___" (2 Sam. 22:37)

26 "Friend, go up ___" (Luke 14:10)
28 Vinegar's acid
30 Abigail's husband had too much of this, perhaps (1 Sam. 25:36)
31 Herbal beverage
32 Abigail "bowed herself on ___ face" (1 Sam. 25:41)
34 The Ten Commandments, e.g.
36 Place of ahhhs

37 Jump

38 Make a mistake

39 Affectionate monikers (2 wds.)

40 Hurt one's toe

42 Abigail "told him nothing, less or ___, until the morning light" (1 Sam. 25:36)

43 Subject of this puzzle, familiarly

45 Encrypted

47 Someone not nice

48 One-celled water creature

50 To escape secretly to marry

52 "Wait upon the LORD our God, ___ that he have mercy" (Ps. 123:2)

53 Abigail became David's (1 Sam. 25:39)

54 High school event

55 Aloha place

57 Medicine amount

58 Blend

60 Dynamite

62 ___ chi

three 3
ABRAHAM:
MAN OF FAITH AND ACTION
by Patricia Mitchell

ACROSS

1 Six-pack muscles (abbr.)
4 Walk on Mt. Sinai, perhaps
8 Lease giver
14 It's put in a horse's mouth (James 3:3)
15 Eve's garden
16 Take a deep breath, then ___
17 "Deliver thyself as a ___" (Prov. 6:5)
18 God promised it to Abraham
19 The Israelites ___ Egypt
20 Progressive decline
22 Ishmael to Abraham (Gen. 17:23)
23 1960s skirt
24 Did Noah use these?
27 Abraham's grandfather (Gen. 11:24–26)
31 Abraham received one from God

33 Pixie
35 Flightless bird
36 Greek goddess of dawn
38 ___ Schwarz, NY toy store
39 Hagar was one (Gen. 16:1)
40 Describes the rock in the wilderness struck by Moses (Num. 20:11)
44 Chemist's tube
46 James the ___, son of Alphaeus (Mark 15:40)
47 Conger
49 What Israelites were with God's Commandments
50 Unrefined metal
51 "Ye shall not surely ___" (Gen. 3:4)
52 Huff
55 "Offer him there for a ___ offering" (Gen. 22:2)

58 Jerusalem to Babylon (dir.)
61 Marrow
63 Lord's Prayer opener
65 Neglected
67 Abraham was rich in these (Gen. 13:2)
70 Condiment
71 Flavor enhancer
72 "I lift up my hands toward thy holy ___" (Ps. 28:2)
73 Swiss mountains
74 A Pharisee might consider himself this in religious law
75 Abraham built an altar between here and Hai (Gen. 12:8)
76 Prophecy is not this (2 Peter 1:21)
77 "Arise, lift up the ___" (Gen. 21:18)

DOWN

1 Abraham's former name
2 Relating to life
3 Relating to Eve's origins
4 "He is our ___ and our shield" (Ps. 33:20)
5 Gem State
6 African nation
7 "The ___ of all flesh is come before me" (Gen. 6:13)
8 "Moab. . .hath settled on his ___" (Jer. 48:11)
9 Gas company

10 Indo-Aryan language
11 "She ___ over against him, and. . .wept" (Gen. 21:16)
12 Grand ___ Opry
13 Israelites crossed the ___ Sea
21 Lubricators
25 The Lord acted as one between Laban and Jacob (Gen. 31:49)
26 Portion of meat

28 "Cold and ___. . .day and night shall not cease" (Gen. 8:22)
29 We may not ___ any part of God's Word (Rev. 22:19)
30 Describes Nabal (1 Sam. 25:3)
32 Abraham's nephew (Gen. 11:27)
34 "My face is ___ with weeping" (Job 16:16)
37 "Unto thy ___ will I give this land" (Gen. 12:7)

39 Tijuana's country
40 Slovenly person
41 South American country
42 Exploiter
43 Tack
45 Sacrificed instead of Isaac (Gen. 22:13)
48 Downwind
53 Ceremonious
54 Soft drink brand
56 Tally marker
57 Net fabric
59 Onion roll (var.)
60 Famine drove Abraham here (Gen. 12:10)
62 "Sharper than any two- ___ sword" (Heb. 4:12)
64 Peter fished with a net instead of this
66 Eat
67 Male swan
68 "___ sure that thou art that Christ" (John 6:69)
69 Make lace
70 Form of address (var.)

four

ABRAHAM: KEEPER OF THE PROMISE

by Patricia Mitchell

ACROSS

1 Composer Johann Sebastian
5 Temple leaders brought Jesus to one
10 Powder
14 Surrounded Jesus at His transfiguration (Matt. 17:2)
15 Cringe
16 Describes the blackish streams in Job 6:16
17 Abraham's seed would number as these (Gen. 22:17) (4 wds.)
20 Canaan flowed with this (Ex. 3:8)
21 British WC
22 Caps
23 Sinai to Syria (dir.)
25 Lyons affirmative
27 "Kings of armies did flee ___" (Ps. 68:12)

30 Fool does this (Prov. 14:9)
35 Actor Alda
36 Jesus of many carols
40 Fanfare
41 Abraham's seed would number as these (Gen. 22:17) (4 wds.)
44 "Herd ran violently down a ___ place" (Mark 5:13)
45 Clump
46 "Take of the ram the fat and the ___" (Ex. 29:22)
47 TV sitcom family
49 Tricksters Jacob and Laban
51 *Missouri* is one
53 Vigor
54 "A wise son heareth his father's instruction" without this (Prov. 13:1)

57 Ice skater Babilonia
59 Part of Ahasuerus's kingdom (Est. 1:1)
64 Abraham's promised position (Gen. 17:4) (3 wds.)
67 Choir section certainly in the king's house (1 Kings 10:12)
68 Ahasuerus would ___ a decree that wives shall honor their husbands (Est. 1:20)
69 Snack on manna, maybe?
70 Laodiceans may have had a salve for this
71 Genesis section, e.g.
72 Might describe a Hobby Lobby customer

DOWN

1 Nabal's feast, e.g.
2 Not what Abram used in Gen. 15:11
3 Berry start
4 Unclean animal (Lev. 11:6)
5 Ark number
6 Burglars might do this
7 Lazarus was carried "___ Abraham's bosom" (Luke 16:22)
8 Cold sound
9 Downwind
10 Kon ___, Heyerdahl ship

11 Phenol
12 "A feast of wines on the ___" (Isa. 25:6)
13 Recording medium
18 We desire to act in ___ with God's will
19 Thin cuts
24 Moab mount (Deut. 32:49)
26 "Lead ___ not into temptation" (Matt. 6:13)
27 Like the dove in Ps. 55:6
28 Jury
29 Chilean mountain range

31 Yellow pigment
32 Unleavened Exodus staple
33 Cain does this
34 "But a ___ between me and death" (1 Sam. 20:3)
35 Business group (abbr.)
37 Fore companion
38 Energy measurement
39 Radio band
42 Sarah to Abraham
43 Fancy case
48 Canadian prov.

50 "They ___ upon" Jesus (Matt. 27:30)

52 God could use this to raise up a child for Abraham (Luke 3:8)

53 Bluish-white metals

54 ___ Sea, biblical site

55 Courtroom figure (abbr.)

56 Abram wouldn't take a lachet of one of these (Gen. 14:23)

58 "Abraham. . .saw the place ___ off" (Gen. 22:4)

60 Little girl (Sp.)

61 Abraham "sat in the tent ___ in the heat of the day" (Gen. 18:1)

62 Smithsonian ___ (abbr.)

63 Sodom and Gomorrah the day after

64 USDA global group

65 Church leader, familiarly

66 Abraham and his visitors did this (Gen. 18:5)

5

ABSALOM: A MONARCH WANNA-BE

by Patricia Mitchell

ACROSS

1 Bilhah or Zilpah (Gen. 30:7, 9)
5 Tamar's appearance (2 Sam. 13:1)
9 Antitraditional artistic movement
13 "Bless me, even me ___, O my father" (Gen. 27:34)
14 "It is a ___ thing that the king requireth" (Dan. 2:11)
15 Absalom felt this way toward his brother (2 Sam. 13:22)
16 It went away and left Absalom hanging (2 Sam. 18:9)
17 Baruch needed these (Jer. 36:18)
18 There were six of these during creation (poet.)
19 "He would not go, but ___ him" (2 Sam. 13:25)
21 Native of former Siam
23 Cereal
24 Qumran to Jerusalem (dir.)

25 ___ of Israel, Absalom's supporters (2 Sam. 17:4)
29 Possible descriptor of Absalom
30 Bible pronoun
32 Jericho's walls fell amid one (Josh. 6:20)
33 Descendants of Benammi (Gen. 19:38)
36 Absalom's servants set Joab's on fire (2 Sam. 14:30)
37 The fool's problem (Prov. 12:15)
38 Descriptor of Absalom
39 Absalom's princely friends
40 Arab leader
41 ___ Baba
42 An angel's trumpet might do this
43 Forest clearing
44 "O Absalom, my ___, my son!" (2 Sam. 19:4)
45 RR org.

46 The kind of tree that held Absalom (2 Sam. 18:9)
47 Pasty in color
49 Choose
50 Colorado winter time zone
53 Tub spread
55 Describes Esau's arms (Gen. 27:11)
57 "Let him turn to his own ___" (2 Sam. 14:24)
60 El ___, TX
62 An earthly disaster could be this (Luke 21:11)
63 Went gently
64 Shield of Zeus (var.)
65 Infant Moses might have held one
66 Doctor's picture
67 "I will put my hook in thy ___" (2 Kings 19:28)
68 Chewy candies

DOWN

1 Cuban dance
2 Bird's "bastard" wing
3 Tiny offshore landform
4 Acts
5 "What a ___ We Have in Jesus"
6 Root beer brand (3 wds.)
7 Annoy
8 "Arise, O LORD, into thy ___" (Ps. 132:8)

9 Absalom's father (2 Sam. 13:1)
10 Jesus and disciples did this in the Upper Room
11 Daniel and lions sat together in this (Dan. 6:16)
12 Commercials, for short
15 Jesus did this often
20 Thames bird
22 Tilts
26 Water retention

27 Taut
28 Saw logs
29 Against
30 Hanging Gardens of Babylon had these
31 Not there
33 Commander of Absalom's rebel army (2 Sam. 17:25)
34 Fruit
35 Northeastern state

36 "Smite Amnon; then kill him, ___ not" (2 Sam. 13:28)
39 Set
40 Antlered animal
42 Paul and shipmates no doubt did this (Acts 27:15)
43 Absalom stood here to greet men (2 Sam. 15:2)
46 Absalom would do this to his father

48 Stroll
49 Water in the wilderness of Zin, e.g. (Num. 27:14)
50 Old timer's office copy, for short
51 Form of trapshooting
52 Leans
54 "Encamped in the ___ fields" (2 Sam. 11:11)

56 Absalom "vowed unto the ___" (2 Sam. 15:7)
57 Balak wanted Balaam to put one on the Israelites (Num. 22:6)
58 "All that handle the ___, the mariners" (Ezek. 27:29)
59 Stars and stripes nation
61 Long ___

6
ADAM: THE FIRST DUDE
by Patricia Mitchell

ACROSS

1 British cop
6 Wound healer
10 UAE native
14 "Oh, come, let us ___ Him!" Christmas refrain
15 Knitting stitch
16 Painter of melting clocks
17 "This is now bone of my ___" (Gen. 2:23)
18 One of the Great Lakes
19 "Grievous words ___ up anger" (Prov. 15:1)
20 Space
21 Adam felt this when hiding from God
23 "With you. . .unto the ___ of the world" (Matt. 28:20)
24 Adam was to do this to the garden
26 Makes noise during sleep
28 Delineated
31 God gave Adam "every herb bearing ___" (Gen. 1:29)
32 There you are!
33 They of Tyre did this (1 Chron. 22:4)
36 Jacob's description of Leah, maybe (Gen. 29:17)
40 Soda
42 God "drove ___ the man" (Gen. 3:24)
43 "Man became a living ___" (Gen. 2:7)
44 Maybe part of Noah's ark
45 What broke out when Samson brought the house down
48 When Eve offered, Adam did this
49 Adam's second son (Gen. 4:1–2)
51 Herb
53 "___ is the ground for thy sake" (Gen. 3:17)
56 Half
57 Adam's helpmeet
58 You can tiptoe through them
61 "Male and female created he ___" (Gen. 1:27)
65 "God formed man of the ___ of the ground" (Gen. 2:7)
67 "The LORD is on my ___" (Ps. 118:6)
68 Leather
69 Choir member
70 "Been faithful over ___ things" (Matt. 25:21) (2 wds.)
71 Small knife
72 Grate upon
73 "Fill the waters in the ___" (Gen. 1:22)
74 "Not good that the man should be ___" (Gen. 2:18)

DOWN

1 Ali ___
2 Isaac was fooled with this (Gen. 27:27)
3 God used one of Adam's
4 God gave Adam the ___ of life (Gen. 2:7)
5 Adam did not say this to God's question (Gen. 3:11)
6 What a foolish man will do with his treasure (Prov. 21:20)
7 Jesus is the ___ for Adam's sin
8 Opera solo
9 "Created he them; and ___ them" (Gen. 5:2)
10 Spots
11 A judgmental Pharisee is one
12 Dress style (2 wds.)
13 Adam named these
21 "I will ___ all that afflict thee" (Zeph. 3:19)
22 Egypt to Canaan (dir.)
25 Snakelike fish
27 Chances of winning
28 Tongues of fire "sat upon ___ of them" (Acts 2:3)
29 "Where art ___?" (Gen. 3:9)
30 "To see what he would ___ them" (Gen. 2:19)
31 Adam's third son (Gen. 4:25)
34 Paul had one (Phil. 3:14)
35 Adam, e.g.
37 "The young lions ___ after their prey" (Ps. 104:21)
38 Accord not meant in Acts 1:14
39 "After one day the south wind ___" (Acts 28:13)
41 Alack's partner

45 Snake-haired women

46 Forbidden fruit was pleasant to these (Gen. 3:6)

47 Member of Mayan people

50 Wager

52 Jewish ceremonial law directed this

53 Solomon's Temple wood (1 Kings 5:10)

54 Throat dangler

55 God does this on the seventh day

56 What God does to the lukewarm (Rev. 3:16.) (var.)

59 Tree of ___, the other tree in the garden (Gen. 2:9)

60 Adam's bite of the fruit was a bad one

62 Abel is a ___ of the faith (Heb. 11)

63 Adam called this home

64 Scant

66 A tower "whose ___ may reach unto heaven" (Gen. 11:4)

68 Relaxing tub

seven

AMOS SPEAKS GOD'S WORD

by Patricia Mitchell

ACROSS

1 Math sign
5 The captives were taken here (Amos 1:6)
9 Soft white cheese
13 Wise men's home
14 No need to take this, according to Matt. 10:10
15 Modern-day Elam
16 "He kept his wrath for ___" (Amos 1:11)
17 Rebekah's ride (Gen. 24:64)
18 "I will ___ the house of Israel among all nations" (Amos 9:9)
19 "The houses of ivory shall ___" (Amos 3:15)
21 Amos was one
23 "They sold. . .the ___ for a pair of shoes" (Amos 2:6)
25 "She is not afraid of the ___ for her household" (Prov. 31:21)

26 Rainbow shape
29 "The LORD will ___ from Zion" (Amos 1:2)
31 "Flight shall perish from the ___" (Amos 2:14)
34 Bambi's mom
35 Santa's helpers
37 Amos's prophecy, e.g. (Amos 1:4)
39 Slitherer
41 Before, (poet.)
42 Alamo location
43 Zarephath widow had a handful of it (1 Kings 17:12)
44 Rebekah's accompanied her (Gen. 24:59)
46 Seers have this
47 Black and white snacks
50 Dent
51 Bashful
52 Cocoon inhabitant

54 The "swift of ___ shall not deliver himself" (Amos 2:15)
56 Attain
59 Paul and Silas's keeper, e.g. (Acts 16:27)
63 Opera solo
64 Mount Everest site
66 Writer Bombeck
67 Look over
68 God put Adam "into the garden of Eden to ___ it" (Gen. 2:15)
69 Highway sight
70 "Their tongue is as an arrow ___ out" (Jer. 9:8)
71 "If my ___ hath turned out of the way" (Job 31:7)
72 Beautiful bird

DOWN

1 "Seek. . .unto wizards that ___" (Isa. 8:19)
2 Wash
3 Consumer
4 "Shall also ___ thee out of thy clothes" (Ezek. 23:26)
5 Airport info
6 Gideon's fleece was this (Judg. 6:38)
7 Beyond the limit (pl.)
8 Fondly remembered fruits (Num. 11:5)
9 Coarse woman nickname
10 Pennsylvania city

11 U.S. president
12 Sluggard's role model (Prov. 6:6)
14 Paul disputed "daily in the ___ of one Tyrannus" (Acts 19:9)
20 "Of how much ___ punishment" (Heb. 10:29)
22 Gun noise
24 Elijah's server (1 Kings 17:6)
26 First name
27 Cowboy show
28 Amorites compared to this tree (Amos 2:9)

30 Summer TV offering
32 God does this to the heart (Ps. 57:7)
33 To Paul, anything other than Christ (Phil. 3:8)
36 Lettering stroke
38 Moses sent Caleb to ___ out Canaan (Josh. 14:7)
40 Memorable animal
42 Amos's town
45 Frowns angrily
48 Parisian's vote
49 The foolish man does this (Prov. 21:20)

53 Israel could not ___ Amos's prophecies

55 One of Samson's seven (Judg. 16:19)

56 Constantine is one in Rome

57 See ya! (It.)

58 Type of what God placed east of Eden

60 Jesus did this on the ground (John 8:6)

61 Austin title

62 "I have withholden the ___ from you" (Amos 4:7)

63 Jesus' ride (John 12:14)

65 It caused Cleopatra's demise

8
ANDREW'S CATCH
by Patricia Mitchell

ACROSS

1 ___ Kong
5 Venomous snake
10 Philip told Andrew the Greeks said, "___, we would see Jesus" (John 12:21)
13 "Man shall not live by bread ___" (Matt. 4:4)
15 Some things do this on Day 6 of creation (Genesis 1:24)
16 "All ye ___ brethren" (Matt. 23:8)
17 He called out to Andrew and his brother (Matt. 4:18)
18 Poem division
19 "The herd ___ violently down a steep place" (Mark 5:13)
20 Son of Rachel, familiarly (Gen. 35:24)
21 Door grip
23 Writing tablet
25 Mote size in brother's eye (Matt. 7:3)
26 With Andrew in upper room (Acts 1:13)
28 "In the ___ of the book it is written" (Ps. 40:7)
31 Plant seen at Easter
32 Idealized mental image
33 Probable author of Acts
34 Lingerie item
37 Today's chariots
38 Description of Andrew's catch
40 "The First ___," carol
41 "He that endureth to the ___ shall be saved" (Matt. 10:22)
42 Parent groups
43 He's blessed who does this in Rev. 1:3
44 St. Andrew's ___, an X
45 Forbidden in Lev. 19:28
46 "A good tree bringeth not forth ___ fruit" (Luke 6:43)
49 Tasks
50 Architect Frank ___ Wright
51 Andrew heard John say, "Behold the ___ of God!" (John 1:36, 40)
52 Rotational speed measurement
55 Mil. rank
56 Religion of those on a 1 Down
59 Ahab's house (1 Kings 22:39)
61 "I was blind, now I ___" (John 9:25)
62 Kind of fish
63 Andrew's brother (Matt. 4:18)
64 Expert, for short
65 Adam does this when God calls (Gen. 3:8)
66 Plateau

DOWN

1 Pilgrimage to Mecca
2 Margarine
3 "The smell of thy ___ like apples" (Song 7:8)
4 African antelope
5 '50s TV family name
6 Many adherents of 56 Across
7 Jesus told Andrew, "I will make you fishers of ___" (Matt. 4:19)
8 Wager
9 Andrew became one
10 Abraham's wife (Gen. 17:15)
11 How Jonah felt when God spared Nineveh (Jonah 4:1)
12 What the Holy Ghost does in Titus 3:5
14 Igloo dweller
22 Jerusalem to Damascus (dir.)
24 Conservation group
25 Pulls
26 He who bears false witness in Prov. 25:18
27 Relating to alkali (abbr.)
28 Sin
29 Muscat's site
30 Fat
31 Grade
34 Vessel of Andrew's trade
35 Make again
36 If you forgive, God "will ___ forgive you" (Matt. 6:14)
38 "No man shall ___ me of this boasting" (2 Cor. 11:10)
39 Andrew did this (Mark 1:16)
40 What Andrew left to follow Jesus (Matt. 4:20)
42 Prissy
43 Masters in John 1:38
44 "At midnight there was a ___ made" (Matt. 25:6)

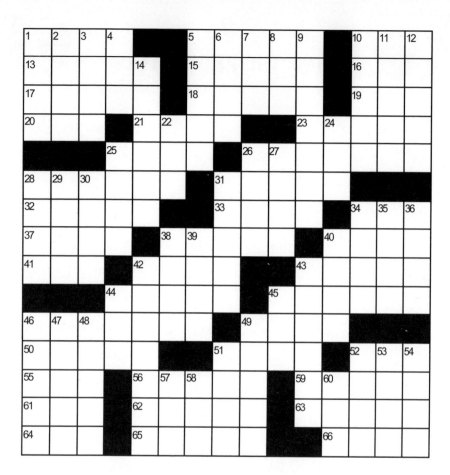

45 Doubting disciple, familiarly
46 You ___ your hands in prayer, maybe
47 Esau in relation to Jacob
48 Juliet's boyfriend
49 Son of Zebedee (Matt. 10:2)
51 Foolish virgins were this to the wedding (Matt. 25:10–11)
52 City of Paul's captivity
53 Not cons
54 Starling
57 Slide on snow
58 Andrew said, "There is a ___ here" (John 6:9)
60 Vitality

nine

ANNA THE PROPHETESS

by Patricia Mitchell

ACROSS

1 City in Judah (Josh. 15:26)
5 One who builds a house on sand, e.g.
10 What the Gardener will do with non-fruitful branches
13 Kind of woman Anna was
14 ___ protector
15 State of unconsciousness
16 Final word in prayer
17 Agitator does this to crowd, as at Jesus' trial (Mark 15:11-13)
18 Feature of God's sign to Noah after the Flood (Gen. 9:16)
19 Winglike part
21 The Garden of Gethsemane and the Temple in Jerusalem, e.g.
23 Anna "served God. . .night and ___" (Luke 2:37)

26 Conger
28 Fish tank growth
29 ___ steroids
32 Ranch guy
33 Man with unclean spirit (Mark 5:4-5) (coll. Sp.)
34 Anna's piety, perhaps
36 Murky
37 Holy ___, source of Anna's inspiration
38 Bearer of the ark of the covenant (2 Sam. 6:3)
42 Hanger-on-er, e.g.
43 Certain idol in Sinai
44 String section instrument
46 Cloth put over Jesus' face in the tomb (John 20:7)
49 Sew with a gathering stitch
51 How you might get across the Sea of Galilee

52 Format for delivering web content
53 Sign shoppers love to see
57 Sock
59 It's often upped
60 San ___, CA
62 Prophet from Tekoa (Amos 1:1)
66 "Play skilfully with a ___ noise" (Ps. 33:3)
67 Genesis 1:1 gives this of life as we know it
68 Promissory notes
69 What Job's comforters do
70 What God does on the seventh day
71 It happens to manna kept overnight (Ex. 16:20)

DOWN

1 When Anna saw Jesus, it was this kind of moment (Luke 2:38)
2 Mary was one
3 The glutton's partner has too much of this (Prov. 23:21)
4 Chatty bird
5 Anna and Simeon waited "for the consolation of ___" (Luke 2:25)
6 Paul and Silas, e.g.
7 Flower with a beard, often
8 David did this when he saw Bathsheba bathing (2 Sam. 11:2)

9 What a God-sent challenge might be
10 Settee
11 "I am Alpha and ___" (Rev. 1:8)
12 So yesterday
15 One presented to the Lord (Luke 2:21-22)
20 Name for tamed beast in Isa. 11:6
22 Tight
23 Painter of melting clocks
24 "And ___ they tell him of her" (Mark 1:30)

25 We should not do this when we pray (Matt. 6:7)
27 Supple
30 One called holy to the Lord (Luke 2:23)
31 Story from Job's comforters, e.g.
32 Morse code element
35 Anna's tribe (Luke 2:36) (var.)
37 Harden
38 Exclamation in Munich
39 Samson was not to cut this (Judg. 13:5)
40 French islands

41 David ___ Goliath with a
   stone (1 Sam. 17:49) (coll.)
42 Anna "gave thanks. . .unto
   the ___" (Luke 2:38)
44 Anna's faithfulness was one
45 Saul felt this way when the
   women praised David
   (1 Sam. 18:7–8)
47 Mechanical agents
48 Top-ranking corporate
   webmaster

49 "They had a few ___ fishes"
   (Mark 8:7)
50 Vietnam capital
54 Jacob fooled Isaac with this
   (Gen. 27:27)
55 Last Supper beverage
56 Loch ___ monster
58 "___ of turtledoves," sacrifice
   choice (Luke 2:24)
61 "___ thee behind me, Satan"
   (Luke 4:8)

63 Pasture sound
64 "Gracious words which
   proceeded ___ of his
   mouth" (Luke 4:22)
65 Sound from the tree in the
   midst of Eden, perhaps
   (Gen. 3:1–4)

10
BARNABAS:
BEARER OF GOD'S WORD
by Patricia Mitchell

ACROSS

1 Barnabas treated people with this
4 "Like ___ that find no pasture" (Lam. 1:6)
9 Jostle
14 Slithery fish
15 God set ___ Barnabas for His work (Acts 13:2)
16 Theologians do this to Bible phrases
17 ___ Maria
18 Barnabas laid this at the apostles' feet (Acts 4:37)
19 Paul and Barnabas discussed these with the apostolic council (Acts 15:20)
20 "Unworthy of everlasting ___" (Acts 13:46)
22 Braces oneself
24 Barnabas was not one of these
25 Prime Meridian clock reading
27 ___ a small world!
29 "Barnabas. . .___ go as far as Antioch" (Acts 11:22)
32 Barnabas took this to Christians in Judea (Acts 11:29–30)
35 Spy org.
36 After a stoning, Paul went here with Barnabas (Acts 14:20)
38 North Pole workshop workers
40 "Hold up my goings. . .that my footsteps ___ not" (Ps. 17:5)
42 24 Across had too much of this
44 "I will perform the ___ which I sware" (Gen. 26:3)
45 Barnabas ___ Mark when Paul refuses (Acts 15:39)
47 Rebekah's husband (Gen. 24:67)
49 "I am ready. . .to ___ at Jerusalem" (Acts 21:13)
50 Grand Turk
52 The disciples did this, then ordained Barnabas as a missionary (Acts 13:3)
54 Farm org.
55 Before (prefix)
56 What Saul hoped to do to David with his javelin (1 Sam. 18:11)
59 Barnabas went to one in Antioch (Acts 11:26)
63 Paul's former name
67 In a tilted position
69 Athenian lawmaker and poet
71 Campus ministry org.
72 "Ye are of more ___ than many sparrows" (Matt. 10:31)
73 The Colosseum in Rome was one
74 ___ Baba
75 Because of Barnabas, "much people was ___ unto the Lord" (Acts 11:24)
76 Old ___ (stubbornly old-fashioned person)
77 Hip

DOWN

1 Greenish blue
2 Barnabas's tribe (Acts 4:36)
3 Notation in music
4 Noah's son (Gen. 5:32)
5 Those who named Barnabas (Acts 4:36)
6 Jeremiah's preaching, to a scorner
7 Mid-Eden feature
8 Eye infection
9 Barnabas took one to Antioch (Acts 15:30)
10 Bearer of barley loaves and fish (John 6:9)
11 James and John, e.g. (Matt. 4:21) (abbr.)
12 Capital of Norway
13 Wild ___
21 Self
23 Ananias and Sapphira told one (Acts 5:3, 8)
26 Wet dirt
28 What a foolish man would fill with grain (Luke 12:16–20)
29 A man chosen along with Barnabas (Acts 15:22)
30 17-syllable poem

31 Run off
32 Summary
33 Jesus did this to those wanting to make Him king (John 6:15)
34 Manna would be this if kept overnight (Ex. 16:20)
35 Kansas City winter hours
37 Vehicle
39 Mourners showed Peter garments Dorcas had made "while ___ was with them" (Acts 9:39)
41 You can't serve God and this

43 Radio receiver
46 Joshua did this with 12 stones in the Jordan (Josh. 4:9)
48 Vehicle
51 It became a boil on man and beast (Ex. 9:10)
53 Barnabas said this to God's call
56 Morning beverage
57 School (abbr.)
58 "Paul and Barnabas waxed ___" (Acts 13:46)
60 Mil. branch

61 Vehicle-accommodating ship
62 Horsefly
64 "All that are ___ off" (Acts 2:39)
65 CA university
66 They "___ their hands on" Paul and Barnabas (Acts 13:3)
68 Jewish opposition was Barnabas and Paul's ___ to preach to the Gentiles
70 "By what law? of works? __: but by the law of faith" (Rom. 3:27)

eleven

BATHSHEBA THE BEAUTIFUL

by Patricia Mitchell

ACROSS

1 "He . . .put them under___"
(2 Sam. 12:31)
5 Black
9 Samson's riddle was this
(Judg. 14:12–13)
14 Noted persecutor of early
Christians
15 Opera solo
16 David and Bathsheba found
they were not ___ God's law
17 Mil. branch
18 Careen
19 Bathsheba bore Solomon,
"and the Lord ___ him"
(2 Sam. 12:24)
20 Terra-___ (type of clay)
22 "___, thou desirest truth"
(Ps. 51:6)
24 U.K. driver's concern
25 Beetle
27 Time periods
31 Opposite of David's attitude
when accused of sin

32 Zero
34 A psalm, perhaps
35 A prophet accused David of
this (2 Sam. 12:9)
38 Movie bio with Will Smith
40 Israel's enemy (2 Sam. 11:1)
42 Uriah ___ his life in battle
(2 Sam. 11:17)
44 "Little ___ lamb"
(2 Sam. 12:3)
46 "A thousand ___ in thy sight
are but as yesterday"
(Ps. 90:4)
47 David was this while his men
went off to war (2 Sam. 11:1)
48 The rich man had many, the
poor man had ___
(2 Sam. 12:3)
50 Prophetess at the Temple
(Luke 2:36) (var.)
51 Pseudonym
52 Roman trio
55 Adultery is this

57 Bathsheba to Solomon
(2 Sam. 12:24)
59 Metal
61 Corn holder
64 Relating to the brain
66 Bathsheba's baby would ___
her guilt
68 Joab would ___ the men to
put Uriah up front
(2 Sam. 11:15–16)
71 Sinai's Peninsula
73 Musical composition
74 Cabled
75 Nathan's story had David on
the ___ of his seat
76 ___ Accords, 1993
agreement
77 David ___ as Bathsheba
bathes
78 David tried to cover up his
guilt, so he did this
(2 Sam. 11:25)
79 David to Uriah: "Go. . .wash
thy ___" (2 Sam. 11:8)

DOWN

1 David and Bathsheba had
done this while Uriah was
gone
2 "Ant and Grasshopper"
author
3 David and Bathsheba
brought about God's ___
(2 Sam. 11:27; 2 Sam 12:7–12)
4 David's accuser was not this
(2 Sam. 12:1–7)
5 David would not do this
while Bathsheba's son lay
dying (2 Sam. 12:17)

6 Joab knew the truth, but was
probably this
7 Tanker
8 Accused David (2 Sam. 12:1)
9 "They would shoot from the
___?" (2 Sam. 11:20)
10 "Uriah ___ in Jerusalem that
day" (2 Sam. 11:12)
11 State official (abbr.)
12 She talked to a serpent

13 David's face may have been
this when he recognized
his sin
21 Communication method
23 Kimono sash
26 Spy org.
28 Paul's citizenship
(Acts 22:25)
29 A bride may ___ herself with
jewels (Isa. 61:10)
30 "They read. . .distinctly, and
gave the ___" (Neh. 8:8)

31 Gaiety

33 David took Bathsheba, and "he ___ with her" (2 Sam. 11:4)

35 Bathsheba's dad (2 Sam. 11:3)

36 Popular spirit in Russia

37 Religion promulgated in the 7th century

39 ___ Jima

41 David prepared this for Uriah (2 Sam. 11:8)

43 ___ Lanka

45 Preservation by silo storage

49 Flightless bird

53 Rich man could give one of these to poor man (2 Sam. 12:4)

54 Uriah said: "___, and Judah, abide in tents" (2 Sam. 11:11)

56 Referee

58 "David's ___ was greatly kindled" (2 Sam. 12:5)

60 ___ Gras

61 Thicket

62 Plant seed

63 Bathsheba's beauty would do this to David (2 Sam. 11:2)

65 Tails

67 Where Bathsheba bathed

68 Punching tool

69 Uriah would not ___ with his wife (2 Sam. 11:11)

70 David's feelings for the rich man (2 Sam. 12:5)

72 "David arose from off his ___" (2 Sam. 11:2)

twelve 12
BENJAMIN: THE YOUNGER BROTHER
by Patricia Mitchell

ACROSS

1 Panicked, Benjamin's brothers needed to send this signal
4 Ziti
9 Pharisees and Sadducees, e.g.
14 Item found in Benjamin's bag (Gen. 44:12)
15 "My lovers and my friends stand ___" (Ps. 38:11)
16 Benjamin couldn't use this to send a message from Egypt
17 What Benjamin and brothers did at Joseph's (Gen. 43:16)
18 God made Joseph "a ___ throughout all the land of Egypt" (Gen. 45:8)
19 "God Almighty give you ___ before the man" (Gen. 43:14)
20 This existed between Hebrews and Samaritans
22 Jacob believed Benjamin's trip was ___ to death (Gen. 43:14)

24 Stand, and have on this (Eph. 6:14) (var.)
25 Off-Broadway award
27 As Isaac ages, his eyesight does this (Gen. 27:1)
31 Huldah was one (2 Kings 22:14)
32 Herodias's daughter's costume, perhaps (Matt. 14:6)
33 If Benjamin "should leave his father, his father would ___" (Gen. 44:22)
34 There was little of this among Jacob's sons
36 Maine sighting
38 Jesus ___ lepers (Luke 7:22)
40 You may find them on the seashore
42 Joseph's brothers expressed this when asked to bring Benjamin (Gen. 42:21)
43 Turn over
44 Son of Benjamin (Gen. 46:21)
45 Epistle of sorts

47 Roman worship service
51 Sometimes it's more
53 Bearing
54 The unjust steward must give this to his master (Luke 16:1) (abbr.)
55 Prominent N.T. member of the tribe of Benjamin (Rom. 11:1)
57 Joseph harbored none toward his brothers (Gen. 50:20)
59 Rain falls mainly on the plain here
62 Messages from Isaiah, e.g.
65 Bard's "before"
66 Rainbows are this
67 Nebuchadnezzar's order to worship an idol, e.g.
68 "___ of thy youth" (Ps. 110:3)
69 Joseph's brothers' dilemma was this
70 Used to hold Simeon, perhaps (Gen. 42:24)
71 White-tailed sea eagle (var.)

DOWN

1 Benjamin's leaving with his brothers ___ his father
2 Interruption of power
3 Coins the brothers used to pay for food, e.g.
4 Standard golf scores
5 Univ. graduate
6 Roman deity

7 Part iron, part clay digit in the king's dream (Dan. 2:42)
8 Benjamin must have felt this when searched (Gen. 44:12)
9 It might be a Mack
10 Make corrections to
11 Jaguar, e.g.
12 Involuntary movement
13 Crafty

21 Jacob's God-given name (Gen. 32:28)
23 "The ___ of the house of David" (Isa. 22:22)
25 Horse food
26 Jacob said, "Go again, ___ us a little food" (Gen. 43:2)
28 Baal, e.g.
29 Overlook

30 "Your eyes ___, and the eyes of my brother Benjamin" (Gen. 45:12)

32 Card game

35 Found at many doors

36 Joseph saw Benjamin and said, "Bring these ___ home" (Gen. 43:16)

37 "We have a father, an ___ ___" (Gen. 44:20) (2 wds.)

38 Jesus would do this often

39 Caps

40 Bridge

41 ___ you!

42 Guy's partner

43 "When ye pray, ___ not vain repetitions" (Matt. 6:7)

45 Flightless bird

46 Kind of cup found in Benjamin's bag (Gen. 44:2)

48 Jacob would reluctantly do this, to Benjamin's journey

49 Goal maker

50 The sower in Jesus' parable had done this to his seeds (Luke 8:5)

52 Joseph accused his brothers of being these (Gen. 42:9)

56 One of Jesus' disciples, familiarly

57 Japanese staple

58 N.T. book

59 O.T. priest, for short

60 Often goes before

61 Health org.

63 How about: "Why make ye this ___, and weep?" (Mark 5:39)

64 Moses put blood on the ___ of Aaron's right ear (Lev. 8:23)

CAIN: FIRST BORN

by Patricia Mitchell

ACROSS

1 "Began ___ to call upon the name of the LORD" (Gen. 4:26)
4 Cain did not feel this as a vagabond (Gen. 4:14)
8 Meat stew
14 Battle tool in 1 Sam. 13:20 (var.)
15 Off-Broadway award
16 Acceptance of Abel's gift would do this to Cain (Gen. 4:5)
17 Owner of the Technicolor Dreamcoat, familiarly
18 "If haply they might ___ after him" (Acts 17:27)
19 First name in mysteries
20 Cain may have felt like one among other men
22 God ___ Cain live
23 God told Cain to "___ over" temptation (Gen. 4:7)
24 Cain was banished east of here (Gen. 4:16)
27 Files
31 Peasant
33 Distress call
35 Forbidden to a Nazarite (Judg. 13:7)
36 God said to Cain's father, "In the sweat of thy face shalt thou ___ bread" (Gen. 3:19)
38 Long time
39 What a student might do the night before a test
40 Adam ___ the blame to Eve for their sin
44 An Iraqi's southern neighbor
46 Wise men came from this direction (Matt. 2:1)
47 Cain's dwelling place (Gen. 4:16)
49 Oxygen
50 Form of communication
51 ___ Giovanni, Mozart opera
52 Dish at many Thanksgiving feasts
55 Cain's brother kept these (Gen. 4:2)
58 "The ___ is not to the swift" (Eccl. 9:11)
61 "There was a swarm of ___ and honey" (Judg. 14:8)
63 ___ Lanka
65 Italian dish
67 Eli was this to Samuel
70 Wrap a flag, e.g.
71 Pastor, familiarly
72 One-celled water creature
73 Soft white cheese
74 Winter hazard
75 God said to Cain, "Now art thou ___ from the earth" (Gen. 4:11)
76 What Gomorrah might have looked like
77 Eve said of Cain, "I have gotten a ___ from the LORD" (Gen. 4:1)

DOWN

1 Isaiah is considered a ___ prophet
2 Second book of the Bible
3 "Eye of a ___" (Mark 10:25)
4 Living room furniture piece
5 White poplar
6 Site of Abel's death (Gen. 4:8)
7 Conger
8 Cain's fear of God's punishment was this
9 God expressed this toward Cain (Gen. 4:10)
10 Persona non ___
11 Horse morsel
12 Good reaction to sin
13 Can be made with a bag
21 Cain felt ___ of hope (Gen. 4:14)
25 Tel Aviv to Jerusalem (dir.)
26 Cranny partner
28 Eastern garment
29 Perhaps what Cain farmed
30 Very large truck
32 Abel gave his best beast "and of the ___ thereof" (Gen. 4:4)
34 How a bug in a rug feels
37 Cain would to this to his crops
39 Sweet melon
40 "Waters called he ___" (Gen. 1:10)
41 Discuss with, over
42 Paphos is on one

43 God warned Cain, "sin lieth at the ___" (Gen. 4:7)

45 Woe to those who "have gone in the ___ of Cain" (Jude 1:11)

48 Genetic code

53 Dizziness

54 Roman statesman

56 ___ Park, Colorado destination

57 God would do this to Cain concerning Abel (Gen. 4:9)

59 There are these on this page

60 Cain said, "Thou hast driven me out. . .from the face of the ___" (Gen. 4:14)

62 Multiple of punishment due a killer of Cain (Gen. 4:15)

64 Cain's grandson (Gen. 4:18)

66 "Every one that findeth me shall ___ me" (Gen. 4:14)

67 Apple computer

68 Flightless bird

69 "Remember not the sins. . . ___ my transgressions" (Ps. 25:7)

70 Org. of aspiring tillers of the field

fourteen 14
DANIEL:
THE LION TAMER

by Patricia Mitchell

ACROSS

1 Daniel chose the ___ of righteousness
5 What Daniel heard as the door to the lions' den closed, maybe
9 Daniel's face was not this after refusing the king's food
13 Great lake
14 "Take thee a ___, and lay it before thee" (Ezek. 4:1)
15 Painting prop
16 Daniel was given a new one of these (Dan. 1:7)
17 "___, Father" (Mark 14:36)
18 Plant part
19 Daniel and his friends "had ___ in them" (Dan. 1:4)
21 Subject of Nebuchadnezzar's dream (Dan. 4:10)
23 Hallucinogen
24 Spy guys' org.
25 Daniel would do this from the lions' den

29 Luke for short (Col. 4:14)
30 Nick
32 "Do they not ___ that devise evil?" (Prov. 14:22)
33 Adam and Eve each made one (Gen. 3:7)
36 Nathan may have done this as he said, "Thou art the man" (2 Sam. 12:7)
37 Man has dominion "over the fowl of the ___" (Gen. 1:26)
38 Subject of Daniel's vision (Dan. 8:5)
39 "He sent divers ___ of flies among them" (Ps. 78:45)
40 Dog food brand
41 Actress MacGraw
42 Daniel's pussycats
43 Marcel Marceau, for one
44 "Prove thy servants. . .___ days" (Dan. 1:12)
45 Sight the king expected would be left in the fiery furnace

46 Where Nebuchadnezzar dreamed (Dan. 2:29)
47 Compositions
49 Beige
50 Tweak
53 "___ of the kingdom" (Matt. 16:19)
55 Daniel could not have this on him (Dan. 1:4)
57 Burnt color
60 Asian country
62 For sure, Daniel was not this (Dan. 1:4)
63 Wall word (Dan. 5:28)
64 Volcano
65 Guards probably did this to the lions' den
66 Psalmist's bed did this (Ps. 6:6)
67 Daniel would ___ it wrong to eat the king's food (Dan. 1:8)
68 Humorist Bombeck

DOWN

1 Inability to interpret the king's dreams was a ___ offense (Dan. 2:5)
2 Persians' neighbors
3 Stepping forward to interpret the king's dreams, Daniel was not this (Dan. 5:17)
4 "Thou shalt bruise his ___" (Gen. 3:15)
5 Lions were this with Daniel

6 African nation
7 Clerical garment
8 "In it was ___ for all" (Dan. 4:12)
9 Recipient
10 Form of communication
11 Downwind
12 Idols were worshipped under this (Hos. 4:13)

15 Daniel was not ___ from the king's decree (Dan. 6:13)
20 Saintly image of sorts
22 "Try my ___" (Ps. 26:2)
26 Darius set Daniel "over the whole ___" (Dan. 6:3)
27 Even Job did this at times
28 Concerning Daniel, there wasn't "any ___ or fault found in him" (Dan. 6:4)

29 Morse code mark
30 Kansas in August descriptor, according to song
31 Wallops
33 Syrian merchandise (Ezek. 27:16)
34 Sticks
35 Blessings are like these in Ezek. 34:26
36 What Daniel could have said to the king's magicians

39 No one could call Daniel this
40 Assist
42 Tiers
43 Wall word (Dan. 5:25)
46 Ointment
48 '80s pro-wrestler, ___ the African Dream
49 Steak
50 African country
51 Muslim religion

52 Animal kingdom division
54 Snow vehicle
56 "I ___ on the work of thy hands" (Ps. 143:5)
57 Down's partner
58 What the lions may have said to Daniel
59 Undergarment
61 Daniel never ___ the king's food

fifteen 15

DAVID:
THE GREAT KING

by Patricia Mitchell

ACROSS

1 Javelin's results, if David hadn't ducked (1 Sam. 18:11)

6 Essence

10 Saul was more than a ___ jealous of David (1 Sam. 18:8)

13 Balloon filler, often

15 Scandinavian capital

16 See 42 Across

17 Saul's changing moods made him one to David

18 "They. . . burn incense unto their ___" (Hab. 1:16)

19 Might accompany "snow, and vapours," as in Ps. 148:8

20 David's strings (1 Sam. 16:23)

22 David's son (2 Sam. 13:37)

24 Describes the scope of David's experiences

26 "Moab. . .hath settled on his ___" (Jer. 48:11)

28 Jonathan's feelings toward David (1 Sam. 18:1)

29 "Fiddlesticks!"

30 David's popularity was ___ for Saul's jealousy

31 Nathan ___ David's guilt (2 Sam. 12:7)

32 Samuel anointed David with it (1 Sam. 16:13)

33 Absalom gathered one to run ahead of him (2 Sam. 15:1)

34 Min. part

35 Shelve again

37 A hose with a hole is ___

41 Gardener's tool

42 Beverage in the hand of a drunkard, perhaps (Prov. 26:9)

43 Snaky scarf

44 The rich man "___ sumptuously every day" (Luke 16:19)

47 "The Philistines. . .___" (1 Sam. 17:51)

48 Because of David and Bathsheba's sin, "the child ___" (2 Sam. 12:18)

49 Greek god of war

50 Campus military org.

51 David's dad, for short (Ruth 4:17)

52 Saul's jealousy would ___ David's life (1 Sam. 18:11)

54 Joseph's coat had many (Gen. 37:3)

56 Battle with no winner

57 Opposing (dial.)

59 Absalom set himself up as a ___ ruler (2 Sam. 15:2–4)

63 "As a ___ doth gather her brood" (Luke 13:34)

64 "Git!"

65 Web cruiser

66 Booming transport

67 Battlefield casualty, often

68 David's weapon (1 Sam. 17:49)

DOWN

1 Referring to Michal (1 Sam. 14:49)

2 "Ascribed unto David ___ thousands" (1 Sam. 18:8)

3 ___ Baba

4 David was one with the crowds (1 Sam. 18:8) (2 wds.)

5 Berried shrub, often poisonous

6 "Defy the armies of the living ___?" (1 Sam. 17:26)

7 "Established him king over ___" (2 Sam. 5:12)

8 Thick slices

9 Jonathan gave David his (1 Sam. 18:4)

10 Dorcas was one (Acts 9:39)

11 Shelf for a religious object, perhaps

12 Saul ___ David too young to challenge Goliath (1 Sam. 17:33)

14 Priests' advice: "Make. . . images of your mice that ___ the land" (1 Sam. 6:5)

21 Sound of Goliath when he fell, maybe (1 Sam. 17:49)

23 Alas! partner

24 Great Lakes city

25 Describes David and Jonathan (1 Sam. 18:1)

27 Brain wave tracker

29 Conquered by Joshua (Josh. 12:23)

30 David's plea to God: "Hide thy ___ from my sins" (Ps. 51:9)

31 "Thy servant kept his father's sheep" from one (1 Sam. 17:34)

33 "He hath requited me evil for ___" (1 Sam. 25:21)

34 Jonathan to David: "The LORD be between me and thee, and between my ___ and thy seed for ever" (1 Sam. 20:42)

36 "David laid up ___ words in his heart" (1 Sam. 21:12)

37 Hanger-on

38 Wading bird

39 Responses to Saul's order to kill David (1 Sam. 19:1-2)

40 David's seer's name (2 Sam. 24:11)

42 Bacon-lettuce-tomato sandwich

44 In Athens, Paul found many (Acts 17:22-23)

45 "The God of the ___ of Israel" (1 Sam. 17:45)

46 What Nathan's story led David to do (2 Sam. 12:13)

47 Folded sheets of paper

48 David's cry: "Render to them their ___" (Ps. 28:4)

50 "David did that which was ___ in the eyes of the LORD" (1 Kings 15:5)

51 David's kingly descendent (Matt. 1:1)

53 Grating sound

55 FedEx competitor

58 East of Eden land (Gen. 4:16)

60 Suspicious aircraft

61 Where Daniel spent time with lions (Dan. 6:16)

62 Silver or gold, e.g.

sixteen 16
DEBORAH: THE JUDGE
by Patricia Mitchell

ACROSS

1 Queen of ___, Solomon's visitor (1 Kings 10:1)
6 Abel's portions offered to the Lord (Gen. 4:4)
10 Deborah's song: "They rehearse the righteous ___ of the Lord" (Judg. 5:11)
14 "Blessed above ___ shall Jael . . .be" (Judg. 5:24)
15 Off-Broadway award
16 "Shall ye not eat of them that ___ the cud" (Lev. 11:4)
17 This does not exist between Deborah and Sisera (Judg. 4:11–17)
18 Cincinnati baseball team
19 Companion of harp, viol, tabret, and wine (Isa. 5:12)
20 The Baptizer's mom, familiarly
21 Barak's response to Deborah would ___ to his fear (Judg. 4:8)
23 Pan mate

24 Jael would go out of her tent and ___ Sisera (Judg. 4:18)
26 Iodine compound
28 Succoth shelters (Gen. 33:17)
31 Barak would not go unless Deborah did this (Judg. 4:8)
32 "They chose new gods; then was ___ in the gates" (Judg. 5:8)
33 Noble's attendant
36 Dutch cheese
40 Highest point
42 "They that handle the ___ of the writer" (Judg. 5:14)
43 God to Gideon: "The people are yet too ___" (Judg. 7:4)
44 Children's love
45 Jael covered Sisera with this (Judg. 4:18)
48 Deborah to Barak: "Take with thee ___ thousand men" (Judg. 4:6)
49 Herod's brother, familiarly (Matt. 14:3)

51 Capital of Canada
53 Jael to Sisera: "___ ___, my lord" (Judg. 4:18) (2 wds.)
56 God will be there you when your hair turns this (Ps. 71:18) (var.)
57 ___ Maria
58 Matthew thru Acts, e.g.
61 Food for your printer
65 Adam and Eve, originally
67 "Out of Ephraim was there a ___ of them" (Judg. 5:14)
68 Priest in Toledo
69 Margarine
70 Wager
71 "Curse ye Meroz, said the ___ of the Lord" (Judg. 5:23)
72 A woman of Deborah's wisdom and courage is this
73 Jabin king of Canaan suffered this (Judg. 4:24)
74 Jesus stood in yours

DOWN

1 You might do it to the deck
2 "That disciple took her unto his own ___" (John 19:27)
3 Give off
4 Deborah dwelt "between Ramah and ___" (Judg. 4:5)
5 "Is there ___ man here?" (Judg. 4:20)
6 "Shield or spear seen among ___ thousand in Israel?" (Judg. 5:8)

7 Sisera hoped Jael would ___ his escape (Judg. 4:18)
8 Wave word
9 Meeting
10 Med. org.
11 Hot stuff
12 Barak was this about fighting Sisera (Judg. 4:8)
13 Scandinavian
21 Sanctuary section
22 Doubting disciple, familiarly

25 Jael was this with Sisera (Judg. 4:17–21)
27 Deborah would ___ Barak's request with disfavor (Judg. 4:9)
28 Jael did more than this to Sisera
29 Folded Mexican sandwich
30 Sisera, captain of Jabin's ___ (Judg. 4:7)
31 Barak basically said to Deborah, "I ___!" (Judg. 4:8)

34 October birthstone

35 Deborah and Jael outshine these in this story

37 Book of Numbers contains these

38 After victory, Israel had peace ___ (Judg. 5:31)

39 Loud bird

41 Sports channel

45 Lot's wife turned to one (Gen. 19:26)

46 "The children of Israel again did evil in the sight of the ___" (Judg. 4:1)

47 LAX info

50 Deborah and Jael were this

52 Herod the Great was this

53 "Go and draw toward mount ___" (Judg. 4:6)

54 Screamer's throat dangler

55 Deborah's song would ___ to the Israelite's victory

56 "People of the LORD go down to the ___" (Judg. 5:11)

59 A commandment might be this

60 Jesus welcomed them (Matt. 19:14)

62 Sisera's soldiers "fell upon the ___ of the sword" (Judg. 4:16)

63 Israel is one

64 Israelites were not to do this with heathen peoples

66 Sisera was Deborah's (Judg. 4:14)

68 Abraham, Isaac, and Jacob, for short

seventeen 17

DORCAS: FULL OF GOOD WORKS

by Patricia Mitchell

ACROSS

1 Flightless birds
5 Corp. ending, often
10 Genetic code
13 Parrot
15 With alms, Dorcas would ___ out to the poor (Acts 9:36)
16 Dorcas did this before her death (Acts 9:37)
17 Many, as the garments Dorcas had made
18 Dorcas's creation, in Spain (Acts 9:39)
19 Card game
20 ___ ___ carte, menu choice (2 wds.)
21 Dorcas's sources of colors for clothing
23 Adar, e.g.
25 Peter took one to reach Joppa
26 Dorcas's Hebrew name (Acts 9:36)
28 Hair style

31 Lox mate
32 Pressing items for Dorcas?
33 Ruler
34 Peter showed this toward Dorcas (Acts 9:41)
37 Dorcas had this in herself (Mark 9:50)
38 One without Christ (Eph. 2:12)
40 Peter's prayer would ___ Dorcas (Acts 9:40)
41 Herod was this, according to Jesus (Luke 13:32)
42 Salvation is God's gift, so we should not do this (Eph. 2:8–9)
43 "Lydda was nigh to Joppa," so Peter didn't have ___ ___ go (Acts 9:38) (2 wds.)
44 Peter presented Dorcas this way (Acts 9:41)
45 Put on something Dorcas made
46 Build up to a level

49 Because of Dorcas, "many believed in the ___" (Acts 9:42)
50 Dorcas's creations (Acts 9:39)
51 Dorcas "was ___, and died" (Acts 9:37)
52 ___ Dolorosa, Jerusalem pilgrimage site
55 Focal point
56 The Apostles' Creed, e.g.
59 Hearers must not do this to God's prophecies (Rev. 22:18)
61 See 59 Across: Anyone who does this surely has a big one
62 New Testament period, e.g.
63 Where the blind leading the blind end up (Matt. 15:14)
64 Where Daniel and the lions spent time together (Dan. 6:16)
65 "Inferno" author
66 Jesus' is light (Matt. 11:30)

DOWN

1 Austin title
2 A tale-bearer is one (Prov. 25:18)
3 West Coast educ. inst.
4 When Dorcas "saw Peter, she ___ up" (Acts 9:40)
5 "A strong man ___" (Luke 11:21)
6 "Waters called he ___" (Gen. 1:10)
7 ___ Francisco

8 Mo. Martin Luther posted *Theses*
9 Dorcas was laid "in an upper ___" (Acts 9:37)
10 Dorcas's condition didn't ___ Peter
11 Topaz was the city walls' ___ foundation (Rev. 21:20)
12 Island "hi"
14 Dorcas's mourners (Acts 9:39)
22 Chat

24 Silly virgins had none (Matt. 25:3)
25 Mockers regarded the disciples' words at Pentecost as this (Acts 2:13)
26 "The tongue can no man ___" (James 3:8)
27 In opposition (dial.)
28 Mourners would ___ Dorcas, a godly woman

29 Peter's words to Dorcas, e.g. (Acts 9:40)

30 Churches received "the comfort of the ___ Ghost" (Acts 9:31)

31 Natural color of Dorcas's fabrics

34 Marine bird

35 "To sit up ___" (Ps. 127:2)

36 Boor

38 Wilderness of Sin, e.g. (Ex. 17:1)

39 Bathe

40 Peter "gave her his ___, and lifted her up" (Acts 9:41)

42 Nabal's condition at his feast (1 Sam. 25:36)

43 A deacon's tongue should not be this (1 Tim. 3:8)

44 KJV verb

45 Luke's profession, for short (Col. 4:14)

46 Dorcas's body may have done this (Acts 9:37)

47 Philistines would ___ out Samson's eyes (Judg. 16:21)

48 Libreville's location

49 Beloved must have been this (Song 2:8–9)

51 Sadducees (Acts 5:17)

52 Peter gave death one, so to speak (Acts 9:40–41)

53 South American empire

54 Developmental diagnosis

57 Regulatory organization

58 Paris negative

60 Cubic measure (abbr.)

eighteen

ELI:
THE GREAT PRIEST

by Patricia Mitchell

ACROSS

1 Sheep's clothing wearer
5 Nebuchadnezzar's nail resembled this (Dan. 4:33)
9 You can chart Paul's missionary journeys on these
13 The ark sat on the "great stone of ___" (1 Sam. 6:18)
14 Fruit
15 Upon
16 "Hannah ___ up after they had eaten" (1 Sam. 1:9)
17 Blend
18 "Hophni and Phinehas, are ___" (1 Sam. 4:17)
19 Eli, Hophni, Phinehas, and Samuel, e.g. (abbr.)
21 18 Across to Eli (2 wds.)
23 Arizona Indian
25 Needs of the "ready writer" in Psalm 45:1

26 What the messenger may have put on himself (1 Sam. 4:12)
29 Part of offering Eli's sons took for themselves (1 Sam. 2:15)
31 Eli's sons' behavior did not ___ God's will for priests
34 Officer in U.S. Armed Forces (abbr.)
35 Gem State
37 Asian country
39 As priest, Eli wore this
41 Shape of God's sign to Noah
42 IHOP condiment
43 "Eli. . .sat ___ a seat by a post of the temple" (1 Sam. 1:9)
44 Terra-___ (type of clay)
46 Tire wall letters
47 Altar builders do this
50 "Spear was like a weaver's ___" (1 Sam. 17:7)

51 Philistines took the ark "and ___ it by Dagon" (1 Sam. 5:2)
52 Eli ___ his sons' disobedience (1 Sam. 23–24)
54 In a parade, but not the Bible
56 Man with the unclean spirit, e.g. (Mark 5:2)
59 Gomer's appearance, perhaps (Hos. 1:2–3)
63 Soft drink
64 Most of the Bible is written in this
66 Eli presided over the Temple ___
67 Stave
68 Jael ___ ___ Sisera (Judg. 4:18) (2 wds.)
69 European river
70 No one could do this to 56 Across (Mark 5:4)
71 Biblical paradise
72 Sunday song

DOWN

1 "How can one be ___ alone?" (Eccl. 4:11)
2 In orchestra, but not the Bible
3 "Knew nothing of all this, ___ or more" (1 Sam. 22:15)
4 "Give ___ to roast for the priest" (1 Sam. 2:15)
5 "Whatsoever. . .cheweth the ___" (Lev. 11:3)
6 Samuel's offering (1 Sam. 7:9)

7 20 Down descriptor
8 Eli's "eyes began to ___ ___" (1 Sam. 3:2) (2 wds.)
9 Eli's sons did not behave this way
10 The Holy Spirit makes hearts ___
11 Parents' school groups
12 Third day creation (Gen. 1:11)
14 At first, Eli ___ to see Hannah (1 Sam. 1:13–14)

20 Fifth day creation (Gen. 1:20)
22 Basketball assoc.
24 Almost sacrificed (Gen. 22:9–12)
26 National rights org.
27 Eli's sons would ___ what they wanted (1 Sam. 2:16)
28 Eli gave more ___ to his sons than to God (1 Sam. 2:29)
30 Heart's motion
32 See 20 Down

33 Eli served in the Lord's ___

36 Musical group, perhaps

38 "Then did they ___ in his face" (Matt. 26:67)

40 Eli's sons were this

42 Dance

45 To make firm

48 Eli took a ___ from Hannah's behavior (1 Sam. 1:13)

49 "The lamp of God went out in the ___" (1 Sam. 3:3)

53 Eli's sons ___ dishonor the Lord

55 Hannah was ___ in grief (1 Sam. 1:7)

56 Fizzy beverage

57 Christ was the second (1 Cor. 15:22)

58 Eli's life ends on a sad ___

60 Hauling cart

61 Printer need

62 "Solomon had horses. . .and linen __" (1 Kings 10:28)

63 Sound-barrier breaker

65 "If a man ___ against the LORD, who shall intreat for him?" (1 Sam. 2:25)

nineteen

ELIJAH HEARD IT

by Patricia Mitchell

ACROSS

1 Elijah's disciple (1 Kings 19:19)
7 Elijah "___ slain all the prophets" (1 Kings 19:1)
10 Abba (familiarly)
14 Cowboy shows
15 Lyric poem
16 Actor Alda
17 Elijah suggested the prophets' idol was this (1 Kings 18:27)
18 Associated with 17 Across
19 Ding's partner
20 "A rod out of the ___ of Jesse" (Isa. 11:1)
21 Singing cowboy Autry
22 "Who may stand. . .when ___ thou art angry?" (Ps. 76:7)
23 Elijah's nemesis
25 Moray

26 Sound from bird Noah sent out (Gen. 8:8)
29 Elijah was not this to Jezebel
30 Popular tape
34 Asian plum
36 Many boomers now
39 Where Elijah discovered God (1 Kings 19:12) (3 wds.)
42 Least fresh
43 The widow's never emptied (1 Kings 17:16)
44 Elijah would do this from Jezebel (1 Kings 19:3)
45 Sports org.
46 Thanks to Elijah, the widow and her son did this (1 Kings 17:15)
47 Place of ahhhs
50 "All the ___ of the earth shall fear him" (Ps. 67:7)

51 God's Commandments are one of these to us
53 George Bernard ___
55 Girl
59 Opera offering
60 The God that sends fire, "___ him be God" (1 Kings 18:24)
61 Highest
63 Plateau
64 "Dress it first; for ye ___ many" (1 Kings 18:25)
65 "O Lord, ___ ___" (1 Kings 18:37) (2 wds.)
66 Rind
67 Yearning
68 Elijah and the heathen prophets ___ to a contest (1 Kings 18:24)

DOWN

1 Time periods
2 The prodigal son was this
3 The heathen prophets' idol was this
4 "If it ___ good to thee, I will give" (1 Kings 21:2)
5 Used by Cain, perhaps
6 Forbidden fruit offerer
7 Elijah went "unto ___ the mount of God" (1 Kings 19:8)
8 Yemini city
9 Districts of ancient Attica
10 Pedestal part
11 Elijah felt this way (1 Kings 19:10)

12 Herodias's daughter did one (Matt. 14:6)
13 Who told Elijah, "Arise and eat" (1 Kings 19:5)
21 Guy's partner
23 Roman god
24 Gretel's friend
26 Bank products
27 Horse chow
28 Leave out
30 Eastern state (abbr.)
31 Disarm a gun
32 Social science
33 Pliers, e.g.

35 Part of Elijah's and the prophets' altars
36 Elijah "came and ___ down under a juniper" (1 Kings 19:4)
37 Omani town
38 Beat it!
40 Colorado Springs zone
41 Before (poet.)
45 Mt. Carmel to Zarephath (dir.)
47 Classic comics pooch
48 Mash
49 God to Elijah: "___, get thee to Zarephath" (1 Kings 17:9)

50 Man of God had done this, and he shouldn't have (1 Kings 13:22)

52 He had no ability to send fire to his altar

53 Widow to Elijah: "Art thou come. . .to ___ my son?" (1 Kings 17:18)

54 "God Was ___," title for 39 Across

55 When he spoke, Elijah was not one of these

56 Land for the two altars, perhaps

57 Elijah proved God was not the ___ as a heathen idol

58 Snow goer

61 Elijah's response to 39 Across?

62 Place to hang Elijah's mantle

20 ELISHA: MAN OF GOD

by Patricia Mitchell

ACROSS

1 "___ of lions" (Dan. 6:16)
4 Moses' burning sight (Ex. 3:2)
9 Pump
14 Cain's mom
15 Naaman "stood at the door of the ___ of Elisha" (2 Kings 5:9)
16 Gehazi made a serious one (2 Kings 5:20)
17 Fluffy's doc
18 Naaman's letter caused the king of Israel this (2 Kings 5:7)
19 Elisha to Gehazi: "Is it a time to receive ___?" (2 Kings 5:26)
20 God is always this (Heb. 10:37) (2 wds.)
22 Candy bar choice
24 Elisha healed many of these
25 Ahaz worshipped "under every green ___" (2 Kings 17:10)
27 Community org.
31 Lydia needed one (Acts 16:14)
32 A "corruptible crown," perhaps (1 Cor. 9:25)
33 A long time
34 Fabled fabler
36 Epistle of Paul, in a way
38 They go along with a Day 3 creation (Gen. 1:10)
40 Gehazi did not tell Naaman the ___ story (2 Kings 5:22)
42 Stones of the altar will become like this (Isa. 27:9)
43 Relating to what Peter cut off Malchus's head (John 18:10)
44 Charged particle
45 Gehazi could have used one to haul his loot (2 Kings 5:23)
47 Elisha's question proved one to Gehazi (2 Kings 5:25)
51 Naaman does this to Gehazi's request (2 Kings 5:23)
53 Gehazi's was a bad one (2 Kings 5:20)
54 Hearing what Elisha said, Naaman "went away in a ___" (2 Kings 5:12)
55 Dueling sword
57 Legendary lady of soul
59 Tylenol's competitor
62 Part of Gehazi's loot (2 Kings 5:26)
65 Conversational computer of film
66 Naaman was one (2 Kings 5:1)
67 Lover's voice was like this (Song 2:14)
68 Samaria to Gilgal (dir.)
69 Bingo
70 How Naaman felt when he heard Elisha's orders (2 Kings 5:12)
71 Business org. ending

DOWN

1 The slothful man is ___ of understanding (Prov. 24:30)
2 Smoothly
3 You'll find one in 1 Down's field (Prov. 24:31)
4 Gehazi's story to Naaman was this (2 Kings 5:22)
5 Under Elijah, Elisha could ___ his skills
6 On the floor of a Syrian's tent, perhaps (2 Kings 7:8)
7 *Missouri* letters
8 "___ than all the waters of Israel?" (2 Kings 5:12)
9 Interstate sight
10 Elisha sent one to Naaman (2 Kings 5:10)
11 The widow may have borrowed one (2 Kings 4:3)
12 "Beloved is like a ___" (Song 2:9)
13 Naaman's servants wanted him to ___ Elisha's instructions (2 Kings 5:13)
21 Where Naaman's wife's maid came from (2 Kings 5:2)
23 The couple in Cana did this (John 2:1)
25 Numbers in which Naaman measured payment (2 Kings 5:23)
26 Music style
28 Costa ___, CA
29 One was kindled by God's fire (2 Sam. 22:9)

30 Widow to Elisha: "Thine handmaid hath not ___ thing in the house" (2 Kings 4:2)

32 Handy communication

35 Deer cousin

36 La Guardia message (abbr.)

37 Summer in Samaria, sometimes

38 "___ thee with badgers' skin" (Ezek. 16:10)

39 Naaman thought Elisha should "strike his ___ over" his scars (2 Kings 5:11)

40 Manner

41 The widow would do this to Elisha (2 Kings 4:1)

42 Hush-hush org.

43 Elisha: "They that be with us ___ more than they that be with them" (2 Kings 6:16)

45 Elisha heard one (2 Kings 5:25)

46 Ukrainian city

48 Wept for her kids (Matt. 2:18)

49 How Syrians felt to hear "noise of a great host" (2 Kings 7:6)

50 Pared

52 How many times the child sneezed (2 Kings 4:35)

56 Caffeine-free beverage brand

57 Fruit

58 Elisha was this until his death (2 Kings 13:19–20)

59 Church garb

60 Downwind

61 Gov. agency

63 Attila was one

64 Would dad offer son a scorpion instead of this? (Luke 11:12)

*twenty*21*-one*
ELISABETH'S JOY
by Patricia Mitchell

ACROSS

1 "Are heavy ___" (Matt. 11:28)
6 Flows partner
10 Two cups make one
14 Greek marketplace in Paul's day
15 The sluggard might do this (Prov. 6:9)
16 Galilee, Samaria, or Judea
17 Breastplate stone (Ex. 28:17)
18 Mary "entered ___ the house of Zacharias, and saluted Elisabeth" (Luke 1:40)
19 The Ten Commandments
20 Caesarea to Nazareth (dir.)
21 Educational inst.
23 Polish port
25 Experts, for short
26 Fido's org.
27 Zacharias felt this way to see Gabriel (Luke 1:12)

30 Judgment, council, and hell fire (Matt. 5:22)
34 Hairdo no-no (1 Peter 3:3)
35 Coastal hazes
36 Climate and natural resources org.
38 Yuck!
39 Bard's before
40 What you want to be when 59 Across
42 Elisabeth and Zacharias, e.g.
43 "Till thou hast ___ the very last mite" (Luke 12:59)
44 Spirits
45 Warriors of 1 Chron. 12:2, perhaps
48 Twain's Tom
49 Elisabeth "brought forth a ___" (Luke 1:57)
50 Je ne ___ quoi (Fr.)

51 "No child, because that Elisabeth was ___" (Luke 1:7)
54 Bethsaida native, familiarily (John 1:44)
55 Large tree
58 Samoan capital
59 Paul was this from Seleucia to Cyprus (Acts 13:4)
61 Ahasuerus reigned from here to Ethiopia (Est. 1:1)
63 Paul's destination in 59 Across (Acts. 13:4)
64 "Then drew ___ unto him all the publicans and sinners" (Luke 15:1)
65 Simeon's sobriquet (Acts 13:1)
66 No doubt Elisabeth couldn't wait to ___ Mary what happened
67 Zacharias couldn't do this for a while (Luke 1:22)
68 Dales

DOWN

1 People wondered why Zacharias was this (Luke 1:21)
2 Dramatic conflict
3 Did Zacharias feel like one to argue with Gabriel? (Luke 1:18)
4 Epoch
5 Where Gabriel went after visiting Zacharias (Luke 1:26)
6 Elisabeth's son would have "power of ___" (Luke 1:17)
7 Paul was in one (Acts 26:29)
8 Deli order

9 Mottos
10 Caiaphas had one (Matt. 26:3)
11 Modern Persia
12 What Gabriel brought (Luke 1:13)
13 Brick making, e.g. (Ex. 5:14)
22 Fish
24 10 grams (abbr.)
25 One with a haughty spirit, e.g. (Prov. 16:18)
27 Laban and Jacob had one (Gen. 31:49–50)

28 Nebuchadnezzar's nails (Dan. 4:33)
29 Elisabeth's tribe (Luke 1:5)
30 Actress Day
31 Both Elisabeth and Zacharias were this (Luke 1:7)
32 Elisabeth's baby would "make ___ a people" (Luke 1:17)
33 Jael's weapon (Judg. 4:21)
35 Gabriel to Zacharias: "___ not" (Luke 1:13)
37 Like a wing
40 Helping

41 Among those devils entered (Matt. 8:31)
43 Team flag
46 Elisabeth's child preached to this people (Luke 1:80)
47 Edgar Allen
48 Okinawan weapon
50 Day 5 creation (Gen. 1:21)

51 Judah took Tamar's (Gen. 38:15)
52 Church section
53 The Jordan River in some places today
54 Church bell might do this
55 Gabriel's appearance put Zacharias on it (Luke 1:12)

56 "One of the people might lightly have ___ with thy wife" (Gen. 26:10)
57 Hill site of Paul's sermon (Acts 17:22)
60 Where 41 Down ran (Matt. 8:32)
62 Our righteousness is this (Isa. 64:6)

twenty22-two
ESAU'S ERROR
by Patricia Mitchell

ACROSS

1 Jacob and Esau had one, big-time (Gen. 27:41)
5 Top story
10 Women's magazine
14 Rebekah was one to Jacob in trickery (Gen. 27:8)
15 Animals in a region
16 Genesis includes these for Esau and Jacob
17 Esau sold it (Gen. 25:33)
19 Orchestra voice
20 Cry softly
21 What Christ did for your sins (Rom. 5:11)
23 Esau's father had lost this sense (Gen. 27:22)
26 Esau's father ___ for Jacob's impersonation of Esau (Gen. 27:27)
28 Esau "came out ___, all over like an hairy garment" (Gen. 25:25)

31 Charged particle
32 What Jesus does (Luke 1:68)
33 Jacob drew this from Esau (Gen. 27:41)
34 Jacob ___ gifts to Esau to appease him (Gen. 32:20)
37 Esau's dad (Gen. 25:26)
39 Crucifix
40 What Jacob told his father was not this
42 Asian capital
45 Incense descriptor
49 Winter river sight, at times
50 Camera stand
53 Computing phrase
54 "Thy dwelling shall be. . . of the ___ of heaven" (Gen. 27:39)
55 "I mean not that other men be ___" (2 Cor. 8:13)
56 Frothy

58 Power controlling device, for short
60 How Esau and Jacob may have addressed their father
61 "___ before men" (Matt. 6:1)
63 Frogs, toads, e.g.
69 What a 63 Across might do
70 Jacob wanted to ___ ___ Esau's inheritance (Gen. 25:31) (2 wds.)
71 Scat!
72 Ezekiel's vision (Ezek. 37:1)
73 Psalmist asks God to do this to his transgressions (Ps. 51:1)
74 Esau does this when Jacob gave him stew (Gen. 25:34)

DOWN

1 Charge
2 Roman count
3 Presidential initials
4 Fido's activity
5 Hairdo
6 Chinese ethnic group
7 Tower
8 Breathe in
9 "Lead on softly, according as the ___" (Gen. 33:14)
10 Black
11 West African country
12 London WC

13 Joppa to Jerusalem (dir.)
18 The meat Jacob served his father, perhaps
22 Element
23 Esau's niece Dinah to his nephew Zebulun, for short (Gen. 30:20–21)
24 Jacob's debt to Esau, e.g.
25 Economic measure
26 Esau to Jacob: "___ me, I pray thee" (Gen. 25:30)
27 "The LORD shall ___ to me another son" (Gen. 30:24)
29 When the patriarchs lived, e.g.

30 Noel month (abbr.)
32 2016 Games city, for short
35 At trickery, Jacob was this
36 Mill about
38 ___ of Galilee
40 Feet did this, KJV style
41 Aaron's budded (Num. 17:8)
42 Jacob ___ from Esau (Gen. 27:43)
43 Whiz
44 Walter Cronkite, e.g.
45 Jacob would ___ Esau (Gen. 27:15–16)

46 Sticky black substance
47 Computer corp.
48 Esau emitted an "exceeding bitter ___" (Gen. 27:34)
51 Esau might ___ Jacob's family in revenge (Gen. 32:6)
52 Chemical compound
56 Nursery item

57 Esau: "Let my father ___, and eat" (Gen. 27:31)
59 Rebekah would ___ her husband's plans to bless Esau (Gen. 27:5)
60 Mount Sinai, e.g.
61 Mass garment
62 MGM's Lion

64 School org.
65 KJV hast
66 What Esau might have said when he realized what Jacob did (Gen. 27:34)
67 Commandment word
68 Distress call

twenty-three
ESTHER:
THE BLESSED QUEEN

by Patricia Mitchell

ACROSS

1 Concorde, e.g.
4 British WC
7 Shushan to 22 Across (dir.)
10 Jews may have used one in defense (Est. 8:11)
12 Tool of trade, perhaps, for Andrew and Peter (Matt. 4:18)
13 Esther's appearance (Est. 2:7)
14 Leah to Joseph and Rachel to Reuben (Gen. 35:23–24)
16 Ahasuerus's exclamation to find Haman at Esther's couch (Est. 7:8)
17 Ahasuerus to Esther: "___ ye also for the Jews" (Est. 8:8)
18 Description of Esther (Est. 2:7) (2 wds.)
21 Ahasuerus's calls for young virgins, for short
22 Abraham's native place (Gen. 11:27–28)

23 Esther may have felt this when urged to intercede (Est. 4:16)
26 Chemical symbol
27 Esther was one (Est. 2:7)
31 Scooby-___
32 Skunklike African animal
35 Haman would ___ the king's decree to destroy Jews (Est. 3:8–9)
36 Mordecai to Esther: "Who knoweth whether thou art come to the kingdom for ___ ___ ___ ___ ___" (Est. 4:14) (5 wds.)
41 Esther's pronoun
42 Fern seed
43 Haman had a lot of it (Est. 6:6)
44 Esther was given Haman's (Est. 8:7)
47 Spielberg's alien

48 Esther must not be this (Est. 4:8)
49 Mordecai acted as this to Esther (Est. 2:7)
50 "Go to the ___, thou sluggard" (Prov. 6:6)
51 Where Haman ended up (Est. 7:10) (4 wds.)
61 Mordecai sent letters to the Jews "with words of ___ and truth" (Est. 9:30)
62 Hospital patients do this
63 Haman's plans could be called this (Est. 3:8–9)
64 63 Across homonym
65 Jerusalem to Damascus (dir.)
66 "Singin' in the Rain" Kelly
67 "They shall not hunger ___ thirst" (Isa. 49:10)
68 Esther asked the Jews not to do this for three days (Est. 4:16)
69 Comprehensive dictionary

DOWN

1 Wound cap
2 Skid
3 Charlie's sort
4 What a sluggard does
5 Honolulu's island
6 The king's command to his servants was this (Est. 1:10)
7 "Cause Haman to make haste, that he may do as Esther hath ___" (Est. 5:5)
8 Shushan is one

9 One might be among those singing (Song 2:12)
11 Energy measurement
13 TGI day (abbr.)
15 A psalm often has one
17 Haman's mind did this, perhaps
19 Haman was one, in the foolish sense
20 Austrian river (var.)
23 Passports are these

24 Particle of dust turned to one under Aaron's rod (Ex. 8:16)
25 Ness and Lomond
27 Bread spread
28 Sukkot shelter
29 Sackcloth partner
30 Mr. Ed's negative, perhaps
33 Jesus would do this on the third day
34 Elf
37 Excited (with up)

38 Christians were martyred in one, at times

39 Ahasuerus would not ___ for Vashti's refusal

40 Chinese sauce

45 Church part

46 Chinese philosophical concept

50 Ornamental stud

51 "I stand. . .and knock: if any man. . .___ the door, I will come in" (Rev. 3:20)

52 Christians' nemesis in Rome

53 Esau had a lot of this (Gen. 27:11)

54 Often in cubes

55 Wax mate

56 One of Columbus's ships

57 In the king's dream, one of these was iron (Dan. 2:33)

58 Black and white treat

59 Ahasuerus enjoyed too much of this (Est. 1:10)

60 "If Mordecai be of the ___ of the Jews" (Est. 6:13)

twenty**24**four

EVE:
THE FIRST WOMAN

by Patricia Mitchell

ACROSS

1 Cave dwellers
5 John the Baptist's food, according to tradition
10 Eve to Serpent: "God hath said, Ye shall ___ eat of it" (Gen. 3:3)
13 God would ___ the sin of Adam and Eve (Gen. 3:14)
15 Eden was this before the Fall
16 Easter mo., often
17 Eve placed this on the serpent (Gen. 3:13)
18 Eve's was a biggie (Gen. 3:6)
19 Serpent to Eve: "Ye shall not surely ___" (Gen. 3:4)
20 Eve had one for the fruit of the tree (Gen. 3:6)
21 Chowder mollusk
23 God clothed Adam and Eve in "coats of ___" (Gen. 3:21)
25 Satan called God this, in effect (Gen. 3:4)
26 Satan preyed on those of Eve (Gen. 3:6)

28 "I will put ___ between thee and the woman" (Gen. 3:15)
31 Satan's temptations are often double ___
32 Adam to God: "I heard thy ___ in the garden, and I was afraid" (Gen. 3:10)
33 Tea choice
34 ___ Squad, classic TV show
37 Eve may have been this, as she had time to speak to a serpent
38 Salome or Delilah, e.g.
40 Pedal-powered transport
41 Eve told God she was ___ astray by the serpent (Gen. 3:13)
42 Mob activity
43 "Shall be called ___" (Gen. 2:23)
44 God's punishment for disobedience (Gen. 2:17)
45 Adam and Eve were these before the Fall (Gen. 2:23)

46 Mexican spirit
49 Colorado's Zebulon Mt.
50 Music genre
51 "Time and ___ wait for no man"
52 Noah's vessel
55 Grand ___ Opry, radio program
56 Church steeple
59 Downtown
61 Formerly (Fr.)
62 Despite Eve's sin, God would ___ a promise (Gen. 3:15)
63 For a covering, Adam and Eve would ___ fig leaves (Gen. 3:7)
64 Climate channel
65 God's promise of a Savior ___ sin's sting (1 Cor. 15:54–57)
66 Eve ___ off God's warning, so to speak (Gen. 3:6)

DOWN

1 God's promise of a Savior would take this form (Luke 2:11–12)
2 52 Down's homonym
3 "The serpent was more subtil ___ any beast" (Gen. 3:1)
4 Ruble replacement in the Kyrgyz Republic
5 Humidor item
6 Eve's hubby
7 Team sports figure, for short
8 Nabal, for one (1 Sam. 25:3)

9 "Male and female created he them; and ___ them" (Gen. 5:2)
10 Lowest point
11 Eve would do this in response to God's question (Gen. 3:13)
12 Eve might have had one
14 Those who memorize Bible verses can do this
22 "Little Lord Jesus ___ down His sweet head" (song)
24 Eve's boy Cain, e.g.

25 Plague pests (Ex. 8:17)
26 Chop
27 Eve's paradise
28 "Tree of knowledge of good and ___" (Gen. 2:9)
29 Stem point
30 Like earth inheritors (Matt. 5:5)
31 God created Adam and Eve on the ___ day (Gen. 1:27, 31)
34 Silent performer

35 Eve's word to the serpent's suggestion, maybe (Gen. 3:6)
36 "In ___ and caves of the earth" (Heb. 11:38)
38 Tube
39 Not one of the law shall remain unfulfilled (Matt. 5:18)
40 "Adam said, This is now ___ of my bones" (Gen. 2:23)
42 Many times in the Bible, God would ___ His promise of a Savior

43 After they sinned, Adam and Eve did this, in a way (Gen. 3:7) (2 wds.)
44 After Adam and Eve sinned, punishment was ___
45 "Adam and his wife ___ themselves from" God (Gen. 3:8)
46 Cut of beef
47 Girl's name
48 Title of Solomon's visitor (1 Kings 10:1)
49 Docks

51 Eve "saw that the ___ was good for food" (Gen. 3:6)
52 Eve's murdered son
53 Eve is the mother of the human ___ (Gen. 3:20)
54 "Adam ___ Eve his wife; and she conceived" (Gen. 4:1)
57 School org.
58 After creation, vegetation produced after ___ kind (Gen. 1:11–12)
60 God made Eve from Adam's ___ (Gen. 2:22)

twenty-five
EZRA: THE SCRIBE
by Patricia Mitchell

ACROSS

1 Dance
4 "Who is there ___ you of all his people?" (Ezra 1:3)
9 Damage
12 "Un bel di vedremo," e.g.
14 Ezekiel may have seen one (Ezek. 37:4)
15 "At ___ in the body. . .absent from the Lord" (2 Cor. 5:6)
16 A good man will do this (Ps. 112:5)
17 Matador's passes at bull
18 Arabian Sea gulf
19 Ezra going to Jerusalem did not rest at one of these (2 wds.)
21 Patron
23 Tool likely used in Temple project (Ezra 5:8) (var.)
24 Ezra "did ___ no bread" in mourning (Ezra 10:6)
25 Cyrus or Artaxerxes

28 Really cool
31 Thin strand
34 Third largest island in the world
36 When Temple construction ceased, the builders could do this (Ezra 4:24)
38 Luau dish
40 Whoremonger (Eph. 5:5)
41 God's gift to the faithful remnant (Ezra 9:8)
43 Hiker's nemesis
44 Brew
45 Building wing
46 Islands off of Portugal
48 "Finished on the third day of the month ___" (Ezra 6:15)
51 Throw
53 On the holy day, everyone does this (Neh. 8:10)
54 Subsidiary (abbr.)

56 Flow mate
58 Ezra was a ready one (Ezra 7:6)
61 "___ the house of the Lord" (Ezra 7:27)
66 Location of 30 Down
67 What an angry mob does
69 Human rights org.
70 Baby pooches
71 Temple vessels were in Babylon because Sheshbazzar did this (Ezra 1:11)
72 All the people enjoyed one (Neh. 8:12)
73 Jerusalem to Dead Sea (dir.)
74 "Then ___ we those elders" (Ezra 5:9)
75 It colored the rich man's garment (Luke 16:19)

DOWN

1 Is there any in Gilead? (Jer. 8:22)
2 Black and white treat
3 Gourmet ice-cream container, often
4 Temple builders would ___ stones and timber (Ezra 6:4)
5 Nebuchadnezzar, an oppressor, was ___ than Cyrus, a benevolent ruler
6 Jews' marriages with heathens was a bad one to Ezra (Ezra 9:1–3)
7 Mother Teresa, e.g.

8 "___ hath been shewed from the Lord" (Ezra 9:8)
9 Style
10 The people's response to Ezra's blessing (Neh. 8:6)
11 Ezra did this to his clothing (Ezra 9:1–3)
13 Festive activities of Neh. 8:10, e.g.
15 Port-au-Prince location
20 Reaction of natives when not permitted to work on the Temple (Ezra 4:4–5)
22 Ezra's expertise (Ezra 7:6)

25 Eucalyptus-loving marsupial
26 Natives were this (see 20 Down)
27 Jerusalem to Babylon (dir.)
29 ___-Saxon
30 Doo ___ Parade, 66 Across event
32 The rock in Horeb did this (Ex. 17:6)
33 Skin features
34 Lingerie item
35 17 Across arena cheer
37 School org.

39 Taxing org.
42 How Ezra felt (see 11 Down)
43 Relative of Eve's tempter
47 Asian humped ox
49 "See ya later!" (Sp.)
50 God took one from Adam (Gen. 2:22)
52 Scarab
55 Vice __
57 Cyrus knew God's Temple was __ in Jerusalem (Ezra 1:2)

58 Several of the items Judas received from Jesus (John 13:26)
59 Small freshwater fish
60 "Offer the first of thy __ fruits" (Ex. 22:29)
61 "Ezra opened the __ in the sight of all the people" (Neh. 8:5)
62 Scottish cap, for short
63 The face of the deep is this (Job 38:30)

64 "He shall __ the burnt offering" (Lev. 1:6)
65 December log
68 "__ a Small World," Disney ditty

twenty-26-six

GABRIEL:
THE ARCHANGEL

by Patricia Mitchell

ACROSS

1 Never say this to Gabriel!
6 Investment choices
9 It's for lovers (abbr.)
11 Rights org.
12 Downwind
13 Tramps
16 Temptation, often
17 Gabriel to Mary: "Elisabeth, she hath also conceived a son in her old ___" (Luke 1:36)
18 How Gabriel might respond if you said 1 Across
19 Gabriel's message, Part 1 (Luke 1:28) (3 wds.)
23 It came to ___: KJV for "when"
24 "Fear not" are words Gabriel would use and ___

25 Pasty glue
29 13th letter of the Greek alphabet
30 Gabriel's promise: "The Lord ___ ___ ___" (Luke 1:28) (3 wds.)
33 ___ voyage (Fr.)
36 Mary and Joseph would ___ Jesus (Luke 1:80)
37 Sports org.
38 Press
40 After His resurrection, Jesus did this with His disciples (Luke 24:43)
41 Design process (2 wds.)
44 Fashionable
45 Post-jail sentence
46 Gabriel's message, Part 2 (Luke 1:28)

50 Car rental agency
52 Joseph might have been doing this during Jesus' birth if Nikon had been around (2 wds.)
58 Cuisine choice
59 Parents should not be this (Prov. 23:13)
60 Connection
61 Wildebeest location
62 Kind of messenger Gabriel was
63 Herodias's daughter needed one (Matt. 14:6)
64 Grizzly bear state (abbr.)
65 Daniel and lions met here (Dan. 6:16)
66 Gabriel's message, Part 3 (Luke 1:28)

DOWN

1 Never do this to Gabriel!
2 Astronomer Sagan
3 "Jealousy is the ___ of a man" (Prov. 6:34)
4 Card series
5 U.K. politician (abbr.)
6 Puts on, KJV style
7 Impressionist painter
8 Huldah was one (2 Kings 22:14)
9 Popularity
10 Sackcloth mate
13 "We should be saved. . .from the hand of all that ___ us" (Luke 1:71)

14 Pacific tourist destination
15 Reuben, Judah, and Simon (abbr.)
20 "They ___ upon him" (Matt. 27:30)
21 "The charity of every one of you all toward ___ other aboundeth" (2 Thess. 1:3)
22 God's Word is this
25 Space station
26 Paul and shipmates were this in a storm (Acts 27:15)
27 Pakistani valley in the news
28 A good soldier of Christ does not do this (2 Tim. 2:3)

29 Rebekah put goat skins on Jacob's (Gen. 27:16)
31 Jacob to Esau
32 Movie 2001's talking computer
33 100 cents in Ethiopia
34 You can fiddle with its middle
35 Gabriel's time in France
39 Bethlehem to Jerusalem (dir.)
41 Angel to shepherds: "This shall be a ___ unto you" (Luke 2:12)
42 ___ and span

43 Mary "___ in her mind what manner of salutation this should be" (Luke 1:29)

46 "The king had ___ ___ a navy of Tharshish" (1 Kings 10:22) (2 wds.)

47 What place God needs to have in your life (Matt. 6:33)

48 Mary was this with Gabriel's message (Luke 1:38)

49 Little girl in Cancun

50 "Kings of armies did flee ___" (Ps. 68:12)

51 Harpy

53 Gabriel's tidings (Luke 1:19)

54 Gabriel was "sent to speak ___" Zacharias (Luke 1:19)

55 Range

56 "They shall fall by the ___ of the sword" (Luke 21:24)

57 "We have ___ his star in the east" (Matt. 2:2)

58 Fido's org.

63 Jericho to Jerusalem (dir.)

twenty-seven

GIDEON:
GOD'S MAN OF VALOR

by Laura Lisle

ACROSS

1 Recedes
5 Inflexible
10 Mountain Time (abbr.)
13 Japanese dress
14 Mockery
15 Soft white cheese
16 "Upon the ___ of the rock" (Job 39:28)
17 "___ be unto thee; fear not" (Judg. 6:23)
18 Consumer
19 Sixth tribe of Israel (abbr.)
21 Gideon's job (Judg. 6:11)
23 Teaspoon (abbr.)
26 "He shall be cast into the ___ of lions" (Dan. 6:7)
28 "The ___ shall not always be forgotten" (Ps. 9:18)
29 It might fall on your head

32 These should be redeemed (Num. 3:48) (pl.)
33 Hyundai is one
34 Author of Acts (Philem. 1:24)(Gr.)
36 "Cast him into the ___ of ground" (2 Kings 9:26)
37 Deborah's right-hand man
38 Syllables used in songs (2 wds.)
42 Drop
43 "The children of Israel did ___" (Judg. 2:11)
44 Midianite prince who lost his head
46 Network
49 Trims
51 "Let all thy wants ___ upon me" (Judg. 19:20)

52 "Gideon went up by the ___ of them" (Judg. 8:11)
53 "I ___ not my heart from any joy" (Eccl. 2:10)
57 ___ Lanka
59 Reverberate
60 Bullwinkle is one
62 She follows Judges
66 "There was no such ___ done" (Judg. 19:30)
67 Lawn tool
68 Paul's mission field ___ Minor
69 "A people that do ___ in their heart" (Ps. 95:10)
70 Sleep disorder
71 Dozes

DOWN

1 Keyboard component
2 It reaches from end to end (Ex. 26:28)
3 Lingerie
4 "Shew me a ___ that thou talkest with me" (Judg. 6:17)
5 Jack the ___
6 Wrath
7 "And one ___ for a sin offering" (Num. 29:38)
8 Give 'em an ___, they want a mile
9 Lydia's profession (Acts 16:14)

10 Joins together
11 Trusty horse
12 "I will ___ until thou come again" (Judg. 6:18)
15 Stuck together
20 "___ to your faith virtue" (2 Peter 1:5)
22 "All the ___ of the world shall remember" (Ps. 22:27)
23 "Let it become a ___" (Ps. 69:22)
24 First king of Israel
25 Falafel holder
27 Mr. Ryan

30 "Israel remembered ___ the Lord their God" (Judg. 8:34)
31 Jewish holiday (Est. 9:26)
32 Tree where Gideon met the angel of the Lord (Judg. 6:11)
35 Biblical ground transportation
37 Baby essential
38 "Many are called, but ___ are chosen" (Matt. 22:14)
39 Assert
40 Italian money
41 Alcoholic (slang)
42 Interlock

44 Psalmist's instrument
45 Gideon's was made of gold
47 Canaanite killed by Deborah
48 Samson to his father: "Get ___ for me" (Judg. 14:3)
49 Swedish citizen
50 Kinder

54 Mrs. Peel
55 Ice-skating maneuver
56 "I will break ___ this tower" (Judg. 8:9)
58 Cyrus's kingdom today (Ezra 1:1)

61 "___ there come people down by the middle of the land" (Judg. 9:37)
63 America (abbr.)
64 Part of ear to be anointed (Lev. 14:17)
65 Owns

HAGAR:
THE OTHER WIFE

by Laura Lisle

ACROSS

1 Nebraska city
6 "___ the right, O Lord" (Ps. 17:1)
10 What to do with swaddling (Luke 2:7)
14 Ishmael dwelt here (Gen. 21:21)
15 Loops' location (Ex. 26:5)
16 Drag (Luke 12:58)
17 Concerning
18 Mystery "hid from ___" (Col. 1:26)
19 Woodwind
20 "I will ___ on softly" (Gen. 33:14)
21 Interfere
22 "___ shall be thy name" (Gen. 35:10)
24 Hagar's job (Gen. 16:2)

26 Grown-ups
27 "Enter ye in at the ___ gate" (Matt. 7:13)
30 Blunder
31 Possessive pronoun
32 Constellation near Taurus
33 ___ Lanka
36 Root beer brand (3 wds.)
37 "Fools ___ for want of wisdom" (Prov. 10:21)
38 Ishmael's brother (Gen. 25:9)
40 "___ me come unto thee" (Matt. 14:28)
41 Relating to birds
43 "Is he a homeborn ___?" (Jer. 2:14)
44 Change direction
45 Stowed
46 Capital of Lesotho

49 "Son of man ___ suffer" (Mark 8:31)
50 Ladies' bow
51 Number of years Abram dwelt in Canaan (Gen. 16:3)
52 Slaps
56 Opera solo
57 Entice
59 In advance, as in Rom. 9:23
60 "I am the first and the ___" (Rev. 1:17)
61 Widows might be (1 Tim. 5:13)
62 Private teacher
63 "I ___ from the face of my mistress" (Gen. 16:8)
64 Heavenly pavement (Rev. 21:21)
65 Thrill

DOWN

1 Australian export
2 Lion's hair
3 Region
4 Hagar, "Sarah's ___" (Gen. 25:12)
5 Sluggard's example (Prov. 6:6)
6 "God hath ___ the voice of the lad" (Gen. 21:17)
7 Innovative
8 "The eyes of Israel were dim for ___" (Gen. 48:10)
9 Remnant (Neh. 11:20)
10 Spiral

11 Capital of Morocco
12 "Garments smell of myrrh, and ___" (Ps. 45:8)
13 Orange exterior
21 Joseph was cast into this for his first trial (Gen. 37:22)
23 Scrapes by
25 Radio signals travel on these
26 "I am an ___ in their sight" (Job 19:15)
27 Thrust
28 Siamese
29 "___ your heart" (Joel 2:13)
30 Monk

32 Goodbye (Fr.)
33 German region
34 Rant
35 Frosted
39 "Desire of the ___ killeth him" (Prov. 21:25)
42 Jumbo (2 wds.)
45 "___, stand thou" (Josh. 10:12)
46 Wall picture
47 "___, shine; for thy light is come" (Isa. 60:1)
48 Last worse than first (Luke 11:26)

49 The Lord "___ out heaven" (Isa. 40:12)

50 Abraham's meal (Gen. 18:8)

51 Plow the earth (Gen. 2:5)

53 Small particle

54 Ride horseback

55 Wizened

58 "Why make ye this ___, and weep?" (Mark 5:39)

59 John "___ the little book" (Rev. 10:10)

HAMAN
TRADES PLACES

by Laura Lisle

ACROSS

1 Wicked fall into (Ps. 141:10)
5 Country facing judgment (Ezek. 30:5)
9 Clang
13 Give off
14 Persona non ___
15 ___ mater
16 Banquet beverage (Est. 5:6)
17 Mordecai's garment material (Est. 8:15)
18 Ball of thread
19 Nut (2 wds.)
21 Vashti and Esther
23 Pod vegetables
24 Pitch
25 Sway
28 Role play

31 Hebrew 12th month (Est. 3:7)
32 "My life is ___ with grief" (Ps. 31:10)
34 A woman should "___ her nails" (Deut. 21:12)
36 Jewish days of fasting (Est. 4:16)
37 "David ___, and stood upon the Philistine" (1 Sam. 17:51)
38 "They shall ___, and not be weary" (Isa. 40:31)
39 Hook site (Job 41:2)
41 Wanderer
43 "At thy rebuke they ___" (Ps. 104:7)
44 "He appointed the moon for ___" (Ps. 104:19)
46 "Who can understand his ___?" (Ps. 19:12)

48 Mordecai's seat (Est. 2:19)
49 Removed as confirmation (Ruth 4:7)
50 Hebrew 10th month (Est. 2:16)
53 Wired for internet
57 "Thy ___ is as a flock of goats" (Song 4:1)
58 Lazy person
60 Extinct bird
61 Defunct football league
62 Month Pur was cast (Est. 3:7)
63 Leave out
64 Goliath's plan regarding Israel (1 Sam. 17:25)
65 Nerd
66 Give out a measure, as in Mark 4:24

DOWN

1 Mr. Gingrich
2 Ruler
3 Prong
4 More abrupt
5 What the Lord hears (James 5:4)
6 "He laid his ___ upon the Jews" (Est. 8:7)
7 Colorado tribe
8 Haman attended (Est. 5:5)
9 Warm-up lap (2 wds.)
10 French pronoun
11 Bible's last word
12 Kept in the heart (Heb. 10:16)
14 Ruth does this (Ruth 2:2)

20 "I ___ Mordecai the Jew" (Est. 5:13)
22 Large vase
24 Tattoo type
25 Adam's eldest son
26 Bye! (Sp.)
27 "I will ___ up a shepherd" (Zech. 11:16)
28 Cleans a hole
29 Monte ___
30 More accurate
33 Flat
35 "Salvation unto the ___ of the earth" (Acts 13:47)
40 Anxiously

41 What Esther required (Est. 2:15)
42 Take away the antlers
43 What Paul obtained (Acts 22:28)
45 Mordecai ___ at the king's gate (Est. 2:19)
47 Beryl on 4th (Ex. 28:20)
49 "___ thou unto the king" (Est. 5:14)
50 Thump
51 "At ___ and quiet" (Job 21:23)
52 Hit
53 Otherwise, as in Ex. 10:4

54 Where Jews departed from (Acts 18:2)

55 Redact

56 Be fond of

59 "Curse God, and ___" (Job 2:9)

thirty 30
HANNAH'S CHILD
OF PROMISE

— by Laura Lisle —

ACROSS

1 Trades
6 It may be gray
10 Carmel to Joppa (dir.)
14 Assistants
15 The ___ should bury their dead (Matt. 8:22)
16 "___ and female created he them" (Gen. 1:27)
17 Stupid
18 "There be now an ___ betwixt us" (Gen. 26:28)
19 Modern-day Persia
20 Actress Moore
21 Large computer co.
22 "Why ___ thou not?" (1 Sam. 1:8)
24 Defensive alliance
26 "Eli the ___ sat" (1 Sam. 1:9)
27 CSI data

30 "From thence they went to ___" (Num. 21:16)
31 Not urban
32 "We are thy bone and thy ___" (2 Sam. 5:1)
33 "___ with the dew of heaven" (Dan. 4:33)
36 Island greeting
37 "He that hath an ___" (Rev. 2:7)
38 Dry measure (1 Sam. 1:24)
40 Crave
41 "Christ must ___ have suffered" (Acts 17:3)
43 "Samuel ___ and went to Eli" (1 Sam. 3:6)
44 "As a ___ that is told" (Ps. 90:9)
45 To think
46 Is appropriate

49 "Hannah ___ up after they had eaten" (1 Sam. 1:9)
50 Roman stoic
51 Yang's partner
52 Rocket builders
56 Alabama's Crimson
57 "Their ___ shall be broken" (Ps. 37:15)
59 Aka buffalo
60 "Barzillai was a very ___ man" (2 Sam. 19:32)
61 "He that gathered little had no ___" (Ex. 16:18)
62 The pride of Vidalia, GA
63 Made of gold and silver (Est. 1:6)
64 Epochs
65 Stone on Aaron's ephod (Ex. 28:19)

DOWN

1 "He is risen, as he ___" (Matt. 28:6)
2 Hannah abstained from this (1 Sam. 1:15)
3 The first man
4 Elkanah's other wife (1 Sam. 1:2)
5 Nazareth to Jerusalem (dir.)
6 Seasoning (Sp.)
7 Enlarge
8 "She wept, and did not ___" (1 Sam. 1:7)
9 Cleaves

10 "Saul sought to ___ David" (1 Sam. 19:10)
11 "Gather up thy ___" (Jer. 10:17)
12 "By the ___ of God they perish" (Job 4:9)
13 "But Hannah ___ not up" (1 Sam. 1:22)
21 "That which groweth of ___ own accord" (Lev. 25:5)
23 Frivolous, silly people
25 Second-largest ocean
26 Equals
27 What Hannah does at Shiloh (1 Sam. 1:9–10)

28 "The greater light to ___ the day" (Gen. 1:16)
29 Canaanite chariot material (Josh. 17:16)
30 First sign of growth (Mark 4:28)
32 Senses
33 Stop!
34 This wind brought the locusts (Ex. 10:13)
35 Formal "you" in KJV
39 Cleaning feathers
42 Edible
45 Charged particle

46 Neutral color

47 "The days of thy mourning shall be ___" (Isa. 60:20)

48 The raven ___ Elijah (1 Kings 17:6)

49 Chances

50 Wound that killed Eglon (Judg. 3:21)

51 YMCA counterpart

53 Paul forbidden to preach here (Acts 16:6)

54 Chimney dirt

55 Green Gables dweller

58 Bashan's were made of oak (Ezek. 27:6)

59 It may be feathery or scaly

thirty 31 *one*

HEROD
THE TETRARCH

by Laura Lisle

ACROSS

1 Kingdom or state treasury (abbr.)
5 Child protection agency
8 "He maketh ___ to cease" (Ps. 46:9)
12 Against
13 Lures
15 Weapons of iron (2 Sam. 12:31)
16 Type of jazz vocals
17 Buick model
18 What Herod did to children in Bethlehem (Matt. 2:16)
19 Fortification
21 She wept for the children (Matt. 2:18)
23 How God spoke to Joseph (Matt. 2:12)
25 Con's opposite
26 Flare

29 Took Isaac's place (Gen. 22:13)
31 Desert plant
35 Designer Laura
37 Scientist playground
39 "And ___ shall be a sign unto you" (Luke 2:12)
40 "If any man will ___ thee" (Matt. 5:40)
41 Fiendish
44 "___, and it shall be given you" (Matt. 7:7)
45 Streetcar
47 Average work performance
48 Dress top
50 It's cut with a pruning hook (Isa. 18:5)
52 Roman number of Herods in the Bible
54 Tetrarch of Galilee (Luke 3:1)

55 Hind's mate (Song 2:9)
57 Heavenly messenger
59 Neckwear (17th cent.)
62 Waterways
65 Newsman Sevareid
66 Animals that heard the Good News first
68 Ivy League school
70 Given to Jesus to drink (Matt. 27:34)
71 It may be past or present
72 Send forth
73 Leer
74 "My time is not ___ come" (John 7:6)
75 "In ___ was there a voice heard" (Matt. 2:18)

DOWN

1 Musical syllables
2 Andes inhabitant
3 Wound in Jesus' side
4 Strong tower of Ps. 61:3
5 He ordered a census (Luke 2:1)
6 One who is slovenly, greedy, or gluttonous
7 Herod tracked it (Matt. 2:7)
8 Failure
9 Shaft
10 The earth will do this one day (Isa. 24:20)

11 Jerusalem to Bethlehem (dir.)
13 French province
14 Smack
20 In Isaiah they clap their hands (Isa. 55:12)
22 What stones might do (Luke 19:40)
24 Infectious disease
26 Times of denial
27 Women should not "___ authority" (1 Tim. 2:12)
28 "Nabal did ___ his sheep" (1 Sam. 25:4)
30 Jesus, the Son of ___

32 Seat
33 IT leader
34 "Saul ___ counsel of God" (1 Sam. 14:37)
36 Yelp
38 Apron top
42 ___ chi
43 Singer Leonard
46 "This is again the second ___" (John 4:54)
49 Impediment
51 Joseph's role in Egypt (Gen. 42:6) (abbr.)

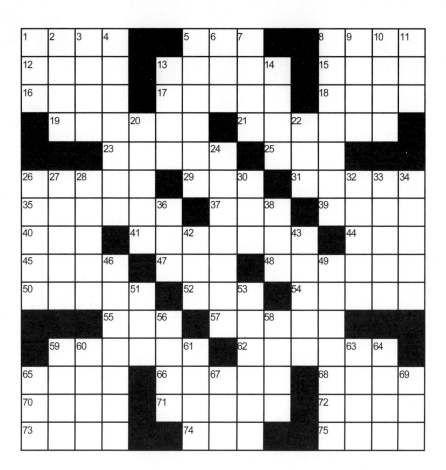

53 Herod Antipas's sin
   (Matt. 14:4)
56 Magi's origin
58 Open-mouthed stare
59 Where the eagle dwells
   (Job 39:28)

60 Rivulet
61 "___ rejoiced with exceeding
   great joy" (Matt. 2:10)
63 "Eli, Eli, ___ sabachthani?"
   (Matt. 27:46)
64 Western actor Pickens

65 Id's companion
67 Bethlehem to Jerusalem (dir.)
69 Seventh Greek letter

HEZEKIAH: JEHOVAH FOLLOWER

by Laura Lisle

ACROSS

1 "Is there no ___ in Gilead?" (Jer. 8:22)
5 Tides
9 China island: ___ Kong
13 Off-Broadway award
14 Saw logs
15 Nighttime (Gen. 19:1)
16 Samuel's role (1 Sam. 9:19)
17 Particle
18 Asian humped ox
19 Plasterwork
21 Hezekiah's water holder (2 Kings 18:31)
23 "My ___ is easy" (Matt. 11:30)
25 Egyptian delicacy (Num. 11:5) (sing.)
26 Christian org. for young athletes

29 "The LORD will ___ me" (2 Kings 20:8)
31 "Salute every ___ in Christ Jesus" (Phil. 4:21)
34 Coffee holder
35 Inches forward
37 Air (prefix)
39 "We shall also ___ with him" (2 Tim. 2:12)
41 "Lot is cast into the ___" (Prov. 16:33)
42 Turkish ruler
43 "They shall ___ as lions' whelps" (Jer. 51:38)
44 Cain's eldest son (Gen. 4:17)
46 Danish krone (abbr.)
47 Material of Heavenly gate (Rev. 21:21)

50 Remain
51 Yes, as in John 11:27
52 Gloomy
54 "A rod out of the ___ of Jesse" (Isa. 11:1)
56 Cleaner brand
59 Tombs
63 The king "___ his garments" (2 Sam. 13:31)
64 Disconcert
66 Shipshape
67 Word of sorrow (Amos. 5:16)
68 Tightly twisted
69 Attacked Hezekiah (Isa. 36:2)
70 Hiding places (Rev. 6:15)
71 Disciple nickname
72 "Rejoicing in ___" (Rom. 12:12)

DOWN

1 Springsteen nickname
2 Aid
3 Instead: "In ___ of"
4 Seat of gold (Ex. 25:17)
5 Bethel to Shiloh (dir.)
6 Pear type
7 Cooking technique from Luke 24:42
8 Senses
9 King who saw a shadow (2 Kings 20:10)
10 "I will pass ___ you" (Ex. 12:13)
11 Gaza to Joppa (dir.)
12 African antelope

14 Food cured
20 Musician Leonard
22 Four o'clock beverage
24 "Fly away as an ___" (Prov. 23:5)
26 God's anger (Isa. 42:25)
27 How beasts move (Ps. 104:20)
28 Senile
30 Rests against
32 The Lord hears them (Isa. 41:17)
33 Three-wheeler
36 What the leopard can't change (Jer. 13:23)

38 Gumbo ingredient
40 "They sang praises with ___" (2 Chron. 29:30)
42 More timid
45 Attention-getting
48 Hind's partner (Prov. 5:19)
49 Zambia capital
53 Batman's partner
55 Asian bird
56 Appearance of death horse (Rev. 6:8)
57 Persia today
58 "God called the dry ___ Earth" (Gen. 1:10)
60 Coffee alternative brand

61 Tap in lightly
62 Eye infection
63 A little bit

65 "So many as the stars of the
___" (Heb. 11:12)

HOSEA: THE LONG-SUFFERING SPOUSE

by Laura Lisle

ACROSS

1 Caribbean dance
6 Jewish calendar month
10 Chimney
14 Jacob's father (Gen. 25:26)
15 "___ not ye unto Gilgal" (Hos. 4:15)
16 Speech defect
17 Playfully romantic
18 "Not an ___ be left behind" (Ex. 10:26)
19 Beehive state
20 "Go quickly, and ___ his disciples" (Matt. 28:7)
21 Exacerbate
23 Self
24 Native ruler in Africa
26 "Moses ___ up the tabernacle" (Ex. 40:18)

28 Citizen of Libya
31 Bible teacher Moore
32 Epoch
33 They are bent to backsliding (Hos. 11:7)
36 "For as in ___ all die" (1 Cor. 15:22)
40 "God waited in the days of ___" (1 Peter 3:20)
42 Charm
43 Tubular pasta
44 "Man doth not live by bread ___" (Deut. 8:3)
45 What Esther wrote regarding Purim (Est. 9:29)
48 An age
49 "The ___ was fair and beautiful" (Est. 2:7)
51 Hosea's son (Hos. 1:9)

53 "Raw" color
56 May be a good or bad sign
57 Body sys. consisting of brain and spinal cord
58 Iraq river
61 Festive party
65 "Go, take ___ thee a wife" (Hos. 1:2)
67 Paul before Damascus Road
68 Absurd
69 "Surely he shall not ___ quietness" (Job 20:20)
70 Gape
71 Male honeybee
72 Flintstone or Astaire
73 "To abound and to suffer ___" (Phil. 4:12)
74 "He reproved kings for their ___" (Ps. 105:14)

DOWN

1 "I will ___ up mine eyes" (Ps. 121:1)
2 John's prison, ___ of Patmos
3 Goliath's coat (1 Sam. 17:5)
4 Hosea's payment for Gomer (Hos. 3:2)
5 Fall mo.
6 Where Achan was destroyed (Josh. 7:24)
7 Achor was a "___ of hope" (Hos. 2:15)
8 Old Testament prophet
9 Umpire
10 Winter malady

11 Liquid measure
12 Utilization
13 Israel didn't have one (Hos. 3:4)
21 "They shall not offer ___ offerings" (Hos. 9:4)
22 Part of the altar (Ex. 27:5)
25 Traveler's aid
27 Son of Jotham (Hos. 1:1)
28 Comedian Jay
29 Og's bedstead material (Deut. 3:11)
30 Israel served ___ (2 Kings 17:16)

31 "___ out all mine iniquities" (Ps. 51:9)
34 "The one ___ five hundred pence" (Luke 7:41)
35 "The fining ___ is for silver" (Prov. 17:3)
37 Carpe ___
38 Particle
39 Short
41 Prelude to Gethsemane (Mark 14:26)
45 Intermediary
46 Trees of sacrifice (Hos. 4:13)
47 "My beloved is like a ___" (Song 2:9)

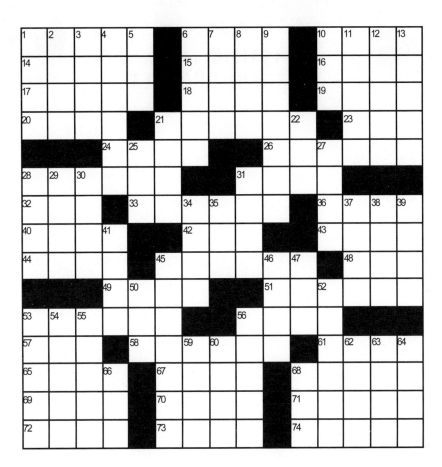

50 "Go to the ___, thou
   sluggard" (Prov. 6:6)
52 Goat or rabbit hair
53 Scratch
54 "The cloud filled the ___
   court" (Ezek. 10:3)
55 Perfume maven Lauder

56 Bread sacrifice type
   (Lev. 8:26)
59 Challenge to combat
60 "The sun to ___ by day"
   (Ps. 136:8)
62 Priest of Jeshua (Neh. 12:7)

63 Rahab "bound a scarlet ___"
   (Josh. 2:21)
64 Experts
66 "Honour the face of the ___
   man" (Lev. 19:32)
68 Savings accts.

ISAIAH: THE FAITHFUL PROPHET

by Laura Lisle

ACROSS

1 Wilderness tree (Isa. 41:19)
6 Fashionable
10 Connect
14 "The LORD ___ shall be exalted" (Isa. 2:11)
15 Crazy (Sp.)
16 Taboo
17 "Your hands are full of ___" (Isa. 1:15)
18 Prayer ending
19 Jainism believer
20 Half
21 "My heart standeth in ___ of thy word" (Ps. 119:161)
22 Phantoms
24 G-man Eliot
26 " ___ for ashes" (Isa. 61:3)
27 Hog side

30 "This people draw ___" (Isa. 29:13)
31 Painting prop
32 Jacob had 10 (Gen. 32:15)
33 Noah's building project
36 Diacritic mark
37 Shortened (abbr.)
38 Netherlands' capital
40 "Come down ___ my child die" (John 4:49)
41 "Unto us a ___ is born" (Isa. 9:6)
43 Musical composition
44 Adjust
45 "Holy One of ___" (Isa. 1:4)
46 His birth foretold in Isaiah (Isa. 9:6)
49 "___ us a son is given" (Isa. 9:6)

50 "___ good tidings unto the meek" (Isa. 61:1)
51 Licensed caregiver
52 Seraphims held (Isa. 6:6)
56 Rejoicing, "The earth ___ again" (1 Sam. 4:5)
57 Bearded or Japanese
59 Transitional state
60 "God hath spoken ___" (Ps. 62:11)
61 "Call his ___ Immanuel" (Isa. 7:14)
62 Askew
63 "He shall ___ his flock" (Isa. 40:11)
64 "Strain at a ___, and swallow a camel" (Matt. 23:24)
65 Sound or mega

DOWN

1 Taxis
2 Women's magazine
3 Gloom and ___
4 "The LORD hath ___ me" (Isa. 61:1)
5 "___ like crimson" (Isa. 1:18)
6 "Nails like birds' ___" (Dan. 4:33)
7 Groom's first-year location (Deut. 24:5)
8 "Out of whose womb came the ___?" (Job 38:29)
9 Coagulate
10 Green-skinned pear

11 "Shall the axe ___ itself?" (Isa. 10:15)
12 "Keep the ___ of the Spirit" (Eph. 4:3)
13 Thousands of pounds
21 Tree the carpenter planted (Isa. 44:14)
23 Most unpleasant
25 Diverse
26 Razor consumes this (Isa. 7:20)
27 Lavish party
28 Hideout
29 "Howl, ye inhabitants of the ___" (Isa. 23:6)

30 "Not many ___, are called" (1 Cor. 1:26)
32 "They shall walk, and not ___" (Isa. 40:31)
33 Water (Sp.)
34 Describes Paul's speech (2 Cor. 11:6)
35 Musical actor Howard
39 Cruelty
42 Muting
45 No room here
46 Chattering bird (Isa. 38:14)
47 Command the idol, "Get thee ___" (Isa. 30:22)

48 "The heathen ___" (Ps. 46:6)
49 Toppled
50 University instructor (abbr.)
51 Peru capital

53 Leave out
54 " Believe ye that I am ___?" (Matt. 9:28)
55 These were cast for Jesus' clothes (John 19:24)

58 "David ___, and stood upon the Philistine" (1 Sam. 17:51)
59 Canine retriever (abbr.)

thirty**35**five
ISHMAEL: THE OTHER SON

by Laura Lisle

ACROSS

1 Astronaut employer
5 "And ___ of the son of the bondwoman" (Gen. 21:13)
9 Small flute
13 Old Testament prophet
14 Groups
15 Carved image (2 Chron. 33:7)
16 Beasts' homes (Job 37:8)
17 Fastener
18 "Set me as a ___ upon thine heart" (Song 8:6)
19 Central African country
21 Ishmael's father (Gen. 17:23)
23 Salad type
25 Ninth month (abbr.)
26 Car speed measurement
29 Hagar "___ from her face" (Gen. 16:6)

31 Leaven
34 Yes, as in Ps. 23:4
35 ___-cotta (clay)
37 Object
39 Bird homes (Luke 9:58)
41 "Give ___ unto my prayer" (Ps. 17:1)
42 Incline
43 Female voice
44 Formal statements
46 Animal companion
47 "Thou God ___ me" (Gen. 16:13)
50 "The Lord hath ___ of them" (Matt. 21:3)
51 "Ye shall not ___ my face" (Gen. 43:5)
52 "Planted in a good ___" (Ezek. 17:8)

54 Restaurant
56 Haunted
59 Dryads
63 Animal out of the wood (Ps. 80:13)
64 Nineteenth U.S. president
66 Realm
67 Cleves or Aragon (var.)
68 "His hand will be against ___ man" (Gen. 16:12)
69 Far Side's Larson
70 Dye color (Ex. 25:5) (pl.)
71 Dried up
72 God opened Hagar's (Gen. 21:19)

DOWN

1 Zilch (Sp.)
2 "The people shall say, ___" (Deut. 27:16)
3 ___ of Solomon
4 Organizational group (abbr.)
5 "Go to the ___, thou sluggard" (Prov. 6:6)
6 Italian currency
7 Jabs
8 Unclean bird (Lev. 11:13) (var.)
9 Back of car swerving
10 Thought
11 What Samaria's king is like (Hos. 10:7)

12 Building extension
14 Useful
20 Eutychus fell from (Acts 20:9) (pl.)
22 Tharshish cargo (1 Kings 10:22) (sing.)
24 Where Hagar and Ishmael rested (Gen. 16:14)
26 Asian starling
27 Apple skins
28 Move quickly, as in Gen. 19:22
30 Empty
32 Red lights

33 Indian lodge
36 Bow-shaped
38 Assign, as in Ps. 108:7
40 Corns (2 wds.)
42 "Wherefore look ye so ___?" (Gen. 40:7)
45 Small
48 Distress call
49 Brought to the storehouse (Mal. 3:10)
53 "Therefore shall a man ___ his father and his mother" (Gen. 2:24)
55 "In the ___ of God made he man" (Gen. 9:6)

56 "The LORD is ___ out against me" (Ruth 1:13)

57 "His___ will be against every man" (Gen. 16:12)

58 Colorist

60 "I ___ thee, go in unto my maid" (Gen. 16:2)

61 "Behold, ___ am I" (Gen. 27:1)

62 Declares

63 Block

65 Before, as in John 4:49

JACOB:
THE USURPER

by Laura Lisle

ACROSS

1 Western state
5 Wise king (abbr.)
8 Musical symbol
12 "I sink in deep ___" (Ps. 69:2)
13 Brief witty speech
15 Jacob held Esau's ___ (Gen. 25:26)
16 Urgent request
17 Learner
18 "Fear not: believe ___" (Luke 8:50)
19 Baltic state
21 Brains (slang)
23 Rental car company
25 "The LORD shall ___ to me another son" (Gen. 30:24)
26 Part of the offering in Lev. 8:26
29 How the rich ruler felt (Mark 10:22)
31 Lettuce and toppings
35 Color between red and yellow
37 Ballet steps
39 Jacob's priestly son (Gen. 34:25)
40 Unrefined metal
41 Country bordering Latvia
44 Convert into leather
45 "Thou hast now ___ foolishly" (Gen. 31:28)
47 Isaac did before blessing his son (Gen. 27:4)
48 Cat food brand
50 Actress Hilary
52 Bookstore section (abbr.)
54 "I will surely give the ___ unto thee" (Gen. 28:22)
55 N.T. author, for short
57 Imitation chocolate
59 Jacob's new name (Gen. 32:28)
62 Jacob's favored son (Gen. 37:3)
65 "The truth shall make you ___" (John 8:32)
66 Legitimate
68 To maintain, as in Gen. 17:9
70 "Eli, Eli, ___ sabachthani?" (Matt. 27:46)
71 Jacob dwelt in these (Gen. 25:27)
72 Paul was forbidden to preach here (Acts 16:6)
73 Troop
74 Springsteen's "Born in the ___"
75 Shofar, as in Josh. 6:5

DOWN

1 Referee (abbr.)
2 Plow, as in Gen. 2:5
3 Region
4 "Among the ___, and I will sing praises" (2 Sam. 22:50)
5 Weightlifting exercise
6 "Get thee ___ of thy country" (Gen. 12:1)
7 "A false witness that speaketh ___" (Prov. 6:19)
8 Harmonic
9 "I have ___ him to the LORD" (1 Sam. 1:28)
10 Morays
11 "He shall ___ away as a dream" (Job 20:8)
13 "Grievous words ___ up anger" (Prov. 15:1)
14 Judgment seat (Gr.)
20 Brink
22 Spots
24 Southern Mexican Indian
26 Where God's people will sleep (Ezek. 34:25)
27 "Their tongue is as an ___" (Jer. 9:8)
28 Matador's passes at bull
30 Jacob's fifth son (Gen. 29:32—30:6)
32 Induct (2 wds.)
33 ___ -garde
34 Jacob's daughter (Gen. 34:1)
36 Shiloh to Jericho (dir.)
38 Drink slowly
42 Sticky black substance
43 Vehicles
46 "I will cause the enemy to ___ thee" (Jer. 15:11)
49 Isaac's wife (Gen. 24:67)

51 Soldier killed while in active service
53 Tortilla rollup
56 "Our hearts did ___" (Josh. 2:11)
58 Decays

59 Cyrus's kingdom today (2 Chron. 36:22)
60 Very large truck
61 Instead: "in ___ of"
63 Mexican money
64 Jesus, "___ of all things" (Heb. 1:2)

65 Winter malady
67 Body sys. consisting of brain and spinal cord
69 "A meat offering baken in a ___" (Lev. 2:5)

thirty 37 even

JAMES THE DISCIPLE

by Laura Lisle

ACROSS

1 "___ that great city Babylon" (Rev. 18:10)
5 Ancient Greek marketplace
10 "Ye ___. . .by works a man is justified" (James 2:24)
13 "Resist the ___, and he will flee" (James 4:7)
15 Small appliance maker
16 Cable network
17 Burning, as in Ex. 3:2
18 Type of offering
19 Sackcloth partner
20 Cable music network
21 Stuck-up person
23 Offspring (Matt. 22:25)
25 "Every good ___. . .is from above" (James 1:17)
26 James to Jesus (Mark 6:3)

28 Tyrannus led one (Acts 19:9)
31 Insolent
32 Constellation (Job 9:9)
33 "Receive ___ meekness the engrafted word" (James 1:21)
34 Unruly crowd
37 Crossing place in Gen. 32:22
38 "Weeping and gnashing of ___" (Matt. 25:30)
40 Musical instrument (Isa. 5:12)
41 Peacock partner (2 Chron. 9:21)
42 Vulture gathers with (Isa. 34:15)
43 Keyed
44 ___ of Olives
45 "A time ___, and a time to heal" (Eccl. 3:3) (2 wds.)

46 Home of the Braves
49 Emaciated
50 "And if children, then ___" (Rom. 8:17)
51 Horsefly
52 Greek letter
55 Suffix meaning direction
56 Shewbread sat upon this (Ex. 25:30)
59 Turn over
61 Is (pl.)
62 Seen at transfiguration (Luke 9:30)
63 Uncanny
64 Father, familiarly
65 Tear, as in John 19:24 (sing.)
66 Unhatched insect

DOWN

1 Eve's husband
2 Goat side (Matt. 25:33)
3 Tel ___ (Israel's capital)
4 What John called the elder (Rev. 7:14)
5 Monastery superior
6 Dig
7 Mariner's tool (Ezek. 27:29)
8 "Eyes of the LORD ___ to and fro" (2 Chron. 16:9)
9 Early church site (Acts 15:35)
10 Hide away
11 Pursue, as in 1 Peter 3:11
12 Anesthetic (arch.)
14 Leprosy scab

22 Football assoc.
24 Pig's home
25 Gift from above (See 25 Across)
26 Lure
27 Wife of Boaz (Ruth 4:13)
28 Divan
29 Prune, as in Lev. 25:3
30 "Labourer is worthy of his ___" (Luke 10:7)
31 Bitter's opposite (James 3:11)
34 Short
35 Australian gemstone
36 Hangs on priest's garment (Ex. 28:34)

38 Tight
39 Volcano
40 Dawdling
42 Creature of Lam. 4:3 (sing.)
43 This is hard to tame (James 3:8)
44 Endanger, as in Ruth 4:6
45 Anointing spot (Lev. 14:28)
46 In the lead
47 ___ firma
48 Covered
49 "___ them which persecute you" (Rom. 12:14)
51 Dressed
52 South American nation

53 Trim
54 Notion

57 Lager
58 Container

60 Vigor

thirty-38-eight

JEHOVAH: THE GREAT AND MIGHTY ONE

by Laura Lisle

ACROSS

1 Will come out of Jacob (Num. 24:17)
5 Try
9 Hungry
14 Coca-___
15 Scent
16 Sifter (Amos 9:9)
17 "Cast me not ___" (Ps. 51:11)
18 Judgment seat (Gr.)
19 Ms. Lauder
20 Deep sleep
21 Bahrain capital
23 "Behold, I ___ an Angel" (Ex. 23:20)
24 Romp around
26 Après ___
28 Business name ending (abbr.)
29 Pine
31 Cooking measurement (abbr.)
34 Pizza brand
37 Noah found this in the eyes of the Lᴏʀᴅ (Gen. 6:8)
39 Snack
40 "Even to your old ___ I am he" (Isa. 46:4)
41 Arab Peninsula country
42 Closes, as in 2 Sam. 13:17
44 "For their ___ is mighty" (Prov. 23:11)
47 Until, as in Job 18:2
48 Exploiter
50 Gov. agency responsible for food and drug regulations
51 Grown in a pod (sing.)
52 Best, as in Ps. 81:16
56 Ali, with 40 Thieves
59 Absolute ruler
63 Fasted's opposite
64 What the trumpets sound (Joel 2:1)
66 Raise, as in John 2:20
67 PC Security card (abbr.)
68 Types, as in Ps. 78:45
69 Ship part (Isa. 33:23)
70 Gas burner used in laboratories
71 "Thou God ___ me" (Gen. 16:13)
72 Prophet of Tekoa (Amos 1:1)
73 Not now

DOWN

1 Kerchief
2 The Lord is a strong one (Ps. 61:3)
3 Crockett battle site
4 R&B singer Charles
5 Southern crop
6 Eve's garden
7 Core
8 Trolley
9 Employ
10 Ending for Jehovah, meaning "Lord our banner" (Ex. 17:15)
11 Lavish party
12 Evening, as in Gen. 19:1
13 "A prophet mighty in __" (Luke 24:19)
21 Cooper automobile
22 Tree of Isa. 44:14
25 "I will make darkness ___" (Isa. 42:16)
27 Cask
29 "His ___ is not turned away" (Isa. 9:12)
30 Dorm dweller
31 "The tongue can no man ___" (James 3:8)
32 Former wound
33 Writing tool in Isa. 8:1
34 What Maaseiah kept (Jer. 35:4)
35 Patmos is one
36 Unusual (Dan. 2:11)
38 Cannot be scourged (Acts 22:25)
39 Jerusalem to Salim (dir.)
43 Take to court, as in Matt. 5:40
45 Exertions
46 Condense
49 Hypocrites' look (Matt. 6:16)
51 "Thou shalt see my back ___" (Ex. 33:23)

53 "God created the heaven and the ___" (Gen. 1:1)

54 "A precious corner ___" (Isa. 28:16)

55 Dallas dweller

56 Deep voice

57 Sweet-smelling herb from Ps. 45:8 (sing.)

58 Gave birth, as in Gen. 4:2

60 Writer Bombeck

61 Jesus' coat was without this (John 19:23)

62 El ___, TX

65 Montana time zone

67 Stroke an animal

thirty39nine

JEREMIAH:
THE GREAT PROPHET

by Laura Lisle

ACROSS

1 Agricultural org.
4 "Believe ye that I am ___?" (Matt. 9:28)
8 Eight ounces
14 He had loaves (John 6:9)
15 Entice
16 Discomfort
17 Israel did this (Jer. 23:13)
18 Volcano
19 Frightened
20 Terrier
22 Pouch
23 What the Ammonites did not have (Jer. 49:1)
24 "Before I formed thee. . .I ___ thee" (Jer. 1:5)
27 Bird's seat
31 Shut, as in Ps. 107:42

33 "___, though I walk through the valley" (Ps. 23:4)
35 French affirmative
36 Made in the ___
38 Word receiver in Jer. 9:20
39 Pixies
40 Unsurpassed to the present (2 wds.)
44 Uncooked nature
46 "The prophets prophesy ___" (Jer. 14:14)
47 Adam's wife
49 Nocturnal flyer (Lev. 11:19)
50 Hovercraft
51 Cut
52 "He maketh the storm a ___" (Ps. 107:29)
55 Earthquake
58 The Lord gives a pleasant one (Jer. 3:19)

61 This was embroidered for a priest (Ex. 28:39)
63 Pod vegetable
65 Small chapel
67 What a woman buys in Prov. 31:16 (2 wds.)
70 What Publius's father has in Acts 28:8
71 Part to dip (Luke 16:24)
72 What Simon did at night (Luke 5:5)
73 Curse
74 Israel to Babylon (dir.)
75 What Israelites were in Babylon
76 Used to write with (Jer. 36:18) (pl.)
77 Hebrews crossed the ___ Sea

DOWN

1 "The LORD, the God of all ___" (Jer. 32:27)
2 Comedies
3 Adept
4 A wager (2 wds.)
5 Hand-dyed fabric
6 Jeremiah's girdle material (Jer. 13:1)
7 Arrival time info.
8 Curse
9 Take off the lid
10 "Thoughts of ___, and not of evil" (Jer. 29:11)

11 Where watchers come from (Jer. 4:16)
12 "___ not vain repetitions" (Matt. 6:7)
13 "Thou hast ___ captivity captive" (Ps. 68:18)
21 Rainbow fish (pl.)
25 "Lift up thine ___" (Jer. 3:2) (sing.)
26 "Waters ___ the stones" (Job 14:19)
28 Paul's destination in Acts 28:14
29 Used to drink in Jer. 52:19

30 Snake speech
32 Greek letter
34 City of Joshua in Josh. 15:52
37 A woman's affirmation (Num. 5:22)
39 Inviolate
40 "___! for that day is great" (Jer. 30:7)
41 Fourth plague (Ex. 8:16)
42 Leah's son (Gen. 29:34)
43 This comes from the north in Jer. 4:6

45 Corps of women serving in the armed forces
48 Gov. agency for environmental regulations
53 Raider
54 Military branch
56 Short period

57 Disturbance
59 Mr. Ryan
60 Princes' state (Jer. 51:57)
62 Used a keyboard
64 Totals
66 Chopping tools (Jer. 46:22)

67 Daniel "___ no pleasant bread" (Dan. 10:3)
68 Herod's nickname in Luke 13:32
69 Roman number of doorkeepers in Jer. 52:24
70 Gov. agency housed in the U.S. Dept. of Justice

40

JEROBOAM: MIGHTY MAN OF VALOR

by Laura Lisle

ACROSS

1 Author Bombeck
5 Zero
10 Volume
14 Complain bitterly
15 "Come, let us ___ him"
16 ___ mater
17 Where Paul wintered (Acts 28:11)
18 Model
19 "Iniquity shall ___ her mouth" (Ps. 107:42)
20 Pickup maker
22 Tan color
23 "Dogs shall ___ Jezebel" (1 Kings 21:23)
24 Female sheep (Gen. 21:28)
26 Color of pottage (Gen. 25:30)

27 Iota, as in Matt. 5:18
30 Divide, as in Ps. 108:7
33 Ladies' undergarment
35 Flightless birds
37 Forms in which Jeroboam's story is told (1 Kings 14:19)
42 This animal chews cud in Lev. 11:6
43 Long time
44 Plow (Gen. 2:5)
45 Not amiable
49 Flexible tube
50 Presidential initials
51 "Thou shalt see it with thine ___" (2 Kings 7:2)
53 "Sing unto him a ___ song" (Ps. 33:3)
54 Pouch

57 Before, as in Ex. 1:19
59 Alias
61 Approximate date
63 Keillor and William Lloyd
69 Twelfth Hebrew month (Est. 3:7)
70 Tower
71 "Every ___ shall bow" (Isa. 45:23)
72 TV host Jay
73 "The ___ of thine eye" (Prov. 7:2)
74 Economics (abbr.)
75 "She ___ not near to her God" (Zeph. 3:2)
76 "Jeroboam ___ by the altar" (1 Kings 13:1)
77 Remove, as in 1 Kings 11:11

DOWN

1 Actor McCormack
2 "Be not ___ with thy mouth" (Eccl. 5:2)
3 Distance in Matt. 5:41
4 Tylenol's competitor
5 Southern Mexican Indian
6 Made of wood and stone (Deut. 29:17) (sing.)
7 "A time to ___; a time to keep" (Eccl. 3:6)
8 Paul's destination in Acts 27:12
9 That girl
10 Aram offspring (Gen. 10:23)

11 Jeroboam made his offering upon this (1 Kings 12:33)
12 Ascended with the prayers in Rev. 8:4
13 Flavorful
21 Elihu kin (Job 32:2)
22 Lotion brand
25 Ephraim to Shechem (dir.)
27 Son of Jehoshaphat (2 Kings 9:14)
28 Gulf nation
29 Territory
31 "___ Jeroboam built Shechem" (1 Kings 12:25)
32 Eat away

34 Hormone
36 Vassal
38 "He ___ of Jeroboam shall come" (1 Kings 14:13)
39 It slew a prophet (1 Kings 13:24)
40 Otherwise, as in Ex. 10:4
41 Killed
46 Belief
47 Stray, as in Ps. 119:118
48 Longed for, as in 1 Kings 3:26
52 Winter sport
54 Blanch
55 Helper
56 Bird of Jer. 8:7

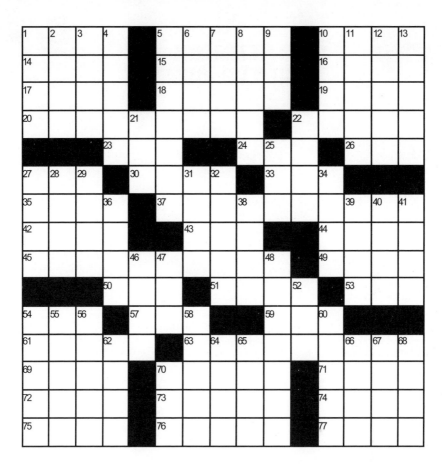

58 Where Jeroboam fled in
   1 Kings 11:40
60 Beggar
62 "Before the cock ___"
   (Luke 22:61)

64 Dog food brand
65 Rolled chocolate candy
   brand
66 "___ in three years came the
   navy" (1 Kings 10:22)

67 Glowing sign
68 "I will ___ rain upon the
   earth" (1 Kings 18:1)
70 Not (Fr.)

JEZEBEL: THE EVIL QUEEN

by Laura Lisle

ACROSS

1 Won't remove iniquity (Jer. 2:22)
5 Bobcat
9 Paul's fleshly messenger (2 Cor. 12:7)
14 Motor vehicle
15 Track
16 Cotton fabric
17 "Praise him for his mighty ___" (Ps. 150:2)
18 "World without end. ___" (Eph. 3:21)
19 "Let us lay ___ every weight" (Heb. 12:1)
20 Patterns
22 Pharisees did this to the weightier matters of the law (Matt. 23:23)
24 Pod vegetable (sing.)
25 The Lord will "___ his people" (Joel 2:18)
26 Ahab and Jezebel worshipped these

28 "___ painted her face" (2 Kings 9:30)
29 NJ neighbor (abbr.)
32 Worker bee
33 Jacob's pillow (Gen. 28:18)
35 Samaria to Jerusalem (dir.)
36 "Bread ___ in secret is pleasant" (Prov. 9:17)
37 Arrest
38 Offered with meat (Lev. 2:13) (pl.)
40 "I ___ no pleasant bread" (Dan. 10:3)
41 "___ the harvest, when the bud is perfect" (Isa. 18:5)
43 The Lord hears these (James 5:4)
44 Esau's color (Gen. 25:25)
45 All the poor man had (2 Sam. 12:3)
46 "Thou shalt not ___ the deaf" (Lev. 19:14)

47 "Immediately the cock ___" (Matt. 26:74)
49 "Why make ye this ___?" (Mark 5:39)
50 Elijah's resting place (1 Kings 17:3)
53 Choked
57 Halos
58 Manasseh put this in the house of the Lord (2 Chron. 33:7)
60 Air (prefix)
61 Tier
62 "The tongue can no man ___" (James 3:8)
63 Jael's weapon (Judg. 4:21)
64 Comforts
65 "Saul ___ David from that day" (1 Sam. 18:9)
66 Elijah rested under this in 1 Kings 19:4

DOWN

1 France and Germany river
2 That hurts!
3 Attorney (abbr.)
4 Defer
5 Alpaca cousins
6 Sweet potatoes
7 Samaria to Galilee (dir.)
8 One scared of foreigners
9 Characteristic
10 "Be not ___ in thy spirit" (Eccl. 7:9)

11 Leave out
12 "In thy majesty ___ prosperously" (Ps. 45:4)
13 "I have ___ to be baptized of thee" (Matt. 3:14)
21 Montana capital
23 Appearance
26 Angry
27 "She ___ upon the Assyrians" (Ezek. 23:12)

28 "They look and ___ upon me" (Ps. 22:17)
29 Cafés
30 ___ Lauder cosmetics
31 "Some more, some ___" (Ex. 16:17)
32 "Followers of God, as ___ children" (Eph. 5:1)
33 1937 Disney classic (2 wds.)
34 Spanish gold
39 Cocky

42 "He will keep the ___ of his saints" (1 Sam. 2:9)
46 "Jesus ___ a little child" (Matt. 18:2)
47 Bird of Isa. 38:14
48 The sun does this each day

50 Point
51 Island dance
52 Epochs
53 "Let fire ___ down from heaven" (2 Kings 1:12)

54 May be in first or park
55 Canal
56 Portion
59 "God called the light ___" (Gen. 1:5)

JOB:
PUT TO THE TEST

by Laura Lisle

ACROSS

1 "His ___ abhorreth bread" (Job 33:20)
5 One-celled creature
10 Jerusalem to Bethlehem (dir.)
13 Beautiful Japanese city
15 "Can that which is unsavory be ___?" (Job 6:6)
16 Boxer Muhammad
17 "Count me for a stranger: I am an ___" (Job 19:15)
18 Canned chili brand
19 Number of Job's children (Job 1:2)
20 First state in U.S. (abbr.)
21 "Lift up thy face without ___" (Job 11:15)
23 "Not ___ your liberty" (1 Peter 2:16)
25 Trade possessions
26 "My ___ scorn me" (Job 16:20)

28 Place of lodging
31 Soak
32 Contract
33 "He maketh peace in his ___ places" (Job 25:2)
34 T.B. vaccine
37 "American Idol" host Seacrest
38 "Upon the ___ of my feet" (Job 13:27)
40 Sore that afflicted Job (Job 2:7)
41 Extension (abbr.)
42 Brand of coffee alternative
43 Main artery
44 "Gat our bread with the ___ of our lives" (Lam. 5:9)
45 Hummed
46 Pre-Columbian civilization
49 "In his ___ remaineth strength" (Job 41:22)

50 Make joyful
51 "He shall not be ___" (Job 15:29)
52 Coloring substance
55 Pig's abode
56 "Who provideth for the ___ his food?" (Job 38:41)
59 "Let mine ___ be as the wicked" (Job 27:7)
61 Twentieth English letter
62 To be
63 "And their children ___" (Job 21:11)
64 "Times ___ not hidden" (Job 24:1)
65 "There is no darkness, nor shadow of ___" (Job 34:22)
66 Parent/teacher groups (abbr.)

DOWN

1 Put ammunition in
2 "Howl, ye inhabitants of the ___" (Isa. 23:6)
3 "But the eyes of the wicked shall ___" (Job 11:20)
4 Stretch to make do
5 Fable writer
6 First Gospel writer, familiarly
7 Airport flight arrival info.
8 "To ___ I am ashamed" (Luke 16:3)
9 "I will speak in the ___ of my spirit" (Job 7:11)

10 Soft shiny fabric
11 Starbucks' daily
12 "Gavest thou the goodly ___ unto the peacocks?" (Job 39:13)
14 "How much less shall I ___ him?" (Job 9:14)
22 VHS alternative
24 "The righteous ___ it" (Job 22:19)
25 Star Trek phaser setting
26 Small fencing sword
27 Toupees (slang)

28 "Thou shalt give him his ___" (Deut. 24:15)
29 Gold and "precious ___" (Job 28:16)
30 Type of jazz vocals
31 Hebrew term for hell
34 "Let the day perish wherein I was ___" (Job 3:3)
35 State your source
36 "The righteous see it, and are ___" (Job 22:19)
38 "Gray hairs are ___ and there" (Hos. 7:9)

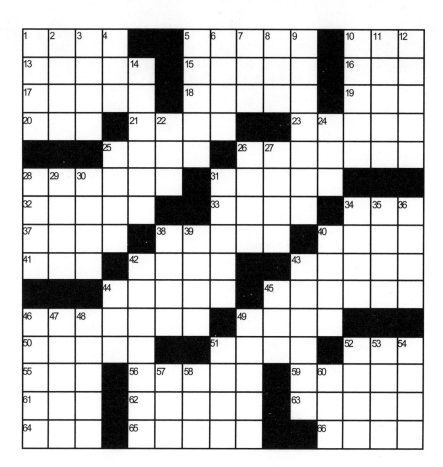

39 Newsman Sevareid

40 "Oh that they were printed in a ___!" (Job 19:23)

42 Tired: ___ out

43 Curved

44 "He maketh the deep to boil like a ___" (Job 41:31)

45 Wintry month (abbr.)

46 Saltine cracker brand

47 "He shall not ___ it, nor change it" (Lev. 27:10)

48 One to whom money is due

49 From the sixth to the ___ hour there was darkness (Matt. 27:45)

51 "My sinews take no ___" (Job 30:17)

52 Make an impression

53 YWCA companion

54 "I made a covenant with mine ___" (Job 31:1)

57 "Abimelech took an ___ in his hand" (Judg. 9:48)

58 Road to the cross: ___ Dolorosa

60 Quick sleep

JOEL:
THE MINOR PROPHET

by Laura Lisle

ACROSS

1 Refuse
6 "___ out the land" (Josh. 14:7)
10 Jesus used this to heal (Mark 7:33)
14 Foolish
15 Used for perfume (Prov. 7:17) (sing.)
16 Comedian Jay
17 "Who shall ___ him up?" (Gen. 49:9)
18 Lilies "___ not" (Matt. 6:28)
19 Cyrus's kingdom today (2 Chron. 36:22)
20 Women's magazine
21 "To the ___ first" (Rom. 1:16)
22 String
24 "That ye be not ___ shaken" (2 Thess. 2:2)
26 "Put ye in the ___" (Joel 3:13)

27 Dog star
30 Gasp
31 "I will ___ thee, O LORD" (Ps. 30:1)
32 Tropical fruit
33 Expression of surprise
36 They are like prophets (2 Kings 17:13)
37 "Neither shall ___ thrust another" (Joel 2:8)
38 Act of kindness
40 Cooking measurement (abbr.)
41 More loyal
43 Fairy-tale writer
44 "Inheritance may be ___" (Luke 20:14)
45 Israel's invaders look like these (Joel 2:4)
46 Astringent chemical

49 Rich man's fate (James 1:11)
50 Whalebone
51 Tree that languisheth (Joel 1:12)
52 Remnant
56 "Believe ye that I am ___?" (Matt. 9:28)
57 Where Paul wintered (Acts 28:11)
59 "They look and ___ upon me" (Ps. 22:17)
60 David made one (1 Sam. 27:10)
61 Christmas (Fr.)
62 Woolen cloth
63 Esau and Jacob (Gen. 25:27)
64 "Be ___ and rejoice" (Joel 2:21)
65 They are withered (Joel 1:12)

DOWN

1 Shrek
2 Says there is no God (Ps. 14:1)
3 "My face is ___ with weeping" (Job 16:16)
4 Tax man
5 Caustic substance
6 Locusts' past activity (Joel 1:4)
7 "Merciful, ___ to anger" (Joel 2:13)
8 Luau dish
9 Shouting
10 Slippery

11 Won't separate us from Christ (Rom. 8:35)
12 Absurd
13 Grasping tool (sing.)
21 Jesus' dad, to friends
23 Disaster due to force of nature (3 wds.)
25 Oil treated whetstone
26 Not as insane
27 For fear that, as in Amos 5:6
28 Iron tools (2 Sam. 12:31)
29 "But a ___ between me and death" (1 Sam. 20:3)

30 Window sections
32 Priests do this in Joel 1:9
33 Car rental agency
34 "Shew piety at ___" (1 Tim. 5:4)
35 God's are everlasting (Deut. 33:27)
39 Policeman
42 Corrupting
45 O.T. prophet (abbr.)
46 Banned
47 Appease

48 "Ye must ___ be subject"
(Rom. 13:5)

49 "The ___ is wasted"
(Joel 1:10)

50 Hook

51 The king of Israel seeks this
in 1 Sam. 26:20

53 "The spirit ___ him"
(Mark 9:20)

54 "Pharisees began to ___
him" (Luke 11:53)

55 Found in a lion's carcass in
Judg. 14:8

58 Solomon, to friends

59 Fast plane

44 forty four

JOHN: THE BELOVED DISCIPLE

by Laura Lisle

ACROSS

1 In ___ (together)
5 Oregon time zone
8 He walked with God (Gen. 6:9)
12 Char
13 Partly frozen rain
15 Ms. Aragon or Cleves (var.)
16 Restrain
17 Egg's fate (Isa. 34:15)
18 Idol
19 "Let us ___ together" (Isa. 1:18)
21 Trinity's home (1 John 5:7)
23 Wave offering (Lev. 23:12)
25 Jordan River to Jerusalem (dir.)
26 Last Supper room (Luke 22:12)
29 Hunted animal (Prov. 6:5)

31 Suffix meaning material-forming
35 Shred (2 wds.)
37 Sphere
39 Family-oriented health ctr.
40 Mad at John and James (Matt. 20:24)
41 Chewy candy
44 Disciples urged Jesus to do this (John 4:31)
45 Nighttime (John 6:16)
47 The Lord delivered David from this (1 Sam. 17:37)
48 Teeter
50 Tree product
52 MGM mascot
54 A pillar of cloud ___ the way (Ex. 13:21)
55 John doesn't write with this (3 John 1:13)

57 Cooking style in Luke 24:42
59 Type of sewer system
62 Mathematical conclusions
65 Crown of glory will not (1 Peter 5:4)
66 Woodworker's tool
68 Stringed instrument (Amos 6:5)
70 "Will of God abideth for ___" (1 John 2:17)
71 He will restore all things (Matt. 17:11)
72 Gospel singer Franklin
73 Beastly homes (Job 37:8)
74 "I write unto you, young ___" (1 John 2:13)
75 "He that was ___ came forth" (John 11:44)

DOWN

1 Super speedy transport (abbr.)
2 "Proclaim the acceptable ___ of the LORD" (Isa. 61:2)
3 "How excellent is thy___" (Ps. 8:1)
4 Folder
5 Two-dimensional
6 "For the joy that was ___ before him" (Heb. 12:2)
7 Virginia ___ University
8 Innocently
9 "Appointed unto men ___ to die" (Heb. 9:27)

10 Immediately, as in Matt. 13:20
11 "As a ___ gathereth her chickens" (Matt. 23:37)
13 Removed this in holy place (Josh. 5:15)
14 "Neither do I condemn ___" (John 8:11)
20 Express indifference
22 Poisonous snake (Rom. 3:13)
24 Ecological food chain (2 wds.)
26 Speak (Lev. 5:1)
27 Annoyance

28 Enclosed sections of windows
30 Sin, as in Ps. 95:10
32 One-celled water creature
33 Hot liquid burn
34 Spouses
36 Baby dog
38 Covenant sign (Gen. 9:13)
42 Last O.T. book (abbr.)
43 Salk's vaccine
46 Pliers
49 "___, let us love one another" (1 John 4:7)

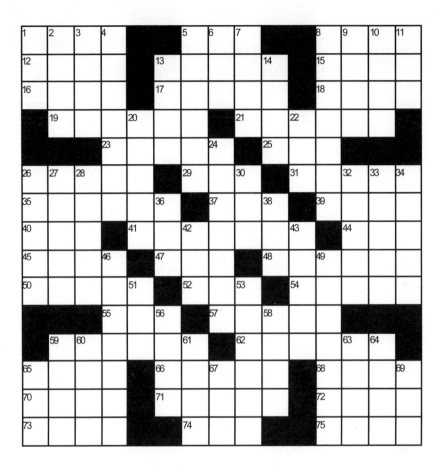

51 Fish holder (John 21:11)
53 Kin to fatherless (Lam. 5:3) (sing.)
56 Pharaoh's river
58 Mined metals
59 Jesus came "to ___ the world" (John 12:47)

60 Nod is east of (Gen. 4:16)
61 Sea after rebuke (Luke 8:24)
63 "It rained ___ and brimstone" (Luke 17:29)
64 Body
65 Nourished

67 "___ them about thy neck" (Prov. 6:21)
69 One with loaves and fishes (John 6:9)

forty-five

JOHN THE BAPTIST: FORERUNNER OF THE LORD

by Laura Lisle

ACROSS

1 Nazareth to Jordan River (dir.)
4 "___ them upon the door posts" (Deut. 11:20)
9 Resort
12 Frilly
14 He arrested John (Matt. 14:3)
15 "___ the sick, cleanse the lepers" (Matt. 10:8)
16 Woodwind instrument
17 Impersonating
18 Leave out
19 They trust in Jesus (Matt. 12:21)
21 Pacific current (2 wds.)
23 Joseph's brother, for short (Gen. 35:24)
24 Tyre to Jerusalem (dir.)
25 Mongolian desert

28 Disciple nickname (Matt. 10:3)
31 Tinter
34 "Thou art ___ the Son of God" (Luke 4:41)
36 "Give us this ___ our daily bread" (Matt. 6:11)
38 Fair weather color (Matt. 16:2)
40 Jonah did this with the fare (Jonah 1:3)
41 "...shall not live by bread ___" (Matt. 4:4)
43 Lion's voice (Ps. 104:21)
44 One (Sp.)
45 Baby essential
46 Trashy
48 Photographer Geddes
51 Animal home

53 "Winds and the sea ___ him" (Matt. 8:27)
54 Snake (Isa. 11:8)
56 Gov. agency for U.S. workforce
58 Afternoon nap (Sp.)
61 Keying in again
66 Hannah made for Samuel (1 Sam. 2:19)
67 Debris
69 "Am I ___, or a whale?" (Job. 7:12) (2 wds.)
70 Askew
71 Mordecai rode (Est. 6:11)
72 Stave
73 Light brown
74 Pledge (Heb. 6:13)
75 Lest, as in John 4:49

DOWN

1 Plod
2 "The ___ leaped in her womb" (Luke 1:41)
3 Economics (abbr.)
4 Large ocean mammal in Ez. 32:2
5 John's message (Matt. 3:2)
6 Rainbow goddess
7 2,000 pounds
8 Sword has two (Rev. 2:12)
9 Prefix meaning half
10 Creation feels this (Rom. 8:22)
11 Singing voice

13 "___ in my flesh shall I see God" (Job 19:26)
15 John ate this in Mark 1:6
20 Wading bird
22 Psychedelic drug
25 African nation
26 Constellation (Job 9:9)
27 "___ me come unto thee" (Matt. 14:28)
29 Seasoning (Sp.)
30 Tribe of Israel (Gen. 49:16)
32 Wear away
33 "Be ye therefore ___ also" (Luke 12:40)

34 Computer part
35 Charges
37 Affirmative, as in Mark 7:28
39 Not wet (Gen. 8:13)
42 John's mother, to friends (Luke 1:57)
43 "Will a man ___ God?" (Mal. 3:8)
47 Jesus baptized with the ___ Ghost
49 Mean-spirited
50 NY time zone
52 West Texas city
55 "Make his ___ straight" (Mark 1:3)

57 Additional, as in Matt. 5:9
58 Scram!
59 Hawkeye State
60 Make money
61 Highly unusual, as in Dan. 2:11

62 French "not"
63 The inhabitant of this can't escape (Isa. 20:6)
64 "Draw ___ with a true heart" (Heb. 10:22)

65 "Enter in at the strait ___" (Luke 13:24)
68 Fourth contained beryl (Ex. 28:20)

JONAH: IN THE BELLY OF THE WHALE

by Laura Lisle

ACROSS

1 Times
5 Moses' brother (Ex. 4:14)
10 Farming org.
13 Exotic bird
15 ___ Arabia
16 This should be made bare (Isa. 47:2)
17 Florida metropolis
18 Clean feathers
19 "___ Father which art in heaven" (Matt. 6:9)
20 Don't do this unto the law (Deut. 4:2)
21 Jonah's ride (Jonah 1:3)
23 Music used as practice
25 Fashionable
26 Counterpart
28 Jonah was this during the storm (Jonah 1:5)

31 Visitor from Sheba (1 Kings 10:1)
32 Pass time, as in Ps. 90:9
33 Beehive State
34 Ministry org. for young athletes
37 Side where Jonah sat (Jonah 4:5)
38 Called to fast in Nineveh (Jonah 3:7)
40 Stubborn Israel's made of brass (Isa. 48:4)
41 "Go to the ___, thou sluggard" (Prov. 6:6)
42 "Light of the ___ is the eye" (Matt. 6:22)
43 Test, as in Ex. 20:20
44 Crimps
45 Appeared, as in Acts 15:25
46 In abundance

49 "The LORD sent out a great ___ into the sea" (Jonah 1:4)
50 What the gourd delivered Jonah from (Jonah 4:6)
51 This ate Jonah's gourd (Jonah 4:7)
52 Morse code "T"
55 Confederate Gen. Robert E.
56 Famous potatoes
59 "___, go to Nineveh" (Jonah 1:2)
61 Found in a nest (Isa. 10:14)
62 Unyielding
63 Lowest point
64 Anointed part (Lev. 8:23)
65 A friend of the world is one (James 4:4)
66 Shamgar's weapon (Judg. 3:31)

DOWN

1 Poetess Lazarus
2 Insect killer
3 Learning institution (abbr.)
4 O.T. prophet to his friends
5 Savory jelly
6 Senior org.
7 Herbal tithe (Luke 11:42)
8 Keats' specialty
9 Wicked city turned good (Jonah 3:5)
10 Cake ingredient (Ex. 29:2)
11 Violent quarrels

12 "___ with thine adversary quickly" (Matt. 5:25)
14 Desired, as in Jonah 4:8
22 Philistines' injury (Judg. 15:8)
24 Lepers cleansed (Luke 17:17)
25 Penny
26 Not ins
27 "Sun ___ upon" Jonah's head (Jonah 4:8)
28 Before God's throne (Rev. 15:2) (2 wds.)
29 Length of measure (Ex. 28:16)
30 For fear that, as in Mark 13:5

31 Wharfs
34 Jonah "fled ___ the presence of the LORD" (Jonah 1:10)
35 Sheltered inlet
36 Reverent
38 Lock, as in 2 Sam. 13:17
39 Baritone Nelson
40 Manna "___" worms the next day (Ex. 16:20)
42 Campsite warmer
43 Scribe
44 Fixed charge
45 Man's title, as in John 12:21

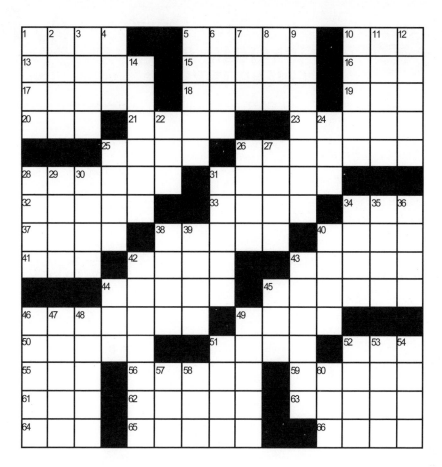

46 Metal tip on the end of a
   lance
47 Ragu's competition
48 Superior
49 *Toy Story* cowboy

51 Sudden fancy
52 Prank
53 Seven churches site
   (Rev. 1:4)
54 Fasted in Nineveh
   (Jonah 3:8)

57 Boom
58 Life, as in Job 11:17
60 Sin is filthy like this
   (Isa. 64:6) (sing.)

forty 47 even

JONATHAN: BEST FRIEND FOREVER

by Laura Lisle

ACROSS

1 Loads
6 Slice
10 "There is none ___ beside him" (Deut. 4:35)
14 Moses' brother (Ex. 4:14)
15 "A thousand ___ with Jonathan" (1 Sam. 13:2)
16 Complain
17 Military groups
18 Grown in Bashan (Isa. 2:13)
19 Went with Saul to Gibeah (1 Sam. 10:26)
20 Limited (abbr.)
21 Geek
23 Practical jokes
25 Jonathan's father hath troubled this in 1 Sam. 14:29
26 To plow, as in 1 Sam. 8:12
27 Stick fast
30 Bedcover
34 Bird of Isa. 38:14
35 Bird appendage
36 Edge
38 Avian homes (Luke 9:58)
39 Burnt offering (Ex. 29:18)
40 Expected, as in Luke 12:46
42 Jonathan would not do this (1 Sam. 20:34)
43 Where jewels may be (Isa. 3:21)
44 Start over
45 "What ___ thou, O sleeper?" (Jonah 1:6)
48 Hinder progress
49 Repetition (abbr.)
50 Type of jazz
51 Affection
54 Sharpen (Ps. 7:12)
55 Vigor's partner
58 Paul visited this place (Acts 19:22)
59 Afghan ruler
61 "___ my heart to fear thy name" (Ps. 86:11)
63 Tear, as in Joel 2:13
64 Walk through water
65 Gets up, as in Ps. 119:62
66 Long narrative
67 David did this to the lion (1 Sam. 17:36)
68 Inspections

DOWN

1 Jonathan's father (1 Sam. 13:16)
2 Trample, as in Amos 2:7
3 Waterless
4 Tater snack
5 Entangles
6 Jonathan gift to David (1 Sam. 18:4)
7 "___ us not into temptation" (Luke 11:4)
8 Stolen by Philistines (1 Sam. 6:18)
9 Ask in advance
10 Begin a journey
11 Elkanah was blessed because of Hannah's (1 Sam. 2:20)
12 Egyptians "___ into the bottom" (Ex. 15:5)
13 Where cherubim stood (Ex. 25:19)
22 Gilgal to Gilead (dir.)
24 "Esau ___ to meet him" (Gen. 33:4)
25 Days before Easter
27 Pimples
28 Pilate's wife suffered many things in this (Matt. 27:19)
29 Hurry, as in 1 Sam. 20:38
30 Animal, as in Gen. 8:19
31 Jonathan's son's condition (2 Sam. 4:4)
32 Rub out
33 Jezebel beautified (2 Kings 9:30)
35 Ringling ___
37 Measure (Mark 4:24)
40 Protective covering
41 David and Jonathan did this (1 Sam. 20:41)
43 Abdon had 30 (Judg. 12:14)
46 Naval fleet
47 Fishing essential for Peter and Andrew (Matt. 4:18)
48 Cast forth like morsels (Ps. 147:17)
50 Shakespeare's was tamed
51 Will hear rumors of (Mark 13:7)

52 Of glass in Rev. 4:6 (2 wds.)
53 Pharaoh gave this to Joseph (Gen. 41:42)
54 "Open thy mouth ___, and I will fill it" (Ps. 81:10)

55 Credit card
56 Detail
57 Benjamin had 5 times more (Gen. 43:34)

60 Minor prophet (abbr.)
62 Call off

JOSEPH: GOD'S MAN IN EGYPT

by Laura Lisle

ACROSS

1 Did well
5 "We cry, '___, Father'" (Rom. 8:15)
9 Tool
13 Favorite (slang)
14 Squirrel's dinner
15 Truth-girded, as in Eph. 6:14 (sing.)
16 Against
17 Infatuate
18 Run easily
19 Savor
21 Joseph's coat had many (Gen. 37:3)
23 Bowed to Joseph (Gen. 37:9)
25 Brass was used to do this (2 Chron. 24:12)
26 The trees of the Lord are full of this (Ps. 104:16)

29 Warm-up activity (abbr.)
31 "Shalt thou indeed ___ over us?" (Gen. 37:8)
34 Kimono sash
35 In worship everyone hath one of these (1 Cor. 14:26)
37 When Joseph dined (Gen. 43:16)
39 Found in sacks (Gen. 42:35)
41 Ball holder
42 Ephod stone (Ex. 39:12)
43 Eve's garden
44 Joseph's brothers "___ him" (Gen. 37:5)
46 Gideon's sign (Judg. 6:37)
47 Organic compound
50 "Midianites ___ him into Egypt" (Gen. 37:36)
51 Concord, e.g.

52 Tubalcain worked with this (Gen. 4:22)
54 Arabian Peninsula country
56 Saloon
59 Wields
63 Dream bovine (Gen. 41:2)
64 Less restricted
66 Sign of dad's favor to Joseph (Gen. 37:3)
67 Asa destroyed this (1 Kings 15:13)
68 ___ Park, CO
69 Metric weight unit
70 "Thou shalt ___ me thrice" (Matt. 26:34)
71 Stagger, as in Ps. 107:27
72 Herod "___ all the children" (Matt. 2:16)

DOWN

1 At a distance, as in Mark 5:6
2 Bird's home (Jer. 5:27)
3 "Ye thought ___ against me" (Gen. 50:20)
4 Jeans fabric
5 Low or high card
6 Pear type
7 Housekeeper's tool
8 Branched horn
9 Referring indirectly
10 "I stand at the ___, and knock" (Rev. 3:20)
11 Fastens
12 Timnah to Gilead (dir.)

14 Hates, as in Rom. 12:9 (sing.)
20 Soaked
22 "The Lord our God is ___" (Deut. 6:4)
24 Under, (poet.)
26 "___ evil beast hath devoured him" (Gen. 37:20)
27 "But his bow ___ in strength" (Gen. 49:24)
28 Trees in the desert (Isa. 41:19)
30 Two in Deut. 17:8
32 "Words of the wise are as ___" (Eccl. 12:11)
33 Scale components

36 Ditto (2 wds.)
38 Former Speaker Gingrich
40 Completely
42 Large whitish antelope
45 Gantry and Bernstein
48 Sin, as in Ps. 95:10
49 Shingler
53 Nordic
55 These were hardened (Neh. 9:16)
56 Wait
57 At once, as in Matt. 13:20
58 Measure
60 Annoy

61 Old wife tells one, as in
   1 Tim. 4:7

62 Store
63 Baby goat (Lev. 4:28)

65 Slippery as an ___

JOSEPH: FATHER OF OUR LORD

by Laura Lisle

ACROSS

1 Coffee (slang)
5 Turf
10 Santa's helper
13 Bad smells
15 Netherlands' capital
16 "Raven" author
17 Lloyd Webber heroine
18 May be barbed, as in Job. 41:7
19 "___ no man any thing" (Rom. 13:8)
20 Type of partnership (abbr.)
21 "Jesus was ___ in Bethlehem" (Matt. 2:1)
23 Caesar decreed that all should be ___ (Luke 2:1)
25 Mary to Joseph
26 "With the blood of the ___ of Jesus" (Rev. 17:6)

28 Broken bone treatment
31 Long, narrow boat
32 Awakened, as in Matt. 2:14
33 Pretentiously artistic
34 Not hers
37 Gripping tool
38 "___, and take the young child" (Matt. 2:13)
40 Wise men's home (Matt. 2:1)
41 Extension (abbr.)
42 Joseph, "___ not to take unto thee Mary thy wife" (Matt. 1:20)
43 Lily type
44 Chisel
45 Resurrection Day
46 Woman's sunshade (arch.)

49 Joseph told to "___ into Egypt" (Matt. 2:13)
50 Gives off
51 Fades
52 Witch
55 Drink slowly
56 Imbecile
59 Indoor football stadium
61 "Voice of ___ crying" (Matt. 3:3)
62 Stairway post
63 To be rebuilt in Amos 9:11
64 "Joseph, thou ___ of David" (Matt. 1:20)
65 "___ to God in the highest" (Luke 2:14)
66 Wicked men set one (Jer. 5:26)

DOWN

1 Old Testament prophet
2 Advertisement (abbr.)
3 Earth at creation (Gen. 1:2)
4 "Blessed ___ thou among women" (Luke 1:42)
5 British county
6 "___ them that are unruly" (1 Thess. 5:14)
7 Hence, as in Acts 10:30
8 "Their feet ___ to evil" (Prov. 1:16)
9 Herod's plan is to ___ "the young child" (Matt. 2:13)
10 Synthetic resin
11 Man to angels (Ps. 8:5)

12 Five loaves and 2 fishes ___ many in John 6:9
14 Texas river
22 Frequently, as in 2 Tim. 1:16
24 Daniel "___ no pleasant bread" (Dan. 10:3)
25 "There came ___ men" (Matt. 2:1)
26 Paul speech site (Acts 17:22)
27 Wager
28 Jesus "shall ___ his people" (Matt. 1:21)
29 Grand ___ race
30 "To save that which was ___" (Matt. 18:11)

31 Marker
34 Jesus healed them (John 5:3)
35 Patmos
36 Wise men's guide (Matt. 2:9)
38 Air (prefix)
39 Insult, as in 2 Chron. 32:17
40 "His soul shall dwell at ___" (Ps. 25:13)
42 Complaining
43 He decreed all should be taxed (Luke 2:1)
44 Flying rodent of Lev. 11:19
45 Tree of Hos. 4:13
46 Cents south of the border
47 Type of acid

48 Mature
49 "Body ___ joined together" (Eph. 4:16)
51 One who does

52 Noah, "___ of the righteousness" (Heb. 11:7)
53 New Testament prophetess
54 Pant

57 First state (abbr.)
58 Battle site ___ Jima
60 Track

50
JOSHUA: THE SUCCESSOR
by Patricia Mitchell

ACROSS

1 Come to ___: KJV for "It will happen" (Gen. 4:14)
5 Sign of despair on Joshua's head (Josh. 7:6)
9 Nonfunctioning smeller (Ps. 115:6)
13 Women's magazine
14 Dueling sword
15 At battle's end, Amalek was this (slang)
16 Joshua went ___ the mount of God (Ex. 24:13)
17 "The LORD said unto Joshua, ___ not, neither be thou dismayed" (Josh. 8:1)
18 One way to accomplish 19 Across
19 "The ___ of the LORD's host said unto Joshua, Loose thy shoe from off thy foot" (Josh. 5:15)
21 Joshua was one
23 Bard's before
24 Presented to the people by Moses, Joshua ___ the Israelites (Num. 27:22-23)

25 Israelites' loot from Ai (Josh. 8:26-27)
29 Joshua said, "How long are ye slack to go to possess the land, which the LORD ___ of your fathers hath given you?" (Josh. 18:3)
30 Deutsche ___, German railway
32 Sweet potato
33 Distribute
36 Southern states, popularly
37 ___ Lanka
38 Baseball glove
39 Rahab ___ ___ the spies (Josh 2:1) (2 wds.)
40 Jericho was one (Josh. 6:1)
41 Swee' ___, Popeye tot
42 Joshua was minister to him (Ex. 24:13)
43 Broadway awards
44 "Is there any taste in the white of an ___?" (Job 6:6)
45 John will not use these to write (3 John 1:13)

46 One of the watchers of Joshua's battle with Amalek (Ex. 17:10)
47 Bean
49 Joshua's dad (Ex. 33:11)
50 "Their works are works of iniquity, and the ___ of violence is in their hands" (Isa. 59:6)
53 "The people served the ___ all the days of Joshua" (Judg. 2:7)
55 Joshua's priest (Num. 27:22)
57 Israelites' dwellings (Josh. 22:6)
60 Mount of 2 Down
62 One of the Ten Commandments, e.g.
63 Ancient Greek marketplace
64 Stringed instrument
65 "I was blind, now ___ ___" (John 9:25) (2 wds.)
66 Star
67 Stravinsky's first name
68 Small amounts, as of paint

DOWN

1 The city of Gibeon "made ___ with Joshua and with the children of Israel" (Josh. 10:4)
2 What Joshua built at 60 Across (Josh. 8:30)
3 Land feature of 60 Across
4 Labor Day month

5 "How shall I defy, whom the LORD hath not ___?" (Num. 23:8)
6 Turn over
7 "The way. . .of the Red ___" (Ex. 13:18)
8 Period of time
9 Feature of a daring aerial escapade (2 wds.)

10 Horse nibble
11 Govt. benefits program
12 Vacation time in Versailles
15 Mississippi university
20 Bible fragrance source (Prov. 7:17)
22 Describes Achan as "all Israel stoned him with stones" (Josh. 7:25)

26 Poultry products producer
27 One of the Stooges
28 Burning incense ___ a fragrance (Gen. 8:20–21)
29 Fishing cord
30 Adder's threats to horse heels (Gen. 49:17)
31 Geometry word
33 A pillar of a cloud would ___ the Israelites to move (Ex. 13:21)
34 Reason "Jericho was straitly shut up" (Josh. 6:1–3)

35 Canned chili choice
36 Writing table
39 Hermit
40 Pro
42 White-flowered plant
43 Piper's product (Matt. 11:17)
46 Nutty tool
48 Extreme prefix
49 Cool!
50 Street of noted 1906 revival

51 Only he and Joshua entered the land (Num. 26:65)
52 Joshua's yuccas
54 Go-to place for a pastrami on rye
56 Sinai wilderness descriptor
57 What Simon could do (Acts 10:6)
58 Pharaoh's problem (Ex. 5:2)
59 Veteran's Day mo.
61 John the Baptist would eat one (Matt. 3:4)

fifty51one
JUDAH:
SON OF PRAISE

by Patricia Mitchell

ACROSS

1 Judah's older brother (Gen. 35:23)
5 Flustered responder to Peter's knock (Acts 12:13–14)
10 Slightly open
14 The brothers saw their treatment of Joseph as one (Gen. 42:21)
15 Judah's reaction when the cup was found in Benjamin's sack (Gen. 44:16)
16 Make again
17 Tamar's attitude, in a way (Gen. 38:25)
18 County in Ireland
19 Joseph made his steward do this to his brothers' sacks (Gen. 44:1)
20 Ceased
22 Benjamin was framed as one of these (Gen. 44:12)
24 Game ref.
25 Judah's sister (Gen. 30:20–21)

27 People like the praying Pharisee (Luke 18:11)
29 With 39 Down, Judah's feelings after he saw Tamar's evidence (Gen. 38:24–26)
32 "The ___ of our house are cedar" (Song 1:17)
35 Reuben was this when he returned to Joseph's pit (Gen. 37:29)
38 Lot's wife would ___ behind, become pillar of salt (Gen. 19:26)
39 Celtic language
40 Before (poet.)
41 Rifle (2 wds.)
43 Time of the patriarchs, e.g.
44 Pineapples in 70 Across
46 French vote
47 Last word in prayer
48 Disband (Brit.)
49 Synthetic fiber

51 Article of Tamar's evidence (Gen. 38:25)
54 Speaking to Eve, Satan would ___ the truth, as in Gen. 3:5
57 Topper
59 Tamar does this to Judah in Gen. 38:25 (slang)
62 RMNP destination
64 Judah's was to sell Joseph to the Ishmeelites (Gen. 37:27)
66 Whimsical
68 British nobleman
69 Popular potted plant
70 German city
71 Joseph to his brothers: Bring your youngest brother, or ___! (Gen. 42:20)
72 Institution (abbr.)
73 Jacob's cuisines (Gen. 25:34)
74 Judah thought to kill Joseph was a bad one (Gen. 37:26)

DOWN

1 What the hind's feet might do (Ps. 18:33)
2 Do not do this to God's Word (Rev. 22:19)
3 Rigoletto composer
4 Describes the brothers' feelings entering Joseph's house (Gen. 44:14)
5 Record label datum
6 "Has" in Scotland (dial.)
7 Judah's son (Gen. 38:4)

8 Bits (dial.)
9 Thieving member of Judah's tribe (Josh. 7:1)
10 Rainbow shape
11 City of Judah (Josh. 15:63)
12 First name
13 Frolic
21 La-de-___
23 Police box in Tokyo
26 Headgear for Gabriel and Michael

28 Bonnet dweller, at times
30 Judah was one
31 The brothers would ___ ___ each other in their plot against Joseph (Gen. 37:20) (2 wds.)
33 Eventually, the brothers found themselves in a ___ of remorse, as in Gen. 44:18
34 Look over

35 Judah took the ___ in entering Goshen (Gen. 46:28)
36 "Rule, Britannia!" composer
37 Truck drivers, often
39 See 29 Across
41 Judah's granddad (Gen. 29:16)
42 Gal's pal
45 Ten Commandments word
47 Flavoring mentioned by Jesus (Matt. 23:23)

50 The brothers would ___ Jacob an explanation for Joseph's absence plotted in Gen. 37:20
52 Joseph's coat does this if washed in hot water? (Gen. 37:3)
53 Er's position among Judah's sons (Gen. 38:3-5)
55 Kept over, manna turned worse than this (Ex. 16:20)
56 Describes Joseph's questions to his brothers (Gen. 44:15)

57 Record player, sometimes
58 Yemeni gulf
60 "___ his life for my sake" (Matt. 16:25)
61 "Er. . .was wicked. . .and the Lord ___ him" (Gen. 38:7)
63 Bob follower
65 Insect commended for foresight (Prov. 30:25)
67 Lancaster PA airport code

fifty 52 two
JUDAS ISCARIOT: THE BETRAYER

by Patricia Mitchell

ACROSS

1 Connery of Bond fame
5 Noah's float
8 Those who "gnash the teeth" might do this, too (Lam. 2:16)
12 Tropical tubers
14 Caesar's seven
15 Clearly, Jesus was not preparing this (John 21:9)
16 Judas to Jesus (Matt. 26:25) (3 wds.)
17 Greek goddess of dawn
18 Judas' money, he thought (Matt. 27:3)
19 Hotel arrangement, for short
20 Aim of Simon Peter's sword (John 18:10)
22 Concorde was one
24 Bravo in Toledo
25 Vivien of Scarlett fame
27 Civil rights org.
29 "If thou hadst ___ here" (John 11:21)

31 "Judas then, having received a ___ of men" (John 18:3)
32 Peter could not do this (Matt. 14:30)
35 To avoid one, Judas identified Jesus (Matt. 26:48) (2 wds.)
37 Jesus identified the soldiers held ___ Him in Matt. 26:57
41 Novelist McEwan
42 Hiram's evergreen gift to Solomon (1 Kings 5:10)
43 "Saw we thee an hungred, and ___ thee?" (Matt. 25:37)
44 Asian starling
46 "O death, where is thy ___?" (1 Cor. 15:55)
48 Chief priests, to hear Judas's proposal (Mark 14:11)
49 Chief priests "sought to ___" Jesus (John 5:16)
51 StarKist fish
53 Very, in music
55 Señora's diacritic

58 Judas would ___ for death rather than repentance (Matt. 27:5)
59 Kansas City summer hour
61 Sodom and Gomorrah were reduced to this (Gen. 19:28)
62 Series ender, often
64 Judas's reaction to see Jesus condemned, maybe (Matt. 27:3)
66 "The sucking child shall play on the hole of the ___" (Isa. 11:8)
68 Jesus' answer to the soldiers (John 18:5) (3 wds.)
70 Daniel's den dwellers (Dan. 6:16)
71 Two in Acapulco
72 Architect Frank ___ Wright
73 Chances of winning
74 Sailed with the navy of Tarshish (2 Chron. 9:21) (sing.)
75 Paul and Barnabas's sailing destination, e.g. (Acts. 13:4)

DOWN

1 "That thou ___ up the gift of God" (2 Tim. 1:6)
2 Artist's item
3 "There shall ___ false Christs" (Matt. 24:24)
4 Modern response to a statement like: "Judas was a nice guy."
5 Jesus would ___, "Thou hast said" (Matt. 26:25)
6 River (Sp.)

7 Judas, betrayest thou the Son of man with a ___?" (Luke 22:48)
8 Jitney
9 Org.
10 Judah: "A lion's ___" (Gen. 49:9)
11 Some ice creams
13 "Draw thee waters for the ___" (Nah. 3:14)
15 "Then entered ___ into Judas" (Luke 22:3)

21 "___, excuse me."
23 Crackle and Pop's pal
26 Computer corp.
28 There was one in the garden when Judas arrived (John 18:4–6)
30 Cool
31 O.T. offerings, often
32 Alike, for short
33 Jesus said, "I am the ___, the truth, and the life" (John 14:6)

34 "There was no room for them in the ___" (Luke 2:7)

36 One dozen, to Felix, the Roman governor (Acts. 23:24)

38 Football assoc.

39 Beverage Pharisees could have made with mint (Luke 11:42)

40 Of the twelve disciples, Judas made himself the ___ man out

45 "An ___ tied" (Matt. 21:2)

46 Jesus to Judas: "Thou hast ___" (Matt. 26:25)

47 Judas did not have the ___ to resist temptation

48 Goes with a guy

50 The Promised Land would have none of these (Deut. 8:9)

52 Nothing

53 Rose pest

54 "Judas also, which betrayed him, ___ with them" (John 18:5)

56 How-to exhibits, for short

57 Pre-1970s gas choice

58 Norwegian capital

60 Christian author Joni Eareckson

61 Church part

63 Judas would ___ his position among the disciples

65 Body coordinator

67 What Jesus gave to Judas at the Last Supper (John 13:26)

69 Last name in boxing

53
LABAN: THE TRICKSTER

by Patricia Mitchell

ACROSS

1 "___ an alarm" (Num. 10:5)
5 "Abraham. . .saw the place ___ off" (Gen. 22:4)
9 Cabbage dish
13 Flot preceder
14 Biblical accounts of the patriarchs, e.g.
15 Sour cream addition, perhaps (sing.)
16 The kingdom of God should be the ___ thing (Matt. 6:33)
17 Paul's physician (Col. 4:14)
18 Lazarus's sores undoubtedly did this in Luke 16:20
19 Laban to Rebekah (Gen. 24:29)
21 Jesus' disciples did not do this (Matt. 9:14)
23 There was no room here for Mary and Joseph (Luke 2:7)
24 Response to Laban's trickery in Gen. 29:25, perhaps
25 After three days, Jacob was ___ by Laban (Gen. 31:22)
29 Brooks are "blackish by reason of the ___" (Job 6:16)

30 Smile
32 Pronoun for Leah or Rachel
33 God to Laban: "___ not to Jacob either good or bad" (Gen. 31:24)
36 Laban "brought [Jacob] to his ___" (Gen. 29:13)
37 "Give me my wife, for my days ___ fulfilled" (Gen. 29:21)
38 Big ships are "turned about with a very small ___" (James 3:4)
39 Taking the gates of Gaza was one of Samson's (Judg. 16:3)
40 Samoan capital
41 LAX info
42 Isaac to Esau: "I am old, I know not the day of my ___" (Gen. 27:2)
43 Basketball player Olajuwon
44 What Laban and Jacob do at the feast in Gen. 29:22
45 God to Moses: "Rehearse it in the ___ of Joshua" (Ex. 17:14)
46 Basketball assoc.

47 A modest woman's hair should not sport these (1 Peter 3:3)
49 "Lift up now thine eyes, and ___. . .I have seen all that Laban doeth unto thee" (Gen. 31:12)
50 Jacob to Isaac: "___ and eat of my venison" (Gen. 27:19)
53 Racetrack activities
55 Oval shape
57 Describes the mob outside Pilate's palace (John 19:12)
60 A sinner does this
62 "Soldiers cut off the ropes of the ___" (Acts 27:32)
63 A craftsman ___ the doors of the temple in 1 Kings 7:50
64 De ___ : anew
65 "The waters thereof ___ and be troubled" (Ps. 46:3)
66 Laban tricked Jacob more than ___
67 Leah when she married Jacob, probably
68 Indian of South America

DOWN

1 Disney deer
2 Laban would ___ (Gen. 30:27)
3 God to Job: "Canst thou. . .loose the bands of ___?" (Job 38:31)
4 Balaam's donkey after abuse: "Was I ever ___ to do so unto thee?" (Num. 22:30)

5 Laban would ___ that Jacob had kidnapped his daughters (Gen. 31:26)
6 Rural club, the long way (2 wds.)
7 Noah's vessel
8 Shallow area
9 The archers' actions (Gen. 49:23)
10 Mary's cuz (Luke 1:36)

11 ___ Maria
12 Jacob proposed to ___ Laban's daughter, Rachel (Gen. 29:18)
15 Trigonometry term
20 Twain boy
22 12 Down went badly ___ for Jacob (Gen. 29:25)
26 "Descended in a bodily ___ like a dove" (Luke 3:22)

27 Scary

28 "God came to Laban the Syrian in a ___ by night" (Gen. 31:24)

29 "___ ___ hath sent me" (Ex. 3:14) (2 wds.)

30 Jacob chose "the spotted and speckled among the ___" (Gen. 30:32)

31 Judges follower

33 Jacob watered these of Laban (Gen. 29:10)

34 A decorative flower in Ex. 25:33 would have had one

35 Rachel would ___ Jacob when he saw her (Gen. 29:10)

36 He who has 45 Across, "let him ___" (Mark 4:9)

39 Laban gathered all the men "and made a ___" (Gen. 29:22)

40 Modern ID: Esau ___ Edom (Gen. 25:30)

42 Jacob and Laban's deceit ___ trust in either one

43 First murder victim (Gen. 4:8)

46 Mandella

48 Laban's invitation to Jacob: "___ with me" (Gen. 29:19)

49 Jacob to Laban: "Did not I ___ with thee?" (Gen. 29:25)

50 Shekel measure (Num. 7:14)

51 Laban's brother-in-law (Gen. 28:5)

52 Tank dweller

54 "Jacob ___ and called Rachel and Leah to the field" (Gen. 31:4)

56 Son of Merari (1 Chron. 24:27)

57 Laban lived long ___

58 Jacob to Laban: "What is my ___, that thou hast so hotly pursued after me?" (Gen. 31:36)

59 Laban and Jacob did not treat each other with this

61 "Asahel was as light of foot as a wild ___" (2 Sam. 2:18)

54
LAZARUS: A NEW LEASE ON LIFE

by Patricia Mitchell

ACROSS

1 Paul's interrogator (Acts 22:27) (abbr.)
5 Shelter for the prodigal son, perhaps (Luke 15:15)
8 Mussolini title
12 Island greeting
14 ___ Jima
15 With 29 Across, shortest verse of the Bible (John 11:35)
16 Not a consonant
17 Wheel tooth
18 Martha hoped for ___ ___ for Lazarus (John 11:21–22) (2 wds.)
19 Bethany to Jericho (dir.)
20 Jesus' sayings would ___ the Pharisees, as in Matt. 15:12
22 "The hole of the ___" (Isa. 11:8)
24 Lazarus does this in John 11:1
25 Jesus went to Lazarus's (John 11:38)
27 Place at which Lazarus sat with Jesus (John 12:2)

29 See 15 Across
31 Mustard seed (Mark 4:31)
32 "Love the Lord thy God. . . with all thy ___" (Matt. 22:37)
35 Sweetener, like the honey Jesus ate in Luke 24:42
37 Psalm valley (Ps. 84:6)
41 Samson's were strong (Judg. 16:29–30) (abbr.)
42 The Lord is not ___ with those He loves, Prov. 3:12, e.g.
43 Business ending, often (abbr.)
44 Roman bye-bye
46 Winds from the north (Job 37:9)
48 Graduate of 39 Down (abbr.)
49 With 68 Across, Jesus' words to Lazarus (John 11:43)
51 Martha served one (John 12:2)
53 Subway
55 Having wings

58 Disciples wanted to ___ Jesus' plan to go to Bethany (John 11:8)
59 Jerusalem to Bethany (dir.)
61 At the sisters' house, there would have been much (John 11:19)
62 Equine nibble
64 Sun Valley resort locale
66 "God shall ___ unto him the plagues" (Rev. 22:18)
68 See 49 Across
70 "Rejoice, because your ___ are written in heaven" (Luke 10:20)
71 Spy guys and gals org.
72 Apollos was one (Acts 18:24–26)
73 Group (abbr.)
74 Pronoun referring to Mary or Martha
75 Condition

DOWN

1 Lazarus lay in one (John 11:38)
2 Mary "rose up hastily" and others went ___ (John 11:31)
3 Jesus displayed this in John 11:43
4 Martha to Jesus: "Thou art ___ Christ" (John 11:27)
5 "A certain man was ___, named Lazarus" (John 11:1)

6 Number of Lazarus's sisters (John 11:1)
7 Exercise
8 Christmas mo. (abbr.)
9 Business as ___
10 Marie ___, chemist
11 JavaScript word
13 Jesus made it clear Lazarus wasn't this (John 11:14)

15 Osaka site
21 We're these for Christ (2 Cor. 5:20) (abbr.)
23 Maybe Martha wanted Mary to do this in the kitchen (Luke 10:40)
26 Tanner's tool, perhaps (Acts 9:43)
28 Baby Jesus' need, perhaps

30 Sheer fabric

31 Proverbs 10:23, e.g.

32 Joey sits in mama's

33 You may see one in 15 Down

34 Red, white, and blue

36 A fool might pull one (Prov. 10:23)

38 Jesus came so "___ men through him might believe" (John 1:7)

39 Chicago seminary

40 Naval figure (abbr.)

45 Halloween mo.

46 Book after Joel

47 People came to "see Lazarus also, whom he had raised from the ___" (John 12:9)

48 ___ ___ carte, menu choice (2 wds.)

50 You can fiddle with their middles

52 Moses held the brass serpent this way (Num. 21:9)

53 He who is "greedy of gain" (Prov. 1:19) might be called one

54 Tests

56 Light cake

57 Drunkard's companion (Prov. 23:21)

58 Girl (Sp.)

60 Jesus loves ___ of us

61 Twelfth month (Est. 3:7)

63 "Jesus saith unto ___, Loose him" (John 11:44)

65 "As a ___ gathereth her chickens" (Matt. 23:37)

67 Jesus knew "what death he should ___" (John 18:32)

69 Jesus "called Lazarus ___" of the tomb (John 12:17)

fifty**55**five
LEAH:
THE UNLOVED WIFE

by Patricia Mitchell

ACROSS

1 Likely in Leah's heart because Jacob did not love her (Gen. 29:30)

5 Rachel would ___ with Jacob over her barrenness (Gen. 30:1)

9 Transport for Leah and the family (Gen. 31:17) (sing.)

14 White fruit

15 ___ Major, Big Dipper locale

16 Leah thought she would ___ herself to Jacob (Gen. 29:32)

17 Laban and Jacob agreed not to cross a boundary "for ___" (Gen. 31:52)

18 Andrew's tools (Matt. 4:18)

19 Feelings Jacob believed Esau had (Gen. 33:1) (abbr./slang)

20 Leah's father-in-law (Gen. 25:26)

22 Leah did not ___ around Rachel's feelings (Gen. 30:15)

24 "Ye have made it a ___ of thieves" (Matt. 21:13)

25 Martha certainly put one on the table (John 12:2)

27 Strap for 9 Across

31 Mongolian desert

32 Bilhah's son (Gen. 35:25)

34 African antelope

35 "Who is a ___ man?" (James 3:13)

38 Transparent sheet (abbr.)

40 Jacob, when he discovered Laban's trick (Gen. 29:25)

42 Awry (Scot.)

44 Rhoda answered Peter's (Acts 12:13)

46 "Noses have they," but they won't smell these (Ps. 115:6)

47 Their covenant was meant to ___ the bitterness between them (Gen. 31:44)

48 "Scatter thou the people that delight in ___" (Ps. 68:30)

50 Stake

51 Luau dish

52 Leah's feelings to know she was not loved (Gen. 29:31)

55 Where Paul would have debarked in Perga (Acts 13:13)

57 They made Leah's heart glad (Gen. 30:20)

59 Of Laban's daughters, Jacob would ___ Rachel (Gen. 29:18)

61 Government dept.

64 Perhaps Leah's was pale (Gen. 29:17)

66 Chocolate substitute

68 Leah's dad (Gen. 29:16)

71 Leah's were weak (Gen. 29:17)

73 Pilate's 13

74 Buckinghamshire village

75 It was sown among the wheat (Matt. 13:25)

76 "If ye ___ to them of whom ye hope to receive" (Luke 6:34)

77 Describes Pharaoh when he refused to let Israel go (Ex. 5:2)

78 "Give me children, or ___ I die" (Gen. 30:1)

79 Jacob was on ___ to see Esau coming (Gen. 33:1)

DOWN

1 Rose bug

2 "We. . .do not ___ to pray for you" (Col. 1:9)

3 "Of ___ are we" (Gen. 29:4)

4 Writer Bombeck

5 In Joseph's dream, it bowed before him (Gen. 37:9)

6 Jacob thought Rachel ___ than Leah (Gen. 29:17–18)

7 Active

8 Perhaps Job did this as he groaned (Job 23:2)

9 "See ya!" in Assisi

10 Leah responded with this when Rachel requested the mandrakes (Gen. 30:15)

11 Pharaoh's cup, maybe (Gen. 40:11)

12 "To ___ from the words of knowledge" (Prov. 19:27)

13 Name for one of Daniel's denizens, maybe? (Dan. 6:16)

21 Head honcho

23 Oolong

26 TV network

28 Laban would ___ ___ Jacob with the promise of Rachel (Gen. 29:26–27) (2 wds.)

29 Jesus was this in the storm (Mark 4:37–38)

30 "Rebekah their sister, and her ___" (Gen. 24:59)

31 Computer expert (slang)

33 Intelligence agency

35 Summer stingers

36 Ice house

37 "The sons of Jacob came upon the ___, and spoiled the city" (Gen. 34:27)

39 The Ten Commandments

41 Twelfth month (Est. 3:7)

43 KJV yea

45 Some home decorators

49 ___-rac, zigzag trim

53 Communication method

54 Do not do this to one word of Scripture! (Rev. 22:19)

56 Series ender, often (abbr.)

58 Spies on (arch.)

60 Crown of life receivers must be this (Rev. 2:10)

61 Cooking method for fish

62 "Thou hast now done foolishly in so ___" (Gen. 31:28)

63 Laban to Jacob: "___ with me" (Gen. 29:19)

65 Green Gables girl

67 Shaft

68 Acid

69 One of the ship's hairy passengers (1 Kings 10:22)

70 Rachel's last, for short (Gen. 35:24)

72 Philip to Nathanael: "Come and ___" (John 1:46)

56

LOT: THE NEPHEW

by Patricia Mitchell

ACROSS

1 Lot's wife's lesson (Matt. 6:33) (Part 1)
4 Describes Lot's choice of Sodom
7 TV initials
10 St. Catherine's city
12 "These ___ the generations of Terah" (Gen. 11:27)
13 Milk mates, often
15 Scarf
16 Hollywood talent org.
17 Artist Andrew
18 Heat unit
19 Abraham did not ___ the Lord by pleading (Gen. 18:32)
21 To rescue Lot, Abram "pursued them unto ___" (Gen. 14:14)
23 Under brimstone, Sodom and Gomorrah would do this (Gen. 19:24–28)
24 Rachel ___ her father's idols (Gen. 31:19)
26 Holy Roman Empire's western border river

28 Salt Lake City site
30 Lot's wife's lesson (Matt. 6:33) (Part 2)
31 One of Lot's choices (Gen. 13:9)
34 The men of Sodom were not interested in these (Gen. 19:5)
36 Ally of Abram (Gen. 14:13)
40 Lot lived a long time ___
41 ___ Jose
42 Borrower's note, as in Ex. 22:14
43 Lot's wife's lesson (Matt. 6:33) (Part 3)
45 Men probably did this as they walked Sodom's streets
47 Lot to his sons-in-law: Go, or ___! (Gen. 19:14)
48 Paul was shipwrecked on one (Acts 28:1)
50 Cell body
52 "Samuel sent. . .every ___ ___ his house" (1 Sam. 10:25) (2 wds.)

54 Lot's wife's lesson (Matt. 6:33) (Part 4)
57 Moving mooer with Abram and Lot (Gen. 13:5)
58 Delivery co.
60 "The ___ was risen. . .when Lot entered" (Gen. 19:23)
61 "___ thee two tables" (Ex. 34:1)
63 Goliath wasn't one (1 Sam. 17:4)
65 Remains of Sodom, Gomorrah
67 The Lord would ___ Sodom for ten's sake (Gen. 18:32)
69 Letter stem
70 Abram didn't ___ with Lot over land (Gen. 13:9)
71 Weight unit for gems as in Ex. 28:18
72 Sea crossed by Israel (Ex. 15:22)
73 ___-time: Revelation's subject
74 Jehu's was notable (2 Kings 9:20)

DOWN

1 Like the flies of Exodus 8:21
2 A Nazarite's hair remained this way (Num. 6:5)
3 Besides Lot, Abram rescued his goods, ___ (Gen. 14:16)
4 How Lot's wife looked (Gen. 19:26)
5 Son of Jether (1 Chron. 7:38)
6 The men of Sodom were ___ in their sins (Gen. 13:13)
7 Lot's hesitation would ___ the angel's patience

(Gen. 19:22)
8 Makes bigger, with "up"
9 Our (Fr.)
10 One who is "slow to speak" doesn't do this (James 1:19)
11 Before wrecking, Paul's ship was this (Acts 27:14)
13 Lot ___ "flocks, and herds, and tents" (Gen. 13:5)
14 The men of Sodom were not this (Gen. 13:13)
20 "Worthy to open and to ___

the book" (Rev. 5:4)
22 It comes before Obadiah
25 "God. . .sent Lot ___" (Gen. 19:29)
27 It has 50 states
29 Angel to Lot: "___ thee, escape thither" (Gen. 19:22)
30 Classification in biology
31 Lot "seemed as one that mocked unto his sons in ___" (Gen. 19:14)
32 To beg the angel, Lot had

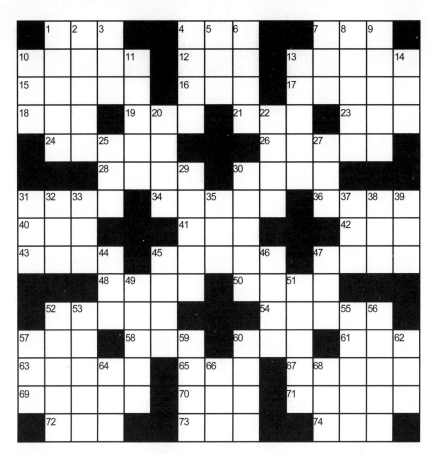

plenty of this (Gen. 19:20)
33 Abram to Lot: "___ we be brethren" (Gen. 13:8)
35 Lot's behavior in many instances would ___ his reputation
37 What was left of Sodom and Gomorrah
38 Aurora
39 Parsed by the Pharisees (Luke 11:42)
44 Surely the fire and brimstone created a big one!
45 What the prodigal son wasn't offered for food (Luke 15:16)

46 Meat alternative
47 Malchus's temporary loss (John 18:10)
49 What Lot's wife may have been concerned about (Gen. 19:26)
51 Capital of Belarus
52 "Wherewith the ___ filleth not his hand" (Ps. 129:7)
53 "Come. . .when he is not ___" (Luke 12:46)
55 "He spreadeth ___ pointed things" (Job 41:30)
56 Lot's granddad (Gen. 11:27)
57 Music choices

59 The Lord would ___ Lot, but he needed to leave Sodom (Gen. 19:20-22)
60 "Reuben said unto them, ___ no blood, but cast him into this pit" (Gen. 37:22)
62 Moses parted the waters so the Israelites didn't get this (Ex. 14:22)
64 "I will ___ evil beasts out of the land" (Lev. 26:6)
66 Men of Sodom's problem (Gen. 13:13)
68 Cooking spray brand

fifty57ven
LUKE: THE BELOVED PHYSICIAN
by Patricia Mitchell

ACROSS

1 Sinai desert climate

5 "Let us go forth therefore unto him without the ___" (Heb. 13:13)

9 "God . . .raised up Jesus, whom ye ___" (Acts 5:30)

13 Way you can memorize Bible verses

14 Philip's preaching, e.g. (Acts 8:35)

15 *Aida* is one

16 First gardener

17 Bloody river (Ex. 7:17)

18 "___ stood up in the midst of the disciples" (Acts 1:15)

19 Luke wrote so readers would do this (Luke 1:1)

21 "All they which dwelt in ___ heard the word" (Acts 19:10)

23 Legume

24 Greek goddess

25 Matthew collected this (Matt. 9:9)

29 Simon tried to ___ the apostles with money (Acts 8:18)

30 Paul's sermons were more than just one of these

32 Paul warned the voyage would ___ the ship not just a little (Acts 27:10)

33 Painter Richard

36 Explore thoroughly

37 Dessert choice

38 He follows Luke

39 "Through the wrath of the Lord of hosts," people are these (Isa. 9:19)

40 Luke was one, for short

41 Perga to Derbe (dir.)

42 Lucre descriptor (1 Tim. 3:3)

43 To some, the first Christians belonged to these

44 Today, Paul and Luke might use this for their journeys

45 Giant of folklore

46 "Thou shalt. . .bring forth a ___" (Luke 1:31)

47 Elijah "made a ___ about the altar" (1 Kings 18:32)

49 Health org.

50 Joseph would pay one in Bethlehem (Luke 2:5)

53 One of these asked Jesus, "What shall I do to inherit eternal life?" (Luke 10:25) (abbr.)

55 47 Across was not this, but around the altar (1 Kings 18:35)

57 Texas tourist site

60 Shopping area

62 Jesus to His followers

63 Seed sower (Luke 8:5)

64 What 63 Across wanted from his labor

65 Craftsman would do this to the four wooden pillars (Ex. 36:36)

66 Tools for 63 Across

67 Luke's second treatise

68 Laodicea, known for its eye salve, may have had a cure for one (Rev. 3:18)

DOWN

1 Some were present at Pentecost (Acts 2:11)

2 Event near 57 Across, perhaps

3 Where Julius planned to take Paul (Acts 27:1)

4 Not quite: prefix

5 Joseph and Mary would have traveled in one for protection on the road in Luke 2:4

6 Ram in the sky

7 Not good: prefix

8 Paul demanded to take his to Caesar (Acts 25:11)

9 Jesus was pierced with one (John 19:34)

10 Agrippa would have ___ Paul go had he not demanded to see Caesar (Acts 26:32)

11 Poet's "before"

12 "What king, going to make ___ against another king, sitteth not down first?" (Luke 14:31)

15 Vinegar given to Jesus on the cross may have acted slightly like this (John 19:29)

20 Snaky fish (pl.)

22 What a sword does (Luke 2:35)

26 The wind would ___ the ship toward Clauda (Acts 27:15–16)

27 "Men ought always to pray, and not to ___" (Luke 18:1)

28 Some people are choked with these and "bring no fruit to perfection" (Luke 8:14)

29 Writing tool

30 "Ye should. . .not have loosed from ___" (Acts 27:21)

31 Mary said, "He that is mighty hath done. . .great things; and ___ is his name" (Luke 1:49)

33 It took 10 plagues before Pharaoh would ___ the Israelites (Ex. 12:31)

34 Threat to whales, often

35 "___ was in the days of Herod" (Luke 1:5)

36 What Daniel heard, maybe (Dan. 6:22)

39 Pharisees: "Let us not ___ against God" (Acts 23:9)

40 What Simon Peter might have drawn today (John 18:10)

42 Luke (Col. 4:14)

43 The young man found the ___ of discipleship too steep (Matt. 19:20–22)

46 The hairy ___ of willful sinners will be wounded (Ps. 68:21)

48 Listings in Matt. 10:2

49 Joshua would ___ land to tribes (Josh. 18:10)

50 "Every tree is known by his own ___" (Luke 6:44)

51 When the women went to Jesus' tomb (Luke 24:1)

52 Jesus would ___ those that would "take him by force, to make him a king" (John 6:15)

54 Christian community org.

56 Prophecy: "As one gathereth ___ that are left, have I gathered all the earth" (Isa. 10:14)

57 Burnt offerings residue

58 WC in London

59 Luke's feeling toward Jesus' ministry (Acts 1:1–4)

61 Shape of God's promise to Noah (Gen. 9:16)

58

MARK:
THE EVANGELIST

by Patricia Mitchell

ACROSS

1 Elisabeth and Mary's needs (Luke 1:41–42)
6 Jesus: "This cup is the new testament in my blood, which is ___ for you" (Luke 22:20)
10 Judas carried one (John 12:6)
13 There was one between Paul and Barnabas about Mark (Acts 15:39–40)
15 East Indian dress
16 Forbidden fruit eater
17 Paul felt this about Mark (Acts 15:37–38)
18 "We know that thou art ___" (Mark 12:14)
19 Pssst!
20 Jesus fed many with two (Mark 6:38)
22 Mark highlights these in his gospel
24 Butcher's hook
26 Eject
28 Swerve
29 Offspring of the beast "like to a bear" (Dan. 7:5)

30 What might have been in Mark's mother's home
31 Tooth-leaved tree
32 Spherical body
33 Pinch
34 "If I should ___ with thee, I will not deny thee" (Mark 14:31)
35 Jesus made great calm on this (Mark 4:39)
37 Mark wanted to show that Jesus was this (Mark 1:1) (2 wds.)
41 Ananias told one (Acts 5:3)
42 Abode
43 Santa's helper
44 Goliath does this to the army of Saul (1 Sam. 17:8)
47 Former Italian magistrate
48 Crucifixion need (John 20:25) (sing.)
49 Fencing sword
50 One may have been thrown over the colt Jesus rode (Mark 11:7)

51 El ___, Texas
52 Mark wrote of Jesus' resurrection to prove His ___ over death
54 Jesus would ___ His disciples "what things should happen unto him" (Mark 10:32)
56 Describes the morsels in Ps. 147:17
57 Paul's vote on taking Mark on a second journey (Acts 15:39)
59 "___ were gathered" (Acts 4:26)
63 The disciples ___ the colt to Jesus (Mark 11:7)
64 God came ___ the mount Sinai (Ex. 19:20)
65 Pilot Earhart
66 Direction Mark traveled from Perga to Jerusalem
67 Pre-Easter season
68 Taken by Samson from Gaza (Judg. 16:3)

DOWN

1 One might be at your desk
2 Perhaps Mark: what the naked young man did (Mark 14:52)
3 Modern job opportunity for Matthew (Matt. 9:9)
4 Features of many coastlines
5 Stems of letters

6 Boomer
7 Scribes and Pharisees did this to Jesus frequently
8 Sound of two who "shall come to poverty," perhaps (Prov. 23:21)
9 Both those mentioned in Prov. 23:21 had a bad one
10 KJV: look!

11 Route
12 One of the "fountains of the great deep," perhaps (Gen. 7:11)
14 KJV yea
21 What cannot stand if divided (Mark 3:25)
23 "Multitude of ___" (Ps. 97:1)

24 Jesus, to some followers

25 Shorten

27 Response to manna kept overnight, as in Ex. 16:20

29 Paul's port on the way to Tyre (Acts 21:1) (var.)

30 Mark might have run one, naked (Mark 14:51-52)

31 Assistant

33 Paul may have stood on one to preach

34 Feature of many cathedrals

36 King Solomon had one in 1 Kings 9:26

37 Paul to Barnabas: I'll ___ ___ someone more reliable than Mark! (Acts 15:37-39) (2 wds.)

38 Sailed by Mark to reach Perga

39 Hodgepodge

40 Sports assoc.

42 What one of "them ye may eat" might do (Lev. 11:22)

44 Mark relates how Jesus "cast out many ___" (Mark 1:34)

45 Tops of Sinai and Ararat, e.g.

46 After Barnabas takes Mark, they ___ from the narrative

47 Ohio city

48 Chili brand

50 Some hearers at Pentecost were from here (Acts 2:11)

51 Seven cows looking like this emerged from the river (Gen. 41:2)

53 Speedway shape

55 Time of the early church was one

58 Paul would ___ for Silas in place of Mark (Acts 15:39-40)

60 Building addition

61 Tigris, e.g. (Sp.)

62 ___ Leandro, Calif.

fifty59nine
MARTHA THE SERVER
by Patricia Mitchell

ACROSS

1 Wise men saw one (Matt. 2:1–2)
5 Martha did this to meet Jesus (John 11:20)
9 Martha to Jesus: "Bid her . . . ___ me" (Luke 10:40)
13 Clearly, an attribute of Martha
14 Beautiful Helen's city
15 Crippling disease
16 Martha's sister's choice (Luke 10:42)
17 Martha to Jesus: "I know that he shall ___ again" (John 11:24)
18 In 9 Across, Martha was this. . .
19 . . .and this
21 Martha to Jesus: ". . .my brother had not ___" (John 11:21)
23 Couldn't Martha's sister ___ the problem?
24 Martha's sister wouldn't lift one ___ finger!

25 Potato brand
29 Martha's motto: Don't just think about it, ___!
30 Bluish-white metal
32 Calais negative
33 Gear for the Bahamas
36 Physicist Marie
37 Pull
38 Jesus was not telling Martha's sister one of these
39 ___ boom
40 Was Martha's kitchen this?
41 Like Martha, it's busy (Prov. 30:25)
42 Actress Day
43 Head covering
44 Blemish
45 Ski destination
46 Temperature in Martha's kitchen, perhaps
47 Blood part
49 Sower's medium (Luke 8:8)

50 San Diego winter hour
53 Martha to Jesus: "Dost thou not ___?" (Luke 10:40)
55 Outspoken Martha didn't do this with words (2 wds.)
57 Ran wild in the desert (Job 24:5)
60 The transfiguration took place___ a high mountain (Mark 9:2)
62 Martha's sister wiped Jesus' feet with this (John 11:2)
63 Martha said Lazarus's body would do this (John 11:39)
64 Aaron used one to fashion an idol (Ex. 32:4)
65 "They cried out all at ___" (Luke 23:18)
66 Belly (Scot.)
67 Pop
68 Martha wanted to ___ her sister into action

DOWN

1 Long stories
2 Cut of beef
3 How Martha felt in the kitchen (Luke 10:40)
4 Martha needed to ___ her to-do list (Luke 10:42)
5 Wall ___
6 Martha probably took this in her housekeeping
7 Goddess known to 14 Across
8 Describes the rich man's garments (Luke 16:19)

9 Crowd
10 Antlered animal
11 Devil is its father (John 8:44)
12 Spacecraft detachment
15 "A sword shall ___ through thy own soul also" (Luke 2:35)
20 Christian community org.
22 Paul would have seen these kinds of columns in Athens
26 The Jews would ___ Lazarus in a cave (John 11:38)

27 Elijah would ___ God's altar with water (1 Kings 18:33–34)
28 What Martha probably suffered concerning what she would serve Jesus
29 Bible patriarch, for short
30 American Indian tribe
31 Rhizome riser
33 One of what a philatelist collects
34 Dug around God's altar, as in 1 Kings 18:35

35 Extreme: prefix

36 Org.

39 Describes "the greater light to rule the day" (Gen. 1:16)

40 "Martha...went and ___ him" (John 11:20)

42 Fabric used in interior decorating

43 Soma

46 Sounds like a lot of this when Lazarus died (John 11:19)

48 Martha's sister caused one anointing Jesus' feet (John 12:3)

49 "Chief priests and scribes ___ and vehemently accused him" (Luke 23:10)

50 Organ substitute in some churches

51 Adhere

52 Martha, her sister and brother

54 Martha, perhaps: Everyone ___ well at my place!

56 Thump

57 Though Martha came out, Jesus needed to___ for Mary (John 11:28)

58 Prodigal son's workplace (Luke 15:15)

59 Martha's sister chose to do this and listen to Jesus (Luke 10:39)

61 Martha's lesson for us: It's possible to be ___ busy (Luke 10:41)

60
MARY:
THE VIRGIN MOTHER
by Patricia Mitchell

ACROSS

1 Most women's response to the plague of frogs, as in Ex. 8:3

4 Mary's pregnancy came ___ of a relationship with a man (Luke 1:34)

9 Jesus said, "Thou shalt not ___ the Lord thy God" (Matt 4:7)

14 ___ chi, martial arts

15 What Jacob could have served Esau's pottage with (Gen. 25:30)

16 Single

17 "Mary kept ___ these things, and pondered them" (Luke 2:19)

18 One was sent to Mary (Luke 1:26–27)

19 What Mary's song of praise was, in a way (Luke 1:46–55)

20 Ships are shifted with a very small one (James 3:4)

22 Mary may have had plans, but accepted God's ___ (Luke 1:38)

24 "The mote that is in thy brother's ___?" (Luke 6:41)

25 "___ ___ Gabriel" (Luke 1:19) (2 wds.)

27 Shape of each ruling light God created (Gen. 1:16)

29 French brandy

32 Pharisees had high, though misplaced, ones (Luke 11:42)

35 Dance

36 Certain roofs

38 The angel appeared to Joseph in one (Matt. 1:20)

40 Mary and Joseph's child is theirs ___, too (Luke 2:23)

42 Comforter

44 The Gospel of Matthew opens with this

45 Usually followed by ruin

47 Ointment ran down Aaron's (Ps. 133:2)

49 Without children, Elisabeth certainly was this (Luke 1:7)

50 Element of Mary's song (Luke 1:46–55)

52 John: unworthy to ___ Jesus' shoes (Luke 3:16)

54 What Lazarus of Jesus' parable did (Luke 16:20)

55 Card game

56 One-sixtieth of a minute (abbr.)

59 It must have been hard for Mary to fully ___ Gabriel's message

63 Apprehends

67 Hosea ___ Israel with sweet words (Hos. 2:14)

69 Likely shape of some of the gems in Ex. 28:18–19

71 There was one in the garden (Song 6:11)

72 Joseph "___, and took the young child" (Matt. 2:21)

73 David's harp playing soothed Saul's (1 Sam. 16:23)

74 Bethlehem to Jerusalem (dir.)

75 "The ___ of the Highest shall overshadow thee" (Luke 1:35)

76 The flight to Egypt was to ___ Herod (Matt. 2:13)

77 Member of a disbelieving generation (Matt. 23:33)

DOWN

1 Beehive State

2 One wouldn't disturb the house built on rock (Matt. 7:25)

3 "Mary. . .went into the ___ country" (Luke 1:39)

4 ___ ___ carte (2 wds.)

5 Mary's description of herself (Luke 1:38)

6 Joseph was on the ___ of leaving Mary (Matt. 1:19)

7 Beverages at Belshazzar's feast (Dan. 5:2–3)

8 Corned beef on rye source

9 The angel's message might have made Mary's face do this (Luke 1:34) (2 wds.)

10 Egypt to Nazareth (dir.)

11 Spice

12 What 64 Down did in the Temple (Luke 2:37)

13 Mary had the ___ of trust we should desire (Luke 1:38)

21 Soviet-era fighter plane

23 "With ___ nothing shall be impossible" (Luke 1:37)

26 "Go to the ___" (Prov. 6:6)

28 Psalmist, in a way

29 Mary would have entered the Temple's (Luke 2:22)

30 Big name in daytime TV

31 Associations

32 Card player's statement (2 wds.)

33 Borrower's option (Prov. 22:7)

34 Jesus' tempter (Matt. 4:10)

35 What the wise men would do (Matt. 2:11)

37 Adam's helpmeet

39 Describes 60 Down's son

41 Wound covering

43 Mary felt this way at Gabriel's greeting (Luke 1:29)

46 One who works with dough

48 Baptized into Christ, do this with Christ (Gal. 3:27)

51 Soviet-era police

53 Mary's baby (Luke 1:31)

56 Servants would ___ Jesus with their hands (Mark 14:65)

57 Continental coin

58 "Before the cock ___, thou shalt deny me thrice" (Matt. 26:34)

60 Father to Jesus: my son "___ vexed" (Matt. 17:15)

61 Track shape

62 Prego's competition

64 She praised Mary's baby (Luke 2:36–38)

65 Hamburger rolls

66 The Lord directs this (Prov. 16:9) (sing.)

68 Emmaus to Jerusalem (dir.)

70 Nazareth to Jerusalem (dir.)

MARY WHO SAT AT JESUS' FEET

by Vicki J. Kuyper

ACROSS

1 There was one between Abraham and the rich man (Luke 16:26)
6 "Paul and Silas prayed, and ___ praises" (Acts 16:25)
10 Organization (abbr.)
14 Main artery
15 Black and white snack
16 Mary's sister said, "The Master . . . calleth for ___" (John 11:28)
17 Pierced Jesus' side
18 "Mary. . .which anointed the ___ with ointment" (John 11:2)
19 Moray and conger
20 Jesus, Mary, and Martha's broke when Lazarus died
22 "Why was not this ointment ___?" (John 12:5)
24 Deli request
25 Church tower song
27 Tiny amounts

29 Martha's hometown (John 11:1)
32 "The ___ of the house of David" (Isa. 22:22)
33 Easter mo., usually
34 Friends assumed Mary went to Lazarus's ___ (John 11:31)
37 Judas made one with the Pharisees (Matt. 26:15)
41 "Fade as a ___" (Isa. 64:6)
43 Traditional bread for a patty melt
44 "Filled with the ___ of the ointment" (John 12:3) (var.)
45 Display
46 "To comfort them concerning ___ brother" (John 11:19)
48 Flightless bird
49 Possible exclamation by crowd when Lazarus' tomb was opened

51 Candidate
54 Pharisees were in one over Jesus
56 Birchlike tree
57 Point
58 Definition resource (abbr.)
60 Travel with
64 Malchus lost one during Jesus' arrest (John 18:10)
66 Mary may have kept her ointment in this
68 Peculiarity
69 Jesus: be born ___ (John 3:3)
70 "Be ye therefore perfect, ___ as your Father" (Matt. 5:48)
71 Monastery superior
72 "It is a ___ thing that the king requireth" (Dan. 2:11)
73 When Jesus arrived, Mary's brother was ___ (John 11:14)
74 Tilts to one side

DOWN

1 What Judas received for his betrayal of Jesus (Matt. 26:15)
2 "Faith, ___, charity, these three" (1 Cor. 13:13)
3 Samaria, e.g.
4 Gravy thickener
5 Mary's sister
6 Sun in Barcelona
7 When Jesus called for Mary "she ___ quickly" (John 11:29)

8 Roman emperor
9 What Baal was not
10 What one did at a feast
11 Queen from this region visited Solomon (1 Kings 10:1–2)
12 In Gen. 37, Judah ___ his brother to traveling merchants
13 Without children, Mary's home was an empty ___
21 "Is any merry? let him ___ psalms" (James 5:13)

23 Roe in KJV
26 Present at Jesus' birth and burial
28 Typed error
29 Describes Elisha (2 Kings 2:23)
30 Fencing sword
31 Trolley car
35 Popeye's yes
36 Surely there are these for silver and gold (Job. 28:1)

38 Room where Mary sat at Jesus' feet, perhaps (2 wds.)

39 Mary told Martha, "The Master is ___" (John 11:28)

40 "I am the ___ vine" (John 15:1)

42 Days Lazarus was dead before Jesus arrived (John 11:17)

46 Boomed

47 Perhaps used by Judas to end his life (Matt. 27:5)

50 "Blessed are the pure in heart: for they shall see ___" (Matt. 5:8)

52 Type of Mexican liquor

53 Cast from Mary Magdalene (Mark 16:9)

54 Female singer ___ Apple

55 Brown

56 What Paul was before he became shipwrecked (2 wds.)

57 Like a wing

59 Where Mary's brother was buried (John 11:38)

61 God's heavenly creations are shaped like these

62 "Faithful children not accused of ___ or unruly" (Titus 1:6)

63 Tater ___

65 "One little ___ lamb" (2 Sam. 12:3)

67 "He loved them unto the ___" (John 13:1)

MARY MAGDALENE:
THE FIRST AT THE TOMB

by Vicki J. Kuyper

ACROSS

1 "[Jesus] appeared ___ to Mary Magdalene" (Mark 16:9)
6 Illegal drug
9 Droops
13 Nice farewell
14 What's easy to see in another's eye (Matt. 7:3)
15 Fake butter
16 What someone was when soldiers bet for Jesus' clothes
17 ___ "the first day of the week" Mary came to the tomb (John 20:1)
18 Pale sherry
19 Brew
20 "He is ___" (Matt 28:6)
22 Could have been used to start fire for breakfast (John 21:9)
23 Synonym for Aramaic *Raca*, as in Matt. 5:22
24 The Israelites burned offerings under this tree (Hos. 4:13)
26 KJV no
27 Skateboard with a handle
30 How some may have responded to Mary before Jesus cast out her demons (Mark 16:9)
32 Created on fourth day (Gen. 1:16)
33 Connect
36 "Many women were there beholding ___ off" (Matt 27:55)
40 The curtain being torn in two was a good one (Luke 23:45)
41 Jesus came to ___ for our sins (Heb. 2:17)
42 Jerusalem to Jericho (dir.)
43 "I write not these things to shame you, but as my beloved sons I ___ you" (1 Cor. 4:14)
44 Despot
45 Cabbage cousin
46 "Why make ye this ___, and weep?" (Mark 5:39)
48 Saul never ___ to be king of Israel (1 Sam. 9:21)
51 Executive director
54 Km/h
56 "The ___ person will speak villany" (Isa. 32:6)
57 What Mary saw at tomb (Matt. 28:2)
59 La Scala is famous for it
61 "Absalom spake . . .neither good nor ___" (2 Sam 13:22)
64 Others thought Mary's words were "___ tales" (Luke 24:11)
65 The women Mary was with had had "___ spirits" (Luke 8:2)
66 A headdress of the ancient Persians, like Queen Esther
68 "Earth shall ___" (Isa. 24:20)
69 Allows
70 One touched Isaiah's lips (Isa. 6:6–7)
71 Chances of winning
72 Seraphim do this (Isa. 6:6)
73 "Therefore ___ I to them in parables" (Matt. 13:13)

DOWN

1 Syllables used in songs (2 wds.)
2 Baal was one (Judg. 2:13)
3 Jesus told his followers he'd ___
4 Angel to Mary: "Come, ___ the place" (Matt. 28:6)
5 Little tower
6 Elisha did this to pull ahead of Ahab (1 Kings 18:46)
7 Mary saw the angel roll this from the tomb (Matt. 28:2)
8 Jesus accused merchants of turning the temple into a "___ of thieves" (Mark 11:17)
9 A divan is one kind
10 The Magi chose to ___ their journey with a star (Matt. 2:9)
11 Birthplace of Columbus
12 Describes those who mourned in sackcloth and ashes
14 Aquatic rodents
21 Cain felt this Abel (Gen. 4:5)
22 Madagascar franc (abbr.)
23 Another woman with Mary at Jesus' tomb (Luke 24:10)
25 Pear-shaped instrument

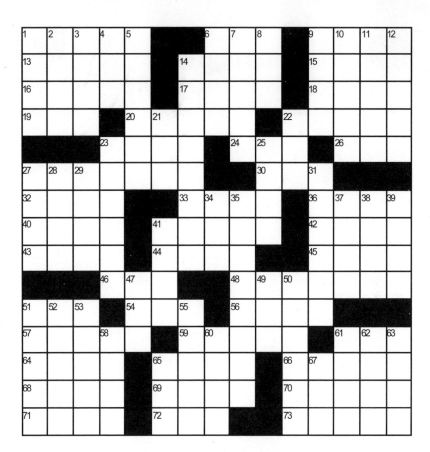

27 The angel Mary saw wore clothes as "white as ___" (Matt 28:3)

28 Cause of unconsciousness

29 "Sitting ___ against the sepulchre" (Matt. 27:61)

31 Handkerchief, for short

34 Type of serpent

35 Jesus' appearance to Mary ___ the mystery of the empty tomb (Mark 16:9)

37 The angel told Mary, "___ not ye" (Matt 28:5)

38 Jesus was ___ to cast seven devils from Mary (Mark 16:9)

39 Put in Jesus' hand instead of a scepter (Matt. 27:29)

41 Gideon built an altar ___ the place of Baal's (Judg. 6:28)

47 Measure of volume (abbr.)

49 Mary addressed risen Jesus, "___" (John 20:15)

50 Silver ones were brought from Tarshish (Jer. 10:9)

51 Egyptian capital

52 Mary thought Jesus' life ___ on the cross (Matt. 27:55–61)

53 David did this to Bathsheba (2 Sam. 11:2)

55 Where widow lived, perhaps (1 Kings 17:12)

58 Snaky fish (pl.)

60 Jonah felt this for a gourd (Jonah 4:10)

61 "Ye shall find the ___ wrapped in swaddling clothes" (Luke 2:12)

62 Palestine, e.g.

63 "Cometh Mary Magdalene early, when it was yet ___" (John 20:1)

65 Fairy

67 Mythical demon, whereas the ones that tormented Mary were real

MATTHEW:
THE TAX COLLECTOR

by Vicki J. Kuyper

ACROSS

1 "By ___ are ye saved" (Eph. 2:8)

6 Elijah was making one for the benefit of Baal's prophets (1 Kings 18:27)

10 Part of a doorway

14 What some Jews felt a taxman, like Matthew, was

15 Matthew learned "the Son of man is Lord ___ of the sabbath day" (Matt. 12:8)

16 Mary's ointment filled the house with this (John 12:3) (var.)

17 "___ in me" (John 15:4)

18 Matthew was one of the "twelve Jesus ___ forth" (Matt. 10:5)

19 Pharaoh was a royal ___ to Moses and God's people

20 "As ___ children" (Eph. 5:1)

21 Dawn

23 School group

24 Chances of winning

26 Matthew did this in Jesus' name (Matt. 10:7)

28 Protrusion of an organ

31 God would ___ out Laodicea (Rev. 3:16) (var.)

32 Passenger on ships from Tarshish (2 Chron. 9:21)

33 Like a leaky faucet

36 Fifth book of the N.T.

40 "Ye have ___ of all these things" (Matt. 6:32)

42 Government spy org.

43 Past times

44 Restaurant

45 "Brother of low ___" (James 1:9)

48 Eve's beginning (Gen. 2:21)

49 Glided

51 Sins

53 In 1 Sam. 17:49, David ___ Goliath with a slingshot

56 "___ the sick" (Matt. 10:8)

57 Number of Bible books by Matthew

58 Tradition says Matthew was one

61 Jesus healed the ___ (Matt. 11:5)

65 "Throughout all ___" (Eph. 3:21)

67 Most Bible scholars believe the wife of Alphaeus ___ Matthew, aka Levi (Luke 5:27)

68 Matthew was in this because of Jesus (Matt. 26:56)

69 Kate ___, model

70 Lazarus "had ___ in the grave" (John 11:17)

71 Joseph "turned ___ into the parts of Galilee" (Matt. 2:22)

72 Esau sold his birthright for this (Gen. 25:30–33)

73 Writer Bombeck

74 Riding a white ___ (Rev. 19:11)

DOWN

1 How Matthew felt after Jesus rose from the dead (John 20:20)

2 The one Jesus was given was scarlet (Matt. 27:28)

3 The Holy Spirit stopped Paul from preaching here (Acts 16:6)

4 Brook Matthew crossed toward Gethsemane (John 18:1)

5 "Come down ___ my child die" (John 4:49)

6 Matthew and the disciples did "as ___ commanded" (Matt. 21:6)

7 "Ye shall not have gone ___ the cities of Israel, till the Son of man be come" (Matt. 10:23)

8 Beano

9 This did not happen to Jesus in the tomb (Ps. 16:10)

10 Regarded as Bible's oldest book

11 Matthew would ___ life of an itinerate preacher (Matt. 10:14)

12 ___ Carlo

13 Disciples forgot this (Matt. 16:5)

21 Twelfth Jewish month (Est. 3:7)

22 "Blessed ___ the poor in spirit" (Matt. 5:3)

25 "The disciples ___ as Jesus had appointed them" (Matt. 26:19)

27 "Will ye also go ___?" (John 6:67)

28 "Dippeth his ___ with me in the dish" (Matt. 26:23)

29 Fencing sword

30 To draw in

31 Box

34 Type of tea

35 Host for demons (Matt. 8:32)

37 Matthew ate this on the Sabbath (Matt. 12:1)

38 Mathematical study of triangles (abbr.)

39 Emmaus to Bethlehem (dir.)

41 God said via the prophets, "I will wipe Jerusalem as a man wipeth a ___" (2 Kings 21:13)

45 Break

46 Perhaps used to fill jars with water at a wedding (John 2:7)

47 Epoch

50 Memory of things long past

52 Ishmael was Abraham's ___ son (Gen. 17:18–19)

53 Fizzes

54 Metal bar

55 Long-necked fowl (pl.)

56 African scavenger

59 "The young lions ___ after their prey, and seek their meat from God" (Ps. 104:21)

60 In Jesus' parable, the virgins awake and ___ their lamps (Matt. 25:7)

62 Canal

63 A disciple, like Matthew, could be regarded as one to Jesus

64 After Jesus' arrest, "all the disciples forsook him, and ___" (Matt. 26:56)

66 Jericho to Bethlehem (dir.)

68 Abraham, Isaac, and Jacob, e.g.

sixt64our

MICAH: THE YOUNGER PROPHET

by Vicki J. Kuyper

ACROSS

1 Samaria was one Micah prophesized against
5 "___ye, O mountains" (Mic. 6:2)
9 "I ___, I shall arise" (Mic. 7:8)
13 Commentators note Micah uses these throughout his prophecies
14 Harvard's rival
15 Organized crime
16 Alcoholic brews
17 Epochs
18 How rainbows are shaped
19 "The ___ of Jacob" (Mic. 5:8)
21 Time in office
23 "___ the spirits" (1 John 4:1)
24 Morse code dash
25 Abraham's was Sarah
29 Butane
30 Joseph's brothers were ___ to him (Gen. 37:23–24)
32 Before (prefix)

33 Saul's was too big for David (1 Sam. 17:38–39) (var.)
36 Ezekiel's valley of bones must have been this (Ezek. 37:7)
37 Jesus' was thirty when he began his public ministry (Luke 3:23)
38 "What is ___" (Mic. 6:8)
39 A righteous person's prayer will ___ much (James 5:16)
40 Possible vessel Samaritan woman left at the well (John 4:28)
41 Samson had strong ones (Judg. 16:29–30) (abbr.)
42 Prophets like Micah did not deliver this kind of message
43 "Thou shalt no more worship the work of thine ___" (Mic. 5:13)
44 Ball holder
45 Aaron, after application of Ps. 133:2's ointment

46 "They hunt every man his brother with a ___" (Mic. 7:2)
47 English class assignments
49 "Ten thousands of rivers of ___?" (Mic. 6:7)
50 School group
53 Pushed with the foot
55 Naaman's ailment (2 Kings 5:1)
57 A Spartan slave
60 Little Mermaid's love
62 Micah compared his mourning to sound of these birds (Mic. 1:8)
63 The Roman Coliseum is one
64 "The LORD require of thee... ___ mercy" (Mic. 6:8)
65 Plateau
66 "Unto the ___ of Jerusalem" (Mic. 1:12)
67 The wicked will drink this from the Lord's cup of wine (Ps. 75:8)
68 "Hear, I ___ you" (Mic. 3:1)

DOWN

1 "The LORD hath set ___ him that is godly for himself" (Ps. 4:3)
2 Micah prophesied a ___ from Bethlehem (Mic. 5:2)
3 "People is risen up as an ___" (Mic. 2:8)
4 Organization (abbr.)
5 Laughing dogs
6 "Now shall he be great unto the ends of the ___" (Mic. 5:4)

7 Pie ___ ___ mode (2 wds.)
8 "Not your ___" (Mic. 2:10)
9 Boaz ___ wheat and barley (Ruth 2:23)
10 Football assoc.
11 Micah said even people who do this are hailed as prophets (Mic. 2:11)
12 Samuel was one when God called him (1 Sam. 3:8)
15 Leatherneck

20 Twelfth Jewish month (Est. 9:1)
22 Electronic messages
26 Produce eggs
27 Micah ___ God's people to return to Him (Mic. 6:9)
28 "Then shall the ___ be ashamed" (Mic. 3:7)
29 "Walk humbly with thy ___?" (Mic. 6:8)

30 Isaac and Esau liked ___ food (Gen. 25:28)

31 Canal

33 Syria traded this in the markets of Tyre (Ezek. 27:16)

34 "Scribes, which desire to walk in long ___" (Luke 20:46)

35 Micah reminded God's people, "I sent before thee ___, Aaron, and Miriam" (Mic. 6:4)

36 "Woe to them that devise iniquity, and work ___ upon their beds!" (Mic. 2:1)

39 "___ and thresh, O daughter of Zion" (Mic. 4:13)

40 Micah to God's people: "Thou shalt ___, but not be satisfied" (Mic. 6:14)

42 Japanese auto maker

43 God called Micah to ___, not hurt, His people (Mic. 6:9)

46 Sister's daughters

48 God's desire is for people to ___ for their sins (Mic. 6:8)

49 Psalm 128 likens children to "___ plants round about thy table" (Ps. 128:3)

50 Micah was "full of ___ by the spirit of the LORD" (Mic. 3:8)

51 Oklahoma city

52 Analyze properties

54 Small wooded valley

56 Sport

57 Old woman in fairy tales

58 Epoch

59 "___ the Lord GOD be witness against you" (Mic. 1:2)

61 Ashael was as light-footed as one (2 Sam. 2:18)

sixty**65**five

MIRIAM:
THE WATCHFUL SISTER
by Vicki J. Kuyper

ACROSS

1 Charges
4 "Then ___ Moses and the children of Israel" (Ex. 15:1)
8 Beetle
14 Conservationist group
15 Symptom of malaria
16 "The tongue of the just is as ___ silver" (Prov. 10:20)
17 Record measure
18 "It is a ___ thing that the king requireth" (Dan. 2:11)
19 Flyers
20 Carrot eaters
22 Deli order
23 Used to preserve Jesus' body (John 19:39) (sing.)
24 Snaky fish (pl.)
27 Russian country cottage
31 "Miriam answered them, Sing ye to the___" (Ex. 15:21)
33 Volkswagen model

35 ___ Sea, site of Miriam's song
36 Possible nickname for Paul's "son in the faith" (1 Tim. 1:2)
38 "God created man in his ___ image" (Gen. 1:27)
39 KJV term for Korah (Jude 1:11)
40 Father, Son, and Holy Spirit
44 When Jesus arrived, Lazarus's tomb was ___ ___ (John 11:38) (2 wds.)
46 "Learn to maintain good works for necessary ___" (Titus 3:14)
47 Cool, in slang
49 "I count all things but loss... that I may ___ Christ" (Phil. 3:8)
50 Chicken ___ ___king (2 wds.)
51 Yang's sidekick

52 Common among soldiers who fight in battle
55 Computer phone
58 Adventure story
61 Land measurement
63 Nickname for doubting disciple
65 Warned troy of equine gift
67 Nathan would ___ David of murder (2 Sam. 12:7)
70 Fix the socks
71 Number of books of the Bible Miriam is mentioned in
72 Card suit
73 What Moses found the Israelites worshipping
74 Business name ending
75 Where Miriam died (Num. 20:1)
76 "___ me thrice" (Matt. 26:34)
77 Type of tree planted in Isa. 44:14

DOWN

1 ___ firma
2 Dismay
3 Tropical grass
4 Mombai dress
5 Stone on ephod (Ex. 28:19)
6 Deborah was Rebekah's (Gen. 35:8)
7 "To the right!"
8 Perhaps Miriam had this as her leprosy healed
9 When we first meet Miriam in the Bible, she's one (Ex. 2:8)

10 Main artery
11 Edge
12 Genius
13 Joseph's baby brother, for short (Gen. 35:24)
21 Beds
25 MGM's Lion
26 "Light is ___ for the righteous" (Ps. 97:11)
28 Farm yield
29 Moses to God: "___ am I" (Ex. 3:4)

30 City in Yemen
32 "All the firstborn in the land of Egypt shall ___" (Ex. 11:5)
34 "Miriam became leprous, white as ___" (Num. 12:10)
37 Miriam is the Hebrew form of this name
39 Brand of cold remedy
40 Small Pacific island
41 Capital of Norway
42 Prayer for Miriam: "Let her not be as one ___" (Num. 12:12)

43 Podium

45 "The ___ of his finger in water" (Luke 16:24)

48 Genetic code

53 Nova ___

54 Israelites pass through the sea; Pharaoh's army ___ (Deut. 11:4)

56 Musical composition

57 Miriam's brother (Ex. 2:7)

59 Forest clearing

60 Miriam's other brother (Ex. 15:20)

62 Cain's eldest son (Gen. 4:17)

64 Tulle

66 Miriam asked, "Hath the LORD indeed spoken ___ by Moses?" (Num. 12:2)

67 "___ for the old paths, where is the good way, and walk therein" (Jer. 6:16)

68 Professional numbers person

69 Villain

70 What God threatened Pharaoh through Moses, He ___

six 66 six
MORDECAI: TRUSTED GUARDIAN

by Vicki J. Kuyper

ACROSS

1 How Esther felt when she saw Mordecai in mourning (Est. 4:4)
4 "Then ___ one of the seraphims unto me" (Isa. 6:6)
8 In John 11:43, Jesus ___ Lazarus from the dead
14 A bonobo is one kind
15 Put on ___; an artificial manner
16 Storm-causing current (2 wds.)
17 Sandwich nickname
18 "Whiter than ___" (Ps. 51:7)
19 Spanish priests
20 "They ___ the passover with fire" (2 Chron. 35:13)
22 ___ Lanka
23 Discharge
24 "Mordecai the Jew was ___ unto king Ahasuerus" (Est. 10:3)
27 Horses' neck hair

31 One color of Mordecai's royal apparel (Est. 8:15)
33 Annoy
35 ___ Maria
36 Weight measurement
38 Roman three
39 Eastern ruler
40 Blotch
44 A person's self
46 "Behold ___ God!" (Isa. 40:9)
47 Conger
49 Haman ___ what he deserved (Est. 8:7)
50 "Mordecai bowed ___" (Est. 3:2)
51 First day of Purim is traditionally known as Mordecai's ___
52 "This is my blood of the new testament, which is ___ for many" (Mark 14:24)
55 Thin paper

58 "When Mordecai perceived all that was done, Mordecai ___ his clothes" (Est. 4:1)
61 Vashti's actions might make wives "despise their husbands in their ___" (Est. 1:17)
63 Hallucinogen
65 Chair support
67 Form ideas
70 Part of Ahasuerus's kingdom (see Est. 1:1)
71 "He maketh me to ___ down in green pastures" (Ps. 23:2)
72 Decorative element on Jews' garments (Num. 15:38)
73 Mordecai did this daily past the women's house (Est. 2:11)
74 "Do not ___" (James 1:16)
75 Mordecai's grandfather (Est. 2:5)
76 Women's magazine
77 Number of chapters in the book of Esther

DOWN

1 Sword
2 Poise
3 Specify
4 Mordecai joined the Jews in a three-day ___ (Est. 4:16)
5 Mordecai's royal garment material (Est. 8:15)
6 Wear away
7 Persia to Sinai (dir.)

8 Spokespersons (abbr.)
9 What Mordecai likely felt hearing of Haman's decree (see Est. 3:6)
10 Part of Ahasuerus's realm (Est. 1:1)
11 "___, give me this water, that I thirst not" (John 4:15)
12 Ethiopia to Shushan (dir.)

13 What Mordecai sent to Esther via Hathach (Est. 4:8)
21 King's probable state after a seven-day feast (Est. 1:5)
25 Caesar's twelve
26 The Kingston ___
28 "Esther certified the king thereof in Mordecai's ___" (Est. 2:22)

29 Describes Mordecai's nemesis, Haman
30 Vassal
32 Savannah time, during winter
34 "The ___ took off his ring. . . and gave it unto Mordecai" (Est. 8:2)
37 Chilled
39 Mordecai's cousin (Est. 2:7)
40 In ___ (together)

41 Part of the Jews' celebration was giving gifts to the ___ (Est. 9:22)
42 Pear-shaped instrument
43 "My voice shalt thou ___ in the morning" (Ps. 5:3)
45 Volkswagen sports car
48 Caustic substance
53 Frilly fabric
54 "LORD, thou has heard the ___ of the humble" (Ps. 10:17)
56 Fluid part of blood (var.)
57 ___ Lauder cosmetics

59 Whining voice
60 Warble
62 Ship section (Acts 27:29)
64 Source for 17 Across
66 Mordecai asked Esther "to ___ supplication" (Est. 4:8)
67 "___ a Small World"
68 Dit's partner
69 Technology that supports Web page components
70 "My heart standeth in ___ of thy word" (Ps. 119:161)

sixty 67 even

NAAMAN, THE LEPROUS COMMANDER

by Vicki J. Kuyper

ACROSS

1 Elisha's farewell to Naaman: "Go in ___" (2 Kings 5:19)
6 "Of them he ___ twelve" (Luke 6:13)
11 U.K. time zone
14 Book of maps
15 "___ among you all, the same shall be great" (Luke 9:48)
16 A small deer in KJV
17 Bird akin to a sandpiper
18 What Naaman took home as a souvenir (2 Kings 5:17)
19 There wasn't room here for Jesus
20 U.S. President William Howard ___
21 "God: incline thine ___" (Ps. 17:6)
22 Metal tip on the end of a lance
24 One billion years
26 Men living among tombs acted this way after meeting Jesus (Matt. 8:28–34)

28 The Ten Commandments, e.g.
31 Naaman was "mighty. . . , but he was a ___" (2 Kings 5:1)
32 Damascus river (2 Kings 5:12)
33 Naaman's chapter in 2 Kings
34 King Saul's was always changing (1 Sam. 16:23)
38 Caesar's seven
39 Stretchy gloves
40 Card game
41 Rev. 22:18 warns one who ___ to God's Word
43 The king of Babylon looked for one (Ezek. 21:21)
44 '70s music
46 Accompanied the prophets in 1 Sam. 10:5
48 The king of Syria sent this on Naaman's behalf (2 Kings 5:5)
49 "Naaman came with his ___ and with his chariot" (2 Kings 5:9)

51 Branches used to make booths in Neh. 8:15
52 Mythical creature
53 Herb the Pharisees tithed (Luke 11:42)
54 Naaman's response to Elisha's instructions: He "went away in a ___" (2 Kings 5:12)
58 Passerby's possible reaction to Naaman's leprous affliction
59 Confess
62 Long, narrow boat
63 Judas's kiss was one for the Roman soldiers (Mark 14:44)
64 To establish as law
65 Coral island
66 "Made he a woman, and brought ___ unto the man" (Gen. 2:22)
67 Gangly
68 Simon ___ Jesus a hand in Matt. 27:32

DOWN

1 "As yesterday when it is ___" (Ps. 90:4)
2 Volcanic mountain
3 First letter of the Arabic alphabet
4 Namaan's position in the Syrian army (2 Kings 5:1)
5 Damascus to Babylon (dir.)
6 "Wash in Jordan. . .and thou shalt be ___" (2 Kings 5:10)

7 "Wise man will ___" (Prov. 1:5)
8 "All that handle the ___. . . shall come down from their ships" (Ezek. 27:29)
9 Fast plane
10 Hydrocarbon
11 What Elisha would do to Gehazi upon his return (2 Kings 5:25–26) (slang)

12 What Gehazi accepted from Naaman (2 Kings 5:23)
13 Structure of the first tabernacle (Ex. 26:12)
21 Volkswagen model
23 Cootie
25 Airport information
26 Times Naaman dipped in the Jordan (2 Kings 5:14)

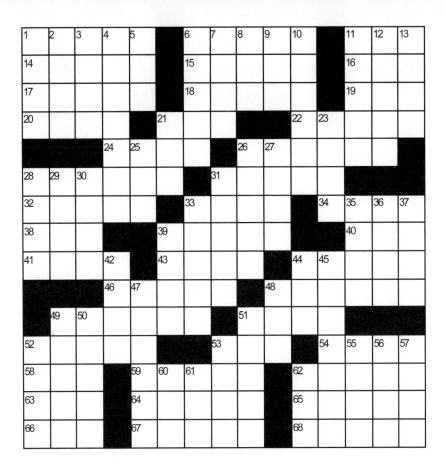

27 Part of Mount Ararat where the ark docked

28 2 Down element

29 Same cite as previous

30 Told Naaman's wife about Elisha (2 Kings 5:2)

31 Cubic decimeter

33 Reputations

35 After 11 Down, what Elisha would do to Gehazi (2 Kings 5:25-27)

36 "___ to die" (Heb. 9:27)

37 Naaman "stood at the ___ of the house of Elisha" (2 Kings 5:9)

39 Run easily

42 Abraham remained this way after a century (Gen. 17:17)

44 Home to Daniel's lions

45 Retell

47 Where Naaman's wife's maid was from (2 Kings 5:2)

48 What Gehazi told to Naaman (2 Kings 5:22)

49 Netherlands' capital

50 After being healed, Naaman promised he'd no longer "sacrifice unto ___ gods" (2 Kings 5:17)

51 Binder

52 "Thou thoughtest that I was altogether ___ an one as thyself" (Ps. 50:21)

53 Alternate nickname for Fred

55 After a while

56 Naaman left Syria with 6,000 pieces of this (2 Kings 5:5)

57 Snaky fish (pl.)

60 God's genetic blueprint

61 According to 2 Kings 5:1, Naaman was a great one

62 Energy measure (abbr.)

sixty**68**ight

NATHAN: TEACHER OF THE LORD'S WILL

by Vicki J. Kuyper

ACROSS

1 David does this to Goliath with a single stone (1 Sam. 17:50)
6 In Nathan's story, Bathsheba was a ___ lamb (2 Sam. 12:1–3)
9 Jesus was upset because people went to ___ in the temple (Mark 11:15)
13 Disloyal
15 To Moses, God's walkway looked like a blue one (Ex. 24:10)
16 "The lilies. . .___ not" (Luke 12:27)
17 Nathan "bowed himself. . . ___" (1 Kings 1:23)
18 Economic measure
19 David to Nathan: "Cause Solomon my son to ride upon mine own ___"(1 Kings 1:33)
20 David's exploits are part of Jewish ___
21 David ___ sorrow before his child died (2 Sam. 12:21)
24 God directed Moses to turn "the ___ into dry land" (Ps. 66:6)

25 Incense to false gods was burned beneath this tree (Hos. 4:13)
26 Middle East sultanate
27 Steak tartare is ___ than steak au poivre
29 Custard dessert
30 Past
31 Bathsheba's died (2 Sam. 12:18)
34 Nocturnal South African dog
38 David to Nathan: "He shall restore. . .because he had no ___" (2 Sam. 12:6)
39 David told Nathan he wanted to build a house for the ___ (2 Sam. 7:2)
40 Cab
41 What people did at the tabernacle (Ex. 38:8)
44 Job was clothed in this (Job 7:5)
45 Nathan knew the ___ story behind Uriah's death (2 Sam. 12:9)
46 University (abbr.)
48 A prophet like Nathan would be a valuable one for a king

50 David's got him in trouble (2 Sam. 11:2)
51 Two of the books Nathan is in are attributed to this prophet (abbr.)
54 Computer co.
55 Nathan to David: "Thou hast ___ Uriah" (2 Sam 12:9)
57 What Peter would do from his boat upon recognizing Jesus (John 21:7)
58 Lake bird
60 How Bathsheba felt after her baby died (2 Sam. 12:24)
61 Utterances meant to be inaudible
63 Pear-shaped instrument
64 ___ God's rules figuratively around your neck (Prov. 6:21)
65 Abana and Pharpar (2 Kings 5:12)
66 KJV pottage
67 Make a mistake
68 Disgusting

DOWN

1 Similar to instrument announcing Solomon as king (1 Kings 1:39)
2 Register (var.)
3 Jesus calmed one (Luke 8:24)
4 Nathan's job was to say what was ___, as in 2 Sam. 12:9
5 Nathan to David: God's judgment would be visible "before all Israel, and before the ___" (2 Sam 12:12)

6 Nathan would ___ ___ Bathsheba to have Solomon become king (1 Kings 1:11–12)
7 "Uriah. . .___ not down unto his house" (2 Sam. 11:9)
8 Nero, e.g.
9 Remembers what just happened
10 "Let the ___ of thy servant David be established" (2 Sam 7:26)
11 Cargo ship

12 David's ___ to God was "forgive me" (Ps. 51:2)
14 Swelling
22 Nathan to David: "Thou art the ___" (2 Sam 12:7)
23 Shina language
26 David "was very ___" (1 Kings 1:15)
28 Children are one (Ps. 127:3)
29 Advertisements
30 Talk
31 Numbers worker

32 "Thou shalt call ___ name JESUS" (Matt. 1:21)

33 "___ a Small World"

34 Nathan, Elisha, and Ezekiel ___ biblical prophets

35 Affirmative in Arles

36 Better than short term memory (abbr.)

37 Nathan saw Adonijah as one (1 Kings 1:9–10)

39 "Solomon in ___ his glory" (Matt. 6:29)

42 Earth inheritors (Matt. 5:5)

43 Thin cloth

44 Vapor

46 Popeye's yes

47 Wood David's home was built from (2 Sam. 7:2)

48 "The angel . . .encampeth round ___ them" (Ps. 34:7)

49 To divert David's attention from "who ___ Abimelech" the messenger mentioned Uriah was dead, as well (2 Sam. 11:21)

50 Though Adonijah was the ___ brother, Nathan helped Solomon become king

51 God concerning Kedar and Hazor: "I will bring their calamity from all ___" (Jer. 49:32)

52 David's repentance could not ___ his son's death (2 Sam. 12:13–18)

53 Sloppy

54 Evils

56 For a time, David's was the cave of Adullam (1 Sam. 22:1)

57 Prima donna

59 "He hath put a ___ song in my mouth" (Ps. 40:3)

62 Nathan helped David own up to his (2 Sam. 12:13)

NATHANAEL CAME AND SAW

by Vicki J. Kuyper

ACROSS

1 David's dad, for short (Ruth 4:17)
5 "The ___ priests answered" (John 19:15)
10 "___ to teach" (1 Tim. 3:2)
13 Dunkable sandwich cookies
15 Island nation
16 Sticky black substance
17 Eastern religion
18 Some believe "Bartholomew" may be Nathanael's ___
19 Jesus stirred this up in many of the Pharisees
20 Even filled with 153 fish, Nathanael's didn't break (John 21:11)
21 Nathanael's friend's ___ was Philip (John 1:45–46)
23 Shampoo brand
25 Peter swam to shore, but Nathanael came "in a little ___" (John 21:8)
26 Eluded
28 Billy ___, evangelist

31 Moses brought water forth from this kind of rock (Deut. 8:15)
32 Nathanael's net was pushed to this in John 21:11
33 Breathing need
34 Metric capacity measure (abbr.)
37 Jesus told Nathanael, "Ye shall see heaven ___" (John 1:51)
38 Canned chili brand
40 Disobeying God would be one
41 What Jacob called his youngest son, for short? (Gen. 35:18)
42 Jesus told Nathanael he'd see angels going up and ___ (John 1:51)
43 More pallid
44 David's sling stones come from one (1 Sam. 17:40)
45 Squirted
46 Stays

49 Nathanael saw one when he came ashore (John 21:9)
50 Women should "___ themselves in modest apparel" (1 Tim. 2:9)
51 "God took one of his ___" (Gen. 2:21)
52 Jetted tub
55 Guileless Nathanael wouldn't do this to anyone (slang)
56 Capital of Afghanistan
59 "Many ___ signs truly did Jesus" (John 20:30)
61 "Out of whose womb came the ___?" (Job 38:29)
62 Socially superior
63 Judas resorted to using one (Matt. 27:5)
64 "That which groweth of ___ own accord" (Lev. 25:5)
65 Side of the ship Jesus told Nathanael and his friends to throw the net over (John 21:6)
66 Dogs, cats, birds, e.g.

DOWN

1 Only gospel Nathanael is mentioned in
2 Canal
3 "Father hath ___ me" (John 20:21)
4 "Jacob ___ pottage" (Gen. 25:29)
5 Rocky Balboa
6 Sound physical condition
7 Caesar's trio

8 Airport info
9 "I go a ___" (John 21:3)
10 Tipped
11 Analyze
12 "Behold, I give unto you power to ___ on serpents and scorpions" (Luke 10:19)
14 Nathanael could have used this while fishing (2 wds)

22 What David did before letting the stone from his slingshot fly
24 None of the disciples asked Jesus, "Who ___ thou?" (John 21:12)
25 Lower leg
26 Counterfeit coin
27 Nathanael told Jesus, "Thou art the ___ of Israel" (John 1:49)

28 Lump

29 "The harvest of the earth is ___" (Rev. 14:15)

30 Last word in the Bible

31 Side

34 Foolish person

35 "At the name of Jesus every ___ should bow" (Phil. 2:10)

36 When Nathanael came ashore, he knew the stranger "was the ___" (John 21:12)

38 "How ___ is the fig tree withered away!" (Matt. 21:20)

39 How animals were grouped for the ark

40 How Philip referred to his friend, perhaps

42 KJV's drunkard

43 "He that deviseth to do evil shall be called a mischievous ___" (Prov. 24:8)

44 "I will break also the ___ of Damascus" (Amos 1:5)

45 Fore-and-aft sail

46 More than one radius

47 One went out from Caesar Augustus (Luke 2:1)

48 "We have found him, of whom ___ in the law. . .did write" (John 1:45)

49 ___ mignon

51 Naomi's daughter-in-law (Ruth 2:22)

52 "The kinsman said unto Boaz, Buy it for thee. So he drew off his ___" (Ruth 4:8)

53 Unwanted insect

54 Greek god of war

57 Boxer Muhammad

58 Jesus' resurrection was this kind of news to Nathanael

60 "The veil of the temple was rent in twain from the ___ to the bottom" (Mark 15:38)

NEHEMIAH: BUILDER OF THE WALL

by Vicki J. Kuyper

ACROSS

1 The ___ of the Apostles
5 Nehemiah didn't take one out to build the wall (Neh. 2:8)
9 Russian country house
14 African tree
15 Writer Bombeck
16 The king agreed to ___ Nehemiah's leave (Neh. 2:6)
17 The descendants of Asaph did this (Neh. 7:44)
18 Swarm
19 "Why is the ___ of God forsaken?" (Neh. 13:11)
20 A plain near one of the towns of Benjamin (Neh. 6:2)
21 Jesus ___ for our sins
23 "My God shall supply all your ___" (Phil 4:19)
24 Glass jar
26 Bethlehem to Bethany (dir.)
28 "Let them shut the doors, and ___ them" (Neh. 7:3)
29 Nehemiah: "Did not I, because of the ___ of God" (Neh. 5:15)
31 Shusan (Susa) to Sinai (dir.)
34 Nehemiah reminded the Jews that when the Israelites ___, God provided (Neh. 9:15)
37 Keeper of king's forest (Neh. 2:8)
39 Nehemiah: "Remember me, O my God, for ___" (Neh. 13:31)
40 After listening to God's law, Nehemiah and all God's people ___ (Neh. 8:10)
41 "We are the ___, and thou our potter" (Isa. 64:8)
42 Nehemiah's list of exiles included their ___ (Neh. 7:68)
44 Railroad car connector
47 "___ the spirits" (1 John 4:1)
48 Philemon author refers to himself as "Paul the ___" (Philem. 1:9)
50 King to Nehemiah: "___ long shall thy journey be?" (Neh. 2:6)
51 There was much of this when the wall was complete (Neh. 12:27)
52 Chinese tea
56 Shorten, for short
59 Heavy cloth
63 Same genus as Eve's tempter (Gen. 3:1)
64 Architect Frank ___ Wright
66 Season leading up to Easter
67 Jerusalem's Jews were deep in this (Neh. 5:3)
68 ___ eel
69 Window glass
70 Patmos is this (Rev. 1:9)
71 Vista
72 Builders didn't ___ their weapons while working (Neh. 4:17)
73 Artaxerxes ___ Nehemiah is upset (Neh. 2:2)

DOWN

1 Organization (abbr.)
2 Porcelain
3 Choir section
4 Droop
5 ___ allowed Nehemiah to travel freely (Neh. 2:7)
6 Dunking cookie
7 The Jews' response to Ezra's blessing (Neh. 8:6)
8 "Blessed be thy glorious ___" (Neh. 9:5)
9 Telegraphic signal
10 The Israelites' declaration: "Thou, art LORD ___" (Neh. 9:6)
11 Hint
12 Elijah could have used one on the trench (1 Kings 18:35)
13 Jesus' miracles left onlookers feeling this (John 2:23)
21 "Joy of Jerusalem was heard even ___ off" (Neh. 12:43)
22 Genetic building block
25 "___ in me, and I in you" (John 15:4)
27 Lingerie item
29 Day-old manna (Ex. 16:20)
30 Eve's garden
31 Nehemiah's plea: "Build up the ___ of Jerusalem" (Neh. 2:17)

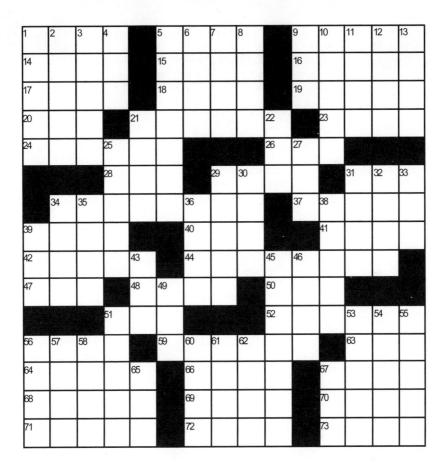

32 Sanballat tried to start one (Neh. 4:1)

33 "___ is the house of God forsaken?" (Neh. 13:11)

34 Nehemiah took one of the Jerusalem's walls (Neh. 2:13)

35 The day the wall was finished was declared ___ unto the Lord (Neh. 8:10)

36 Nehemiah to Sanballat: "Let us ___ counsel" (Neh. 6:7)

38 Sanballat probably overdid this (Neh. 4:1)

39 London time zone (abbr.)

43 Before Nehemiah "had not been beforetime ___" in the king's presence (Neh. 2:1)

45 Haunted

46 Ezra read the ___ of the law aloud upon the wall's completion (Neh. 8:1)

49 "___ shall fight" (Neh. 4:20)

51 Indo-European

53 Describes Eglon, king of Moab (Judg. 3:17)

54 Describes Felix (Acts 24:3)

55 "The ___ thereof are burned with fire" (Neh. 1:3)

56 "When thou doest thine ___" (Matt. 6:2)

57 Coalition

58 "His ear through with an aul" (Ex. 21:6)

60 Swiss mountains

61 Tower of Jerusalem's wall (Neh. 3:1)

62 Green Gables dweller

65 Lydia needed this (Acts 16:14)

67 Roman god

seventy-one

NICODEMUS:
SEEKER OF SALVATION

by Vicki J. Kuyper

ACROSS

1 Soldier's risk
5 Paul felt one when bit by a viper (Acts 28:3)
9 Plateau
13 Basmati
14 Tub spread
15 Church governing board
16 Homophone for Esau's other name (Gen. 36:1)
17 "___ of jewels" (Song 1:10)
18 Children of Israel feared they would become these in the wilderness (Num. 14:3)
19 Pharisees asked Nicodemus, "Art thou also of ___?" (John 7:52)
21 "Noah. . .became ___ of the righteousness" (Heb. 11:7)
23 Nicodemus: "How can a man be born when he is ___?" (John 3:4)
24 Ship initials
25 There was a theological one between Samaritans and Jews (John 4:9)

29 Jesus asked Nicodemus, "___ thou a master" (John 3:10)
30 God's answer to prayer is never this
32 Resort hotel
33 Slip
36 Soldiers directed these at Jesus during the crucifixion
37 "The LORD thy God ___ thee" (Deut. 8:2)
38 Homer's "Odyssey"
39 Beer
40 Royal (Sp.)
41 "Ye do ___" (Matt. 22:29)
42 Time of day when Nicodemus came to Jesus the first time (John 3:2)
43 Hazardous
44 Prayer can be a form of this, at times
45 Establishment (abbr.)
46 "Thou art a teacher come from ___" (John 3:2)

47 "If sinners ___ thee" (Prov. 1:10)
49 Expression of surprise
50 Cool (slang)
53 "God ___ not his Son into the world to condemn" (John 3:17)
55 Metal cap on tip of cane
57 Accumulate
60 We're not to do this with one word of scripture (Rev. 22:19)
62 Zealous Christians have it
63 Destroyed
64 Describes the drink Jesus was offered on the cross (John 19:29)
65 The disciples left these when they followed Jesus (Matt. 4:20)
66 Wager
67 Brand of sandwich cookie
68 "Every ___ is known by his own fruit" (Luke 6:44)

DOWN

1 Ragu's competition
2 Large wave
3 Hot liquid burn
4 ___ Moore
5 "Every beast of the ___" (Ps. 50:10)
6 Nicodemus brought these for Jesus' burial (John 19:39)

7 Nicodemus laid Jesus in a ___ sepulcher (John 19:41)
8 Mild slang expression for surprise
9 Present at Jesus' birth and burial (Matt. 2:11; John 19:39)
10 Bethlehem to Bethany (dir.)
11 Chinese sauce
12 Spots

15 Wound with cloth around Jesus (John 19:40)
20 Potiphar's wife tried to ___ Joseph (Gen. 39:7)
22 Seventeenth Bible book (var.)
26 Hawaii, e.g.
27 "We ___ that we do know" (John 3:11)
28 How Nebuchadnezzar behaved in Dan. 4:33: ___

29 Football org.

30 "I am the ___" (John 8:12)

31 Soldiers placed on Jesus' clothes (John 19:24) (2 wds.) (sing.)

33 Birds with webbed feet

34 Eve's first clothing (Gen. 3:7)

35 "___ and the last" (Rev. 1:17)

36 Jokes

39 "Then took they the body of Jesus, and wound it in ___ clothes" (John 19:40)

40 "Deliver the poor and needy; ___ them out of the hand of the wicked" (Ps. 82:4)

42 Friendliest

43 "The LORD will ___ from Zion" (Amos 1:2)

46 Slum

48 "Waters ___ out" (Ezek. 47:8)

49 Moses' bush was in this condition (Ex. 3:2)

50 Nicodemus was a "___ of the Jews" (John 3:1)

51 Having wings

52 Thick

54 Dorothy's dog

56 "Veil was ___" (Mark 15:38)

57 Precedes an alias

58 "No ___ can do these miracles" (John 3:2)

59 "The servant of the Lord must not strive; but be gentle unto all men, ___ to teach" (2 Tim. 2:24)

61 "I cannot redeem it for myself, lest I ___ mine own inheritance" (Ruth 4:6)

NOAH:
THE GREAT BUILDER
by Vicki J. Kuyper

ACROSS

1 Publicist, slang
6 "The Pharisees began to ___ him vehemently" (Luke 11:53)
10 Trick
14 Northern Egyptian city
15 Person, place, or thing
16 California univ.
17 Noah built one (Gen. 8:20)
18 "As the ___ of Noah were" (Matt 24:37)
19 "Sun and ___" (Ps. 148:3)
20 KJV's roe
21 "They shall ___ thee until thou perish" (Deut. 28:22)
23 What manna would do if kept overnight (Ex. 16:20)
24 "God is ___" (2 Cor. 9:8)
26 African country
28 Walk quietly

31 Noah remained in the ark this long after the dove's return (Gen. 8:12)
32 Ninevah to 4 Down (dir.)
33 "That the ___ of Noah" (Isa. 54:9)
36 Evils
40 Passed (slang)
42 Precedes alias
43 Orderly
44 Rice wine
45 Pancakes in Paris
48 By means of
49 "Noah found grace in the ___ of the LORD" (Gen. 6:8)
51 Leif Erikson, e.g.
53 Merchant, as in Gen. 37:28
56 Quote
57 Movie 2001's talking computer

58 Nap raiser
61 European mountains
65 Shine
67 Sinai or Goshen, e.g.
68 Ermine
69 "Noah was ___ hundred" when he became a dad (Gen. 5:32)
70 "Ye are forgers of ___" (Job 13:4)
71 Bulgarian capital
72 Mary is believed to have been one when she gave birth to Jesus
73 Nebuchadnezzar was not this when he ate grass (Dan. 4:33)
74 Palm Sunday celebrates Jesus' ___ into Jerusalem

DOWN

1 University (abbr.)
2 The valley of Shaveh was the king of Sodom's (Gen. 14:17)
3 One of the generous widow's (Luke 21:2)
4 Ark's stopping place (Gen. 8:4)
5 "Ye do err, not knowing the scriptures, ___ the power of God" (Matt. 22:29)
6 Soldiers came with ___ force to arrest Jesus (Luke 22:52)
7 "Let the sea ___" (1 Chron. 16:32)

8 Gals' partner
9 Christ's sacrifice ___ our forgiveness
10 Sticky stuff
11 Nut
12 "A ___ of waters" (Gen. 6:17)
13 Soft drink brand
21 "Just As I Am, Without One ___"
22 Baaaad critter on the ark
25 "I do set my ___ in the cloud" (Gen. 9:13)
27 Similar

28 What Celestial Seasonings makes
29 South American Indian
30 The ark's window in Gen. 6:16 afforded Noah one
31 Noah's robe: AKA
34 Noah does this to the ark (Gen. 6:14)
35 Stretch to make do
37 Jacob's son (Gen. 34:25)
38 "Had ___ in the grave four days already" (John 11:17)
39 Deer

41 "All flesh ___ " (Gen. 7:21)
45 Grains
46 "___ from his youth" (Gen. 8:21)
47 "It is vain for you to rise up early, to ___ up late" (Ps. 127:2)
50 "He stayed ___ other seven days; and sent forth the dove" (Gen. 8:12)
52 Batman actor

53 Joseph accused his brothers of this (Gen. 44:11-15)
54 Synthetic fabric
55 "Noah only remained ___ " (Gen. 7:23)
56 "Day and night shall not ___ " (Gen. 8:22)
59 Opera solo
60 "For thee have I ___ righteous before me" (Gen. 7:1)

62 Eutychus fell from the third one (Acts 20:9)
63 There was a ___ of each animal on the ark
64 "___ upon his God" (Isa. 50:10)
66 Number of God's commandments
68 Jerusalem to Bethany (dir.)

seventy three

OBADIAH: WORSHIPPER OF JEHOVAH

by Tonya Vilhauer

ACROSS

1 "___, she is broken" (Ezek. 26:2)
4 Southwestern American tribe
8 "___ in me a clean heart" (Ps. 51:10)
14 Make bare the ___ (Isa. 47:2)
15 Obtain
16 "I cried by ___ " (Jonah 2:2)
17 Time period
18 Similar
19 Fished
20 Dwelled
22 Hair product
23 "___ thee like a ball" (Isa. 22:18)
24 "Set thy ___ among the stars" (Obad. 1:4)
27 "Three full ___" (Dan. 10:2)
31 "The house of Jacob shall be a ___ " (Obad. 1:18)

33 Doctors for car safety
35 "Thou shalt ___" (Mic. 6:15)
36 "Neither shall be ___ more" (Joel 2:2)
38 Option (abbr.)
39 Painter of melting clocks
40 "Thou that savest by thy right hand," as in Ps. 17:7, does this
44 Best pitcher award (2 wds.)
46 Military leave without permission
47 "Esau may be ___ off" (Obad. 1:9)
49 Tracking electrical impulses of the brain
50 "All the ___ of thy confederacy" (Obad. 1:7)
51 "Behold the fowls of the ___ " (Matt. 6:26)

52 Mount Sinai in Arabia (Gal. 4:25)
55 "The ___ is full" (Joel 3:13)
58 Classification
61 Experts
63 Stretch to make do
65 Interpreter
67 A worshipper of God, as in John 9:31
70 France and Germany river
71 Day of the week (abbr.)
72 Skinnier
73 California univ.
74 Make angry
75 "The ___ of the rock" (Obad. 1:3)
76 "The spreading of ___ in the midst of the sea" (Ezek. 26:5)
77 Nervous sys.

DOWN

1 Notify
2 "The fame ___ went abroad" (Matt. 9:26)
3 Tennis player Andre
4 "Thy reward shall return upon thine own ___" (Obad. 1:15)
5 Made of oak
6 "The ___ of thine heart hath deceived thee" (Obad. 1:3)
7 "There was no room for them in the ___" (Luke 2:7)
8 "Upon the ___ of the rock" (Job 39:28)

9 "___ a right spirit within me" (Ps. 51:10)
10 "Exalt thyself as the ___" (Obad. 1:4)
11 Communication method
12 "The great ___ of his right foot" (Lev. 14:28)
13 "An utter ___ of the place" (Nah. 1:8)
21 Captivity of the children of ___ (Obad. 1:20)
25 Resort hotel
26 Baby powder

28 "The house of ___ for stubble" (Obad. 1:18)
29 Cologne (Gr.)
30 Quick drink
32 Bethlehem to Bethany (dir.)
34 Eye infection
37 Song by the Village People
39 Muzzle (2 wds.)
40 Freeway entrance
41 Earthen vessel, perhaps, as in Lev. 6:28
42 "As thou hast ___, it shall be done unto thee" (Obad. 1:15)

43 "Many shall make ___ unto thee" (Job 11:19)
45 "___, they shall drink" (Obad. 1:16)
48 "Will ___ them as gold is tried" (Zech. 13:9)
53 Vinegar is this
54 "For dust thou art, and unto dust shalt thou ___" (Gen. 3:19)
56 Stems of letters
57 Trapshooting
59 "The men that were at ___ with thee" (Obad. 1:7)
60 To glorify, as in Obad. 1:4
62 Searches
64 Goofs
66 Time periods
67 TV station
68 Pain measurement
69 "Even thou wast as ___ of them" (Obad. 1:11)
70 God will cause the ___ to go down at noon (Amos 8:9)

seventy four

PAUL:
THE PERSECUTOR

by Tonya Vilhauer

ACROSS

1 Path cut through grass
6 Nails
10 Period
13 Composer Roy
15 Band instrument
16 "Sir, come down ___ my child die" (John 4:49)
17 End of performance cheer
18 Part of speech
19 Large vessel
20 "He was accused of the ___" (Acts 22:30)
22 Paul was sent to ___ (Acts 15:22)
24 African country
26 Paul "preached the ___ of the LORD" (Acts 15:36)
28 "Let the peace of God ___ in your hearts" (Col. 3:15)
29 Blintz
30 "The ___ also calved" (Jer. 14:5)
31 Bishop's headdress
32 Paul was taken ___ of the temple (Acts 21:30)
33 Citizen of Denmark
34 "There ___ a great earthquake" (Acts 16:26)
35 Disgusting
37 Bomb tip
41 The one with 5 loaves and 2 fishes (John 6:9)
42 "And we know that all things ___ together" (Rom. 8:28)
43 "For a ___ and for a snare" (Isa. 8:14)
44 Legal
47 Paul did not spend ___ in Asia in Acts 20:16
48 Cola
49 "The first man ___ was made a living soul" (1 Cor. 15:45)
50 "Who is ___ into heaven" (1 Peter 3:22)
51 Arch
52 Cattle house (2 wds.)
54 "Baptized in the ___ of the Lord" (Acts 10:48)
56 With an high ___ he brought them out of Egypt (Acts 13:17)
57 Soap opera
59 "Neither have I desired the ___ day" (Jer. 17:16)
63 Ball holder
64 Depart quickly
65 Enclose
66 White-tailed sea eagle
67 The head cannot say to the feet "I have no ___ of you" (1 Cor. 12:21)
68 Paul was filled with the Holy ___ (Acts 13:9)

DOWN

1 "And this did ___ many days" (Acts 16:18)
2 Weak and sickly
3 Curve
4 Like the wooden horse
5 Paul stayed in his own ___ house (Acts 28:30)
6 "___ his son" (1 Chron. 7:27)
7 "We went ___, and set forth" (Acts 21:2)
8 "Felix…left Paul ___" (Acts 24:27)
9 Paul was ___ away (Acts 17:14)
10 Pious soldier in Acts 10:7
11 "Lift up my hands toward thy holy ___ (Ps. 28:2)
12 Horse's leash
14 Jacob used stones for these (Gen. 28:11)
21 "Husks that the ___ did eat" (Luke 15:16)
23 U.K. members
24 Guild
25 Beats
27 "___, who is called Christ" (Matt. 1:16)
29 Ghost's greeting
30 Paul beckoned with this (Acts 13:16)
31 "Press toward the ___" (Phil. 3:14)
33 Jesus pronounced Lazarus ___ in John 11:14
34 Article of merchandise
36 Hike a mountain
37 "Honorable ___ which were Greeks" (Acts 17:12)

38 Id's counterparts
39 Military officer
40 Genetic code
42 "That I may ___ Christ" (Phil. 3:8)
44 Abandon
45 Admirer
46 Peacekeepers

47 "Hear we every man in our own ___" (Acts 2:8)
48 Moses: "Slow of ___" (Ex. 4:10)
50 "___ of God" (Acts 15:40)
51 Paul tarried ___ them (Acts 25:6)
53 Group

55 "Stand in ___" (Ps. 4:4)
58 Rachel: "The LORD shall add to me another son" (Gen. 30:24)
60 ___ Schwarz, toy store
61 Ship initials
62 "___ my people go" (Ex. 5:1)

PETER: THE ROCK

by Tonya Vilhauer

ACROSS

1 Large department store
6 First letter of the Arabic alphabet
10 Animal covering
13 Jesus went into the ___ of the high priest (John 18:15)
15 Do it again
16 Jerusalem to Jericho (dir.)
17 Mount Sinai is in ___ (Gal. 4:25)
18 "For they ___ that he was Christ" (Luke 4:41)
19 Sixth sense
20 Wine bottle
22 The "disciples went away into ___" (Matt. 28:16)
24 Penny
26 Welcome rugs
28 "Ye have ___ him go into heaven" (Acts 1:11)

29 Governing authority (abbr.)
30 Waistband
31 "Noah offered ___ offerings on the altar" (Gen. 8:20)
32 Alias (abbr.)
33 Jesus gave them ___ and bread (John 21:9)
34 Twelve (abbr.)
35 Dogmas
37 Injuries
41 Laden with fish, Simon's ___ broke in Luke 5:6
42 The vine's "blossoms ___ forth" in Gen. 40:10
43 Moose relative
44 "His ___ is not changed" (Jer. 48:11)
47 Peter gets into this to go fishing in John 21:3
48 "The ___ Ghost" (Matt. 1:20)

49 Egyptian river
50 "The fallow ___" (Deut. 14:4–5)
51 Damp
52 Bitter tasting
54 Dreadful
56 Pastor (abbr.)
57 Wager
59 "Thou waterest the ___ thereof abundantly (Ps. 65:10)
63 Before (poet.)
64 Competition at the Greek games
65 Happenings
66 "God. . .hath glorified his ___ Jesus" (Acts 3:13)
67 "___, thou art God" (Acts 4:24)
68 Elicit

DOWN

1 Resort hotel
2 Peter cut off Malchus's right ___ (John 18:10)
3 Wing
4 Jack or bunny follower
5 Descendant
6 "The ___ of the covenant" (Heb. 9:4)
7 "___ of days is in her right hand" (Prov. 3:16)
8 Thoughts
9 "Winged ___ after his kind" (Gen. 1:21)
10 Toucher
11 Undetected

12 "Peter said unto them, ___, and be baptized" (Acts 2:38)
14 "Rise, Peter. . .___" (Acts 10:13)
21 Accumulate
23 Car manufacturer
24 Pepsi rival
25 Elliptic
27 "Planteth an ___" (Isa. 44:14)
29 Idle talk
30 Satan wants to ___ as wheat (Luke 22:31)
31 Fishing trade necessity

33 Peter to Jesus: Wash not only my ___ but also my hands and head (John 13:9)
34 "The mountains shall ___ down new wine" (Joel 3:18)
36 Outer's opposite
37 "Go to Caesarea. . .at the ___ hour of the night" (Acts 23:23)
38 Cry like a cat
39 Associate
40 "The ___ is red" (Matt. 16:2)
42 "___ knew Peter's voice, she opened not the gate for gladness, but ran in" (Acts 12:14)

44 "Depart from the ___ of
death" (Prov. 13:14)
45 Roman statesman
46 Jesus had ___ disciples
(Matt. 28:16)
47 Land plot
48 Listened to

50 Wild dog
51 "When the ship was caught...
we let her ___" (Acts 27:15)
53 There were 450 prophets of
this (1 Kings 18:19)
55 Fierce wrath, as in Ps. 88:16

58 God to Noah: "The ___ of
all flesh is come before me"
(Gen.6:13)
60 African antelope
61 And so forth (abbr.)
62 Directional points

seventy-six

PHARAOH: THE HARD-HEARTED RULER

by Tonya Vilhauer

ACROSS

1 Couches
6 Time period
9 "Shalt ___ a son" (Gen. 16:11)
13 Lower
14 "___ shall give Pharaoh an answer of peace" (Gen. 41:16)
15 ___ ___ of Two Cities (2 wds.)
16 "Whose soever sins ye ___" (John 20:23)
17 Root vegetable
18 "Shall I go and call to thee a ___?" (Ex. 2:7)
19 Opera solo
20 "Fountains. . .that ___ out of valleys and hills" (Deut. 8:7)
22 "Jacob ___ pottage" (Gen. 25:29)
23 Charged particle
24 Winged mammal
25 Shallow area in the sea

27 Birthmark
29 Sarah's husband (Gen. 20:2)
33 Government tax agency
34 Brew
35 Ripped up
36 "___ of ten shekels" (Num. 7:14)
39 Cancer research org.
40 Shininess
41 Duke
42 Jesus took the ___, and gave thanks (Matt. 26:27)
43 Tint
44 People without color
46 "Ten ___ of vineyard shall yield one bath" (Isa. 5:10)
49 Cool
50 "I wrote them with ___ in the book" (Jer. 36:18)
51 One-sixtieth of a minute (abbr.)

53 And so on (abbr.)
56 The Lord to Moses: "With a ___ hand shall he let them go" (Ex. 6:1)
58 Blemish
59 After God smote Pharaoh, "a ___ cry in Egypt" (Ex. 12:30)
61 "There was no room for them in the ___" (Luke 2:7)
62 Jonathon felt bad for David because "his father had done him ___" (1 Sam. 20:34)
63 Covers with gold
64 "I ___ no pleasant bread" (Dan. 10:3)
65 Golden oil empties from "two golden ___" (Zech. 4:12)
66 Joseph's brothers ___ him to the Ismeelites (Gen. 37:28)
67 Neither's partner
68 Concerning

DOWN

1 Abram's wife (Gen. 12:5)
2 Titania's husband
3 Egypt's lack of food will be this (Gen. 41:36)
4 Continent
5 Joseph ___ his father before Pharaoh (Gen. 47:7)
6 Famine shall consume this land in Gen. 41:30
7 Young lions ___ after their prey (Ps. 104:21)
8 Naval leaders

9 Heat unit
10 He that has these, let him hear (Matt. 11:15)
11 "I will ___ draw for thy camels" (Gen. 24:44)
12 "This bruised ___" (2 Kings 18:21)
15 "Let not thy ___ burn (Gen. 44:18)
20 Back talk
21 Nazareth to Tiberias (dir.)
24 "Let us make brick, and ___ them thoroughly" (Gen. 11:3)

26 "Leave his ___ and his mother" (Gen. 2:24)
28 Orchestra instrument
30 Garden tool
31 Pharaoh to Moses: "Who ___ they that shall go?" (Ex. 10:8)
32 "Pharaoh commanded his ___" (Gen. 12:20)
34 Police officer talk
36 The Israelites crossed the ___ on dry ground (Ex. 14:22)
37 Chum

38 Ball
39 People from Vienna
40 "He made him to ___ honey out of the rock (Deut. 32:13)
42 Joseph's father made him a ___ of many colors (Gen. 37:3)
43 "Pharaoh. . .shall ___ thee on a tree" (Gen. 40:19)

45 Foxes have holes, and birds have these (Matt. 8:20)
47 They smote them and let none ___ (Josh. 8:22)
48 Mariners
50 Solomon "built the ___ court" with stone (1 Kings 6:36)
52 Crown

53 Partridge sits on these (Jer. 17:11)
54 Triad
55 Jail room
57 Upon
58 Lower leg
60 "___ to your faith" (2 Peter 1:5)
62 Whirlpool

seventy 77 *seven*

PHILEMON: THE AFFECTIONATE ONE

by Tonya Vilhauer

ACROSS

1 Thespian's job (abbr.)
5 Tap in lightly
9 The Holy ___ is a witness to us (Heb. 10:15)
14 The shepherds "were ___ afraid" (Luke 2:9)
15 Thought
16 The tree of life yielded fruit every ___ (Rev. 22:2)
17 "I ___ have written it with mine own hand" (Philem. 1:19)
18 Liturgy of the Eucharist
19 Scholar
20 The brooks are blackish "by reason of the ___" (Job 6:16)
21 Vegetable
23 "___ to honour" (2 Tim. 2:20)
24 Jesus (Philem. 1:3)
26 "___ hospitality" (1 Peter 4:9)

28 Dit's partner
29 Stoles
31 Tint
34 Male dairy worker
37 "I ___ my God" (Philem. 1:4)
39 Abraham, "when he was called ___ ___ out. . . obeyed" (Heb. 11:8) (2 wds)
40 "___ affliction to my bonds" (Phil. 1:16)
41 Parlay
42 "If he. . .___thee ought" (Philem. 1:18)
44 ___ da Vinci
47 "The beginning and the ___" (Rev. 22:13)
48 Breastplate
50 Game presider (abbr.)
51 Not against

52 Misters
56 "___ from idolatry" (1 Cor. 10:14)
59 Suppress
63 Listen in
64 Reliable
66 "Every man a ___" (Rom. 3:4)
67 Peter, for short
68 Put up
69 Ancient Indian
70 "We launched, meaning to ___ by the coasts of Asia" (Acts 27:2)
71 "The Lord ___ to the church daily" (Acts 2:47)
72 "They might ___ after him, and find him" (Acts 17:27)
73 "Offered unto an ___" (1 Cor. 8:7)

DOWN

1 Molded salad
2 Trainer
3 Not as false
4 Solidify
5 "___ our brother" (Philem. 1:1)
6 First man (1 Cor. 15:45)
7 Plateau
8 Present's opposite
9 U.K. time zone
10 Abraham's servant to Rebekah: "Is there room in thy father's ___ ?" (Gen. 24:23)

11 Upon
12 "The ___ of Jesse" (Isa. 11:1)
13 "I do not say to ___ how thou owest unto me" (Philem. 1:19)
21 An emperor
22 "God ___ Father" (Philem. 1:3)
25 Imbecile
27 Concord, e.g.
29 Dims
30 "___ the heavy burdens" (Isa. 58:6)

31 Noah "put forth his ___" (Gen. 8:9)
32 "I wrote ___ thee" (Philem. 1:21)
33 To supplement: ___ out
34 "He laid ___ his life" (1 John 3:16)
35 "The ___ women likewise" (Titus 2:3)
36 African nation
38 "With singing, and with ___" (1 Chron. 13:8)
39 "The great ___ of his right foot" (Lev. 14:28)

43 Pronoun

45 Number representer

46 "The grace of. . .Christ be with your spirit. ___" (Philem. 1:25)

49 "I thank my ___" (Philem. 1:4)

51 Grace and ___ (Philem. 1:3)

53 "In thy ___he might have ministered" (Philem. 1:13)

54 Relationship

55 Short period of time

56 "The king of Israel is come out to seek a ___" (1 Sam. 26:20)

57 "The ___ be with you all" (2 Thess. 3:16)

58 "Saul ___ David from that day and forward" (1 Sam. 18:9)

60 First letter of the Arabic alphabet

61 "I have lift up ___ hand unto the LORD" (Gen. 14:22)

62 Walk back and forth

65 Ford vehicle

67 23rd letter of the Greek alphabet

PHILIP:
THE HORSE LOVER

by Tonya Vilhauer

ACROSS

1 Snow gliders
5 The disciples were ___ ___ in John 21:1 (2 wds.)
10 Make lace
13 Capital of France
15 "A ___ in the flesh" (2 Cor. 12:7)
16 Lyric poem
17 Having wings
18 "Sin which doth so easily ___ us" (Heb. 12:1)
19 "David hastened, and ___ toward the army to meet Goliath" (1 Sam. 17:48)
20 Both ___ and women were baptized in Acts 8:12
21 "For ___ was first formed, then Eve" (1 Tim. 2:13)
23 "God created man in his own image___" (Gen. 1:27)
25 After being baptized, Philip was "caught ___" by the Spirit of the Lord (Acts 8:39)
26 Isaiah, e.g.
28 "Thou shalt not let him_____ empty" (Deut. 15:13) (2 wds.)
31 "___ not the unclean thing; and I will receive you" (2 Cor. 6:17)
32 Backstreet
33 Abraham. . .spake unto the sons of ___ (Gen. 23:3)
34 Seize
37 He ___ the book of the covenant (Acts 8:32)
38 "Philip opened his ___. . .and preached unto him Jesus" (Acts 8:35)
40 Idiot
41 "I believe that Jesus Christ is the ___ of God" (Acts 8:37)
42 "The angel of the ___ spake unto Philip" (Acts 8:26)
43 The Lord to Noah: "Come thou and all thy ___ into the ark" (Acts 8:3)
44 Baits
45 Young swan
46 "There shall be ___, and pestilences" (Matt. 24:7)
49 Identical
50 Open mouthed
51 "Philip went ___. . .to Samaria" to preach (Acts 8:5)
52 Before (prefix)
55 Physician, for short
56 "___ is among the mountains" (Jer. 46:18)
59 Leading
61 Epoch
62 "The thought of ___ heart may be forgiven" (Acts 8:22)
63 Metric measurement (Brit.)
64 The eunuch ___ Philip no more (Acts 8:39)
65 Nosher
66 Viewed

DOWN

1 Canned meat brand
2 Cabbage cousin
3 Iraq's neighbor
4 "Come up and ___" (Acts 8:31)
5 Treed (2 wds.)
6 "Simon offered ___ money" so he could have the power of the Holy Spirit, too (Acts 8:18)
7 Distress call
8 Before, (poet.)
9 Barnabas should go as far as ___ (Acts 11:22)
10 Jewish scripture
11 Expression
12 Belief of the truth
14 Sea route
22 God called light this (Gen. 1:5)
24 Speed measurement
25 Reverent
26 Poem creator
27 Naomi's daughter-in-law (Ruth 2:22)
28 Long fish
29 Fake butter
30 Actor Alda
31 Bumps
34 Sentence part
35 Niche

36 Purple vegetable

38 To a greater degree

39 Mined metals

40 Former magistrate of Venice

42 Crescent-shaped object

43 Book of hymns

44 "The ___ of truth shall be established for ever" (Prov. 12:19)

45 Crow's cry

46 Dims

47 One hundred of these makes a shekel in Israel

48 Parrot

49 More irritated

51 Simon was amazed at the "signs which were ___" (Acts 8:13)

52 Petroleum engineer, for short

53 "It is a ___ thing that the king requireth" (Dan. 2:11)

54 Adam and Eve's garden

57 "___ I am warm" (Isa. 44:16)

58 "With ___ and bridle" (Ps. 32:9)

60 "He went on ___ way rejoicing" (Acts 8:39)

PILATE: THE GOVERNOR OF JUDAEA

by Tonya Vilhauer

ACROSS

1 Pantomime (abbr.)
5 Regional plant life
10 "The heavens shall give their ___" (Zech. 8:12)
13 Imitation chocolate
15 Isaac blessed ___ (Gen. 27:21–23)
16 Time period
17 Creed
18 "Even to the ___ court" (Ezek. 10:5)
19 Tiger
20 Ball holder
21 Shina
23 "Multitude. . .___" and led Jesus to Pilate (Luke 23:1)
25 Pilate: "I ___ no fault in this man" (Luke 23:4)
26 One who obeys

28 Talisman
31 Stingy
32 Pilate was "willing to release ___" in Luke 23:20
33 Wander
34 Basketball assoc.
37 Middle Eastern dweller
38 Architect Frank ___ Wright
40 Fines
41 Sport's official (abbr.)
42 The ship in Acts 27:41 was run aground "where two ___ met"
43 Writings
44 Pilate washed his ___ to show his innocence in Matt. 27:24
45 Asian country
46 Dog food brand (2 wds.)

49 Some people murmured, "He is a ___ man" in John 7:12
50 "Upon the ___ of his right hand" (Lev. 14:28)
51 Endure
52 Investigation agency
55 "___ thou the King?" (John 18:33)
56 Malicious burning
59 Synthetic fiber
61 Downwind
62 "Pilate wrote a ___" (John 19:19)
63 Predictors of the future
64 "Little ___ lamb" (2 Sam. 12:3)
65 Houses
66 Herod ___ Jesus "again to Pilate" (Luke 23:11)

DOWN

1 "Give an ___ of thy stewardship" (Luke 16:2) (abbr.)
2 Samaritan: "Take ___ of him" (Luke 10:35)
3 God raised up Jesus "whom ye. . .hanged on a ___" (Acts 5:30)
4 "The Christ, the Son of ___" (Matt. 26:63)
5 Narrow inlet between cliffs
6 "Praise the Lord. . .and ___ him" (Rom. 15:11)
7 Halloween mo.
8 KJV's deer

9 Isaac was the son of ___ (Luke 3:34)
10 Decoration
11 Take off
12 Out of Jesus' side came "blood and ___" (John 19:34)
14 The ___ should not remain upon the cross (John 19:31)
22 "Go to the ___" (Prov. 6:6)
24 Representative (abbr.)
25 Foul-up
26 Sailors' "hey"
27 "He is not a God of the ___, but of the living " (Luke 20:38)

28 Partially opened
29 Bare livelihood
30 Military branch
31 Mary stood by the ___ (John 19:25)
34 Following
35 Second letter of the Greek alphabet
36 Organization (abbr.)
38 Comedian Jay
39 Woman
40 Isaac, Rebekah, Esau, and Jacob had a family ___ (Gen. 27:15)

42 "When the ___ was past" Mary went to Jesus' tomb (Mark 16:1)

43 "Crown of ___" (Mark 15:17)

44 One of Noah's sons (Gen. 5:32)

45 Snake

46 ___ ___ of Two Cities (2 wds.)

47 The poor widow "___ in two mites" (Mark 12:42)

48 Scholar

49 Units of heredity

51 Tree trunk

52 "Who hath warned you to ___ from the wrath?" (Matt. 3:7)

53 Jesus to Pilate: "To this end was I ___" (John 18:37)

54 Influential org.

57 "By a ___ side" (Acts 16:13) (Sp.)

58 Remember only recent events

60 "___, Lord" (Mark 7:28)

eighty 80

RACHEL, THE BEAUTIFUL WIFE

by Tonya Vilhauer

ACROSS

1 Rachel's father (Gen. 29:10)
6 Last day of the work wk.
9 On top
13 Saying
14 Abraham "took the ___" (Gen. 22:13)
15 Swelling
16 "___ stones at him, and cast dust" (2 Sam. 16:13)
17 Referee (abbr.)
18 Individualist
19 "Restore all that was ___" (2 Kings 8:6)
20 Telephoned
22 Trinitrotoluene, for short
23 Before, (poet.)
24 Rachel ___ upon the images in Gen. 31:34
25 "Am I ___ ___" (Job 7:12) (2 wds.)
27 Legate
29 Recite
33 Spots
34 Heat measurement
35 "And left ___" (Gen. 29:35) (var.)
36 Cliff debris
39 Transport
40 Uncovered
41 Jacob put a pillar ___ Rachel's grave (Gen. 35:20)
42 "It is ___ high day" (Gen. 29:7)
43 Chassis, for short
44 Caves
46 Mid-Eastern dwellers
49 Sego lily's bulb
50 Sea eagle
51 Rachel ___ and told her father what Jacob said (Gen. 29:12)
53 School group
56 "All their ___ ones" (Gen. 34:29)
58 "Let him not ___" (Gen. 31:32)
59 Therefore
61 ___ chi
62 Fizzy drinks
63 "All the ___ of his sons" (Gen. 46:15)
64 Lengthen (abbr.)
65 ___-garde
66 "Prick," as in Acts 2:37
67 Rachel wanted children or wanted to ___ (Gen. 30:1)
68 Becomes liquid

DOWN

1 Machine tool
2 Bind
3 Rachel was ___ (Gen. 29:31)
4 Glory to Jesus "throughout all ___" (Eph. 3:21)
5 "There arose. . .a ___ king over Egypt" (Ex. 1:8)
6 God withheld from Rachel "the ___ of the womb" (Gen. 30:2)
7 "In ___ was there a voice heard" as Rachel wept (Matt. 2:18)
8 Embeds
9 "Why make ye this ___, and weep?" (Mark 5:39)
10 Laban "entered into Rachel's ___" (Gen. 31:33)
11 Bode
12 "An omer is the tenth ___ of an ephah" (Ex. 16:36)
15 Laban's ___ daughter's name was Leah (Gen. 29:16)
20 "Give me my wife, for my ___ are fulfilled" (Gen. 29:21)
21 Jacob's brother (Gen. 32:6)
24 Turfs
26 Fleet
28 Boasts
30 "Any winged fowl that flieth in the ___" (Deut. 4:17)
31 Ball holder
32 When "Isaac had made an ___ of blessing Jacob," Esau returned (Gen. 27:30)
34 Leah was tender eyed; "___ Rachel was beautiful" (Gen. 29:17)
36 Pull
37 Interest rate
38 Water closet
39 Stupefied

40 "Rachel had ___ Joseph" (Gen. 30:25)

42 Bear or Berra

43 "Rachel saw that she ___ Jacob no children" (Gen. 30:1)

45 Expresses

47 Nuptial

48 Scholar

50 Privileged

52 "Where the birds make their ___" (Ps. 104:17)

53 "It came to ___" (Gen. 29:10)

54 Gait

55 Roll the stone from the well, then "___ the sheep" (Gen. 29:8) (Sp.)

57 Cab

58 To Jacob, seven years seemed like nothing "for the ___ he had" for Rachel (Gen. 29:20)

60 Loose gown worn at mass

62 ___ Walton

RAHAB'S SCARLET RIBBON

by Laura Lisle

ACROSS

1 Scent
5 Brews
9 Secondhand
13 Abba, familiarly
14 The Alps' Mont ___
15 Leaf bud
16 Adam's garden
17 Singer Ronstadt
18 Chapter piece
19 Secret meeting
21 "Ye have ___ iniquity" (Hos. 10:13)
23 Rahab's advice: "___ yourselves" (Josh. 2:16)
24 Group

25 Assuage, as in Gen. 8:1
28 Female deer pelt
31 Assert
32 Swagger
34 Between David and death (1 Sam. 20:3)
36 Passover hour (abbr.)
37 Anointing essential (Ex. 29:7)
38 Govt. environmental agency
39 Leprosy sign, as in Lev. 13:2
41 Trapshooting
43 Saudi Arabia neighbor
44 Paid for someone
46 Tease
48 Eagerness

49 Proper
50 Icy
53 People from Faero Islands
57 Describes garden walking time (Gen. 3:8)
58 Australian marsupial
60 "Though he ___ me, yet will I trust in him" (Job 13:15)
61 Colt's mom
62 "I ___ not from thy precepts" (Ps. 119:110)
63 Patmos
64 "Unto the ___ of the earth" (Acts 13:47)
65 Meat to eat (Deut. 14:4–5)
66 Mustard is one (Matt. 13:31)

DOWN

1 Iran and Iraq are members
2 Pedestal part
3 "I will ___ my mouth in a parable" (Ps. 78:2)
4 Cowman
5 "Joshua saved Rahab the harlot ___" (Josh. 6:25)
6 Small street in Luke 14:21 (sing.)
7 "World without ___" (Eph. 3:21)
8 Rahab's thread (Josh. 2:18)
9 Does with suitcases
10 The Lord is like "fullers' __" (Mal. 3:2)
11 "___ of the sword" (Josh. 6:21)
12 Jesus, "Mighty in ___ and word" (Luke 24:19)

14 They spring up (Matt. 13:26) (pl.)
20 Priest put a hole in this (2 Kings 12:9)
22 Aurora
24 Greek government
25 Horns blown in Jericho (Josh. 6:5)
26 Expel
27 Lebanon wood
28 "God ___ up the waters of Jordan" (Josh. 4:23)
29 Objects
30 Everest home
33 Rahab required one (Josh. 2:12)
35 Glass window section

40 Edible insect (Lev. 11:22) (pl.)
41 How corn is stored, as in Ex. 22:6 (past tense)
42 Rahab window hanging (Josh. 2:18)
43 Diffusion of water
45 Boxer Muhammad
47 "Birds of the ___ have nests" (Matt. 8:20)
49 More wan
50 Peak
51 Colored horse
52 Spies' escape route in Josh. 2:15
53 Jonah paid this in Joppa (Jonah 1:3)
54 "I am the LORD; and there is none ___" (Isa. 45:18)

55 Its price according to years (Lev. 25:50)

56 "Leah was tender ___" (Gen. 29:17)

59 Miner's goal

REBEKAH: THE MOTHER OF TWINS

by Tonya Vilhauer

ACROSS

1 "A man ___ number the dust of the earth" (Gen. 13:16)
4 "___ was a plain man" (Gen. 25:27)
9 Doughnut-shaped roll
14 "Neither do thou ___ thing unto him" (Gen. 22:12)
15 Birds "thumb"
16 Man should not be ___ (Gen. 2:18)
17 Disorderly crowd
18 Rebekah drew ___ from the well in Gen. 24:45
19 Isaac ___ Rebekah (Gen. 24:67)
20 Impress
22 Rebekah "___ upon the camels" in Gen. 24:61
24 "Grow as the ___" (Hos. 14:5)
25 Space defined by boundaries

27 "And he ___, Speak on" (Gen. 24:33)
31 Meets
32 Deluxe
33 Spanish "one"
34 Threesome
36 "The LORD hath blessed thee ___ my coming" (Gen. 30:30)
38 Dull from fatigue
40 Jacob to Rebekah: "I am a ___ man" (Gen. 27:11)
42 "All over like an ___ garment" (Gen. 25:25)
43 "Make the trumpet ___" (Lev. 25:9)
44 Clumsy person
45 "___ foolish questions" (Titus 3:9)
47 Thought

51 Delight
53 Spring of water
54 Person, place, or thing
55 Evils
57 Dinner drink
59 Utilization
62 Native American lodge
65 "A time to rend, and a time to ___" (Eccl. 3:7)
66 "For my ___ are many" (Lam. 1:22)
67 "One ___ unto all" (Eccl. 9:3)
68 Specifies an alias
69 Composer Francis ___ Key
70 "Isaac was comforted after his mother's ___" (Gen. 24:67)
71 "___ not thine hand upon the lad" (Gen. 22:12)

DOWN

1 "I will give thy ___ drink also" (Gen. 24:14)
2 Absence of values
3 Half a byte
4 "My tongue cleaveth to my ___" (Ps. 22:15)
5 "___, my lord. . .lay not the sin upon us" (Num. 12:11)
6 "Neither shall all flesh be ___ off any more" (Gen. 9:11)
7 Roberto's yes
8 Rebekah was ___ (Gen. 29:31)

9 A man whose hair has fallen out is ___ (Lev. 13:40)
10 "The trees of lign ___" (Num. 24:6)
11 Executive head of a state
12 Vane direction
13 "Which had ___ me in the right way" (Gen. 24:48)
21 Pearl maker
23 "Jacob hid them under the ___" (Gen. 35:4)
25 "They sent ___ Rebekah" (Gen. 24:59)
26 Cool (slang)

28 "She is thine ___" (Lev. 18:14)
29 Type of worm
30 Buck's mate
32 "O ___, we came indeed down" (Gen. 43:20)
35 Manta
36 "Take a wife unto my ___ Isaac" (Gen. 24:4)
37 Salt addition
38 "High places of ___" (Num. 22:41)
39 Rebekah was weary of her ___ (Gen. 27:46)

A crossword puzzle grid with numbered cells (1–71).

Grid numbers visible: 1, 2, 3, 4, 5, 6, 7, 8, 9, 10, 11, 12, 13, 14, 15, 16, 17, 18, 19, 20, 21, 22, 23, 24, 25, 26, 27, 28, 29, 30, 31, 32, 33, 34, 35, 36, 37, 38, 39, 40, 41, 42, 43, 44, 45, 46, 47, 48, 49, 50, 51, 52, 53, 54, 55, 56, 57, 58, 59, 60, 61, 62, 63, 64, 65, 66, 67, 68, 69, 70, 71

40 "A good ___ by great water" (Ezek. 17:8)
41 Soil
42 Pig
43 Sun's name
45 Punching tool
46 Empowered
48 Type of fin
49 Gold finder's exclamation
50 Anyhow
52 "These ___ Milcah did bear to Nahor" (Gen. 22:23)
56 Isaac to Abimelech: "___ I die for her" (Gen. 26:9)
57 "Have ___ thee away in peace" (Gen. 26:29)
58 "From the children of ___" (Gen. 49:32)
59 Ship initials
60 Attack
61 "Many years ___" (Ezra 5:11)
63 "The serpent beguiled ___" (2 Cor. 11:3)
64 Green pod vegetable

RUTH: THE FAITHFUL DAUGHTER-IN-LAW

by Tonya Vilhauer

ACROSS

1 Play
6 "It is but a ___: and he shall. . . be clean" (Lev. 13:6)
10 "Is this house. . .become ___ ___of robbers" (Jer. 7:11) (2 wds.)
14 Tiny amounts
15 Women's magazine
16 "Forty ___, and ten bulls" (Gen. 32:15)
17 Flying insects
18 "___ of the right ear" (Lev. 14:28) (pl.)
19 Surrender
20 Coiffed
22 Pout
24 "A full reward be given thee of the LORD ___ of Israel" (Ruth 2:12)
25 Toothbrush brand (2 wds.)
27 Nudge

29 Naomi came to live "in the ___ of Moab" (Ruth 1:1)
32 Precedes an alias
33 Reduced (abbr.)
34 "When Boaz had eaten and ___" Ruth came and lay at his feet (Ruth 3:7)
37 In the dove's mouth was "an olive ___" (Gen. 8:11)
41 Type of lily
43 This fell on all the congregation in Josh. 22:20 (var.)
44 Jesus' ___ was Mary (familiar)
45 The garden that God planted (Gen. 2:8)
46 Pimpled
48 Call for help
49 "He took ___ men of the elders of the city" (Ruth 4:2)

51 Most costly
54 "Let me. . .gather after the reapers ___ the sheaves" (Ruth 2:7)
56 Treatment of something
57 "___ it for thee" (Ruth 4:8)
58 "Ye shall eat. . .the fallow ___" (Deut. 14:4–5)
60 Boaz to his servant: "Whose ___ is this?" (Ruth 2:5)
64 Goofs
66 Awkward person
68 Saudi Arabia citizen
69 Tropical edible root
70 Extremely long time periods
71 Makes music vocally
72 Colorless
73 "She told. . .all that the man had ___ to her" (Ruth 3:16)
74 Set in

DOWN

1 Fades
2 "He shall ___ up Israel out of this good land" (1 Kings 14:15)
3 Lawyer (abbr.)
4 Ruth's husband that died (Ruth 4:10)
5 Insist
6 The servant was ___ over the reapers (Ruth 2:6)
7 "___ up upon the rocks" (Jer. 4:29)
8 Dog food brand

9 Engage beforehand
10 Animal organization
11 San ___, CA
12 "He shall surely ___ her to be his wife" (Ex. 22:16)
13 "Lend him sufficient for his ___" (Deut. 15:8)
21 A group of Indic languages
23 Deer relative
26 Set to music
28 The Ishmeelites came "bearing spicery and ___" (Gen. 37:25)

29 "In any ___ thou shalt deliver him the pledge" (Deut. 24:13)
30 Ruth's son (Ruth 4:16–17)
31 "Began to ___ him" (Luke 11:53)
35 Urn
36 "This scripture must ___ have been fulfilled" (Acts 1:16)
38 "Trode them down with ___" (Judg. 20:43)
39 "___, O thou seer" (Amos 7:12)

40 "Abide here ___ by my maidens" (Ruth 2:8)
42 Upon
46 "They ___ him" (Ps. 106:32)
47 "Ruth. . .the wife of the ___" (Ruth 4:5)
50 "Thou hast shewed more kindness in the latter ___" (Ruth 3:10)

52 Tennis player Andre
53 "How shall we do for wives for them that ___?" (Judg. 21:16)
54 Distinctive qualities
55 "With oil of ___" (Est. 2:12)
56 Relating to a city
57 ___ carotene; found in carrots

59 European monetary unit
61 Phoenix's basketball team
62 Saul's army "destroyed all the people with the ___ of the sword" (1 Sam. 15:8)
63 Itemize
65 Chinese sauce
67 Compass direction

SAMSON: THE STRONG MAN BECOMES WEAK

by Tonya Vilhauer

ACROSS

1 "He ___ the withs" (Judg. 16:9)
6 Saloon
9 "Puah, the son of ___" (Judg. 10:1)
13 Clark's partner
14 Flightless bird
15 "Samson's wife was ___ to his companion" (Judg. 14:20)
16 Their cattle will not ___ (Ps. 107:38) (var.)
17 TV station
18 "Samson our ___" (Judg. 16:23)
19 "___ Iram" (Gen. 36:43)
20 The thread was ___ (Judg. 16:9)
22 Tyrannosaurus ___
23 Stretch to make do
24 Snakelike fish
25 Samson ___ a thousand men (Judg. 15:15)

27 Puffy
29 Russian Kathy
33 Verve
34 "That I may ___ Christ" (Phil. 3:8)
35 Chilled
36 "___ that I will cease" (Judg. 15:7)
39 "He shall be cast into the ___ of lions" (Dan. 6:7)
40 Soups
41 Samson about the pillars: "That I may ___ upon them" (Judg. 16:26)
42 Shirt protector
43 Garden tool
44 Jezebel "wrote ___ in Ahab's name" (1 Kings 21:8)
46 No want in the ___ (Judg. 18:10)

49 "Samson ___ unto his father, Get her for me" (Judg. 14:3)
50 Samson took the ___ and all (Judg. 16:3)
51 Tap
53 Dismayed expression
56 "Because there. . .was he ___" (Deut. 33:21)
58 Card game
59 Gravy
61 Charged particle
62 Handgrips
63 Map collection
64 Not (prefix)
65 Mete out
66 "The house ___ upon the lords" (Judg. 16:30)
67 "The ___ is red" (Matt. 16:2)
68 Make ___ from cedar (Ezek. 27:5)

DOWN

1 "The haft. . .went in after the ___" (Judg. 3:22)
2 This is a day of ___ (2 Kings 19:3)
3 "He ___ out of his sleep" (Judg. 16:14)
4 "The vulture, and the ___" (Lev. 11:14)
5 Compass direction
6 "___ of great price" (Matt. 13:46)
7 Convex shape
8 Hunting prize

9 Obnoxious noises
10 "The Philistines had dominion ___ Israel" (Judg. 14:4)
11 Interbreeding population within a species
12 "___ stones" (Ex. 25:7)
15 Civet cat's cousin
20 Samson went away with the pin of the ___ (Judg. 16:14)
21 Eagerness
24 Native ruler in Asia

26 "The pen of the ___" (Judg. 5:14)
28 "One ___ to the righteous" (Eccl. 9:2) (pl.)
30 The waters are blackish "by reason of the ___" (Job 6:16)
31 Delilah used ___ ropes (Judg. 16:12)
32 Spots
34 Weave my locks with the ___ (Judg. 16:13)
36 Samson to Delilah "___ his heart" (Judg. 16:17)

37 "Will they not pay ___" (Ezra 4:13) (var.)

38 Slang for tattoo

39 Despises

40 Fly

42 Soft cheese

43 Not a razor has come upon my ___ (Judg. 16:17)

45 Comforts

47 Tracks

48 Samson "saw there an ___" (Judg. 16:1)

50 Joon's friend (movie character)

52 Samson took "the two ___" (Judg. 16:3)

53 Military division

54 Six hundred men "stood by the entering of the ___" (Judg. 18:16)

55 Structure Noah would have needed

57 Samson "___ firebrands" (Judg. 15:4)

58 Syllables used in songs (2 wds.)

60 State by Pacific Ocean (abbr.)

62 "Or for a ___" (Num. 15:6)

SAMUEL: GOD WAS CALLING

by Tonya Vilhauer

ACROSS

1 "Why make ye this ___" (Mark 5:39)
4 Yellow cabs
9 Heart rate measurement
12 David chose "__ smooth stones" (1 Sam. 17:40)
14 Samuel offered a ___ offering (1 Sam. 7:10)
15 Ladies' magazine
16 Hannah: "There abide for ___" (1 Sam. 1:22)
17 Japanese city
18 Existing
19 Buyer risk insurance
21 Samuel had his face to the ___ (1 Sam. 28:14)
23 Eli could not ___ (1 Sam. 3:2)
24 "The ark of ___" was in the Lord's temple (1 Sam. 3:3)

25 Hannah ___ a son (1 Sam. 1:20)
28 Sport assoc.
31 Angus
34 "Ruler of ___" (Neh. 3:19)
36 Slang for cool
38 Cc
40 Astringent
41 "They are without ___" (Rom. 1:20) (var.)
43 Settee
44 Denmark currency
45 New Jersey's neighbor (abbr.)
46 Haughty
48 Prophet (1 Sam. 9:9)
51 "___ the priest sat upon a seat" (1 Sam. 1:9)
53 The people refused to ___ Samuel (1 Sam. 8:19)

54 "___, my sons" (1 Sam. 2:24)
56 Samuel found favor with the ___ (1 Sam. 2:26)
58 Decadent
61 "The LORD ___ again in Shiloh" (1 Sam. 3:21)
66 Chowder ingredient
67 Muslim's God
69 "Go ye every man unto his ___" (1 Sam. 8:22)
70 "Vessels of the young men are ___" (1 Sam. 21:5)
71 2:1, e.g.
72 Cornbread
73 "I am like an ___ of the desert" (Ps. 102:6)
74 "Samuel said, As thy ___ hath made women childless" (1 Sam. 15:33)
75 Little bit

DOWN

1 "Borrow not ___ ___" (2 Kings 4:3) (2 wds.)
2 Prima donna
3 "My mouth is enlarged ___ mine enemies" (1 Sam. 2:1)
4 Cut of beef
5 Author of Sense and Sensibility
6 Doctor's picture
7 "I wrote them with ___" (Jer. 36:18)
8 Canned chili brand
9 ___ cheese dressing

10 Method
11 Combine
13 "Manasseh made...the inhabitants of Jerusalem to ___" (2 Chron. 33:9)
15 Wear away
20 At sea
22 "___ not the poor" (Prov. 22:22)
25 Cheats
26 Blue
27 A tachometer measures this
29 Adornment

30 Scientist's office
32 Show emotions
33 Noah lived "nine hundred and ___ years: and he died" (Gen. 9:29)
34 David "feigned himself ___" (1 Sam. 21:13)
35 "Hannah ___ conceived" and bare a son (1 Sam. 1:20)
37 Insult (slang)
39 Samuel "went and ___ down" (1 Sam. 3:5)
42 Downwind
43 Bawl

47 "___ like him" (1 Sam. 10:24)
49 Samuel: "The LORD. . .is become thine ___?" (1 Sam. 28:16)
50 Rodent
52 Spoil
55 Eli was ninety-eight ___ old (1 Sam. 4:15)

57 Samuel was girded with an ___ (1 Sam. 2:18)
58 Reverberate
59 "His goods shall ___ away in the day of his wrath" (Job 20:28)
60 "Saul thought to make David ___" (1 Sam. 18:25)
61 Singing voice

62 Where doctors study
63 "To ___ in the day time" (2 Peter 2:13)
64 Volcano
65 "Who is this. . .with ___ garments?" (Isa. 63:1)
68 "Glory is departed. . .because of her father in ___" (1 Sam. 4:21)

eighty86six

SARAH:
THE MIRACLE MOM

— by Tonya Vilhauer —

ACROSS

1 Florida city
6 "To the right!"
9 Tigers
13 Arrive at
14 Brat
15 Abram "Dwelt in the plain of ___" (Gen. 13:18)
16 "Make ready. . .___ measures of fine meal" (Gen. 18:6)
17 By way of
18 Advertiser
19 Tropical wood
20 "At the time appointed I will ___ unto thee" (Gen. 18:14)
22 "God shall ___ to place his name there" (Deut. 26:2) (var.)
23 ___ Lanka
24 Sarah will have a ___ (Gen. 18:10)

25 "He ___ unto him" (1 Kings 13:18)
27 Alters
29 The sun was risen when Lot ___ Zoar (Gen. 19:23)
33 "___; but thou didst laugh" (Gen. 18:15)
34 Type of partnership
35 Not any
36 Prepare
39 Old-fashioned fathers
40 Metric capacity unit
41 Recess
42 Israel "sat upon the ___" (Gen. 48:2)
43 "I will ___ his face" (Gen. 32:20)
44 Upset (2 wds.)
46 "A people ___ with iniquity" (Isa. 1:4)
49 Shina

50 Dit's partner
51 "Put a covering upon his upper ___" (Lev. 13:45)
53 Energy unit
56 Campanile
58 Sarah made cakes with "___ meal" (Gen. 18:6)
59 Jacket part
61 "And ___ the lamp of God went out in the temple" (1 Sam. 3:3)
62 "I am ___ old" (Gen. 18:12)
63 "I called him ___, and blessed him" (Isa. 51:2)
64 Arbiter (abbr.)
65 1996 Madonna movie
66 "The wicked ___ their bow" (Ps. 11:2)
67 Sarah conceived at the ___ time (Gen. 21:2)
68 Transparent gem

DOWN

1 Baseball gloves
2 Not in there! (2 wds.)
3 Sarah was ___ (Gen. 18:15)
4 "The ___ shall inherit the earth" (Ps. 37:11)
5 "His ___ was kindled" (Gen. 39:19) (var.)
6 "Hath he ___ all that he hath" (Gen. 24:36)
7 Discharge
8 Ornaments for military uniforms
9 Bounder

10 Ammunition, for short
11 "They set a ___" (Jer. 5:26)
12 The king ___ for Sarah (Gen. 20:2)
15 Impressionist painter
20 Pinkish
21 Orange peel
24 "Trust in the. . .Lord, and ___ upon his God" (Isa. 50:10)
26 Sarah ___ laughing (Gen. 18:15)
28 Sarah will bear a son ___ (Gen. 17:19)

30 Gnawer
31 "Thou made us to ___" (Isa. 63:17)
32 Change color
34 "God heard the voice of the ___" (Gen. 21:17)
36 "Abraham went and took the ___" (Gen. 22:13)
37 Environmental agency (abbr.)
38 Eleazar "shall ___ counsel for him. . .before the Lord" (Num. 27:21)

39 Mongers

40 "There I buried ___"
(Gen. 49:31)

42 Sarah ___ Abraham a son
(Gen. 21:2)

43 Abraham: "They will ___ me
for my wife's sake"
(Gen. 20:11)

45 Type of fur

47 Tonic

48 "Sarah, that is ___ years old"
(Gen. 17:17)

50 Laundry detergent brand

52 Move a bike

53 Tell

54 "___ of the bricks" (Ex. 5:8)

55 "Abraham fell ___ his face,
and laughed" (Gen. 17:17)

57 "The oppressed go ___"
(Isa. 58:6)

58 Favorite for short

60 "One end of the borders. . .to
the other ___" (Gen. 47:21)

62 "Weave the spider's ___"
(Isa. 59:5)

eighty87even

SAUL:
THE PEOPLE'S KING

by Patricia Mitchell

ACROSS

1 Cuban drum
6 Feature of Mount Lebanon
10 Damascus to Joppa (dir.)
13 O.T. trumpet sounds, often (Jer. 4:19)
15 Former monetary unit in Guinea
16 What David's men may have said when Saul entered their cave (1 Sam. 24:3–4)
17 Saul's kingdom, e.g.
18 Samuel to Saul: "Stay, and I will ___ thee" (1 Sam. 15:16)
19 Hearing David praised, "Saul ___ very wroth" (1 Sam. 18:8)
20 "Saul said, Cast ___ between me and Jonathan" (1 Sam. 14:42)
22 Samuel's assessment of Saul's behavior (1 Sam. 13:13)
24 Potter's tool
26 Goliath would ___ himself as invincible (1 Sam. 17:10)

28 Stake
29 Ziphites to Saul: "Doth not David ___ himself" (1 Sam. 26:1)
30 David to Jonathan: "Thou shalt ___ kindly with thy servant" (1 Sam. 20:8)
31 Author Poe
32 ___ Jima
33 Regular church attender
34 Blvd.
35 Lager beer
37 Glimmered
41 What David and Jonathan may have done upon parting (1 Sam. 20:41)
42 "Saul took a sword, and ___ upon it" (1 Sam. 31:4)
43 Samuel's mentor (1 Sam. 3:1)
44 Groundcovers
47 Saul wanted to ___ David (1 Sam. 19:11)
48 Describes Saul (1 Sam. 9:2)

49 ___ qua non
50 Become less distinct
51 "Saul thought to ___ David fall by the hand of the Philistines" (1 Sam. 18:25)
52 What Jesus would do giving the Spirit (John 20:22)
54 "Saul cast the javelin," intending to ___ David (1 Sam. 18:11)
56 Wiser than a sluggard (Prov. 6:6)
57 Samuel was one (1 Sam. 9:19)
59 Saul vented his ___ on the oxen (1 Sam. 11:6–7)
63 Joppa to Shechem (dir.)
64 Volcanic rock
65 Jonathan to David: "If it ___ my father" (1 Sam. 20:13)
66 300 men would do it (Judg. 7:6)
67 Eve's garden
68 Ahasuerus's new queen (Est. 2:17) (var.)

DOWN

1 Today's chariot
2 Arena cry in Spain
3 The brawling woman, perhaps (Prov. 21:9)
4 Ornamental screen grate
5 Saul fought "against the children of ___" (1 Sam. 14:47)
6 Los Angeles winter hour
7 Bathsheba gave David one as she bathed (2 Sam. 11:2)

8 God to Joshua: ___ the land by lot (Josh. 13:6)
9 Metric measure
10 Hiram's cedars needed this (1 Kings 5:10)
11 It has a 6 Across
12 Abigail offered to be this for David's servants (1 Sam. 25:41)
14 "It repenteth me that I have ___ up Saul" (1 Sam. 15:11)

21 Jonathan's words would ___ David away from Saul (1 Sam. 20:37)
23 Jesse sent "an ass ___ with. . . wine" to Saul (1 Sam. 16:20)
24 Fruit
25 House where Saul's head would be displayed (1 Sam. 31:9)
27 Noah didn't need one

29 One among the dry bones, perhaps (Ezek. 37:4)
30 Saul's main servant (1 Sam. 22:9)
31 Nature of Saul's troubling spirit (1 Sam. 16:15)
33 African antelopes
34 Jonathan would ___ with David against Saul (1 Sam. 19:2)
36 Saul kept the best of these for himself (1 Sam. 15:9)

37 Mechanisms
38 Tropical wood
39 Women's magazine
40 1990 Hindi movie
42 Fever, chills indicator
44 Saul's kingdom (1 Sam. 13:1)
45 Austrian capital
46 Shoe part
47 Part of Joseph's coat, perhaps (Gen. 37:3)
48 God to Moses: "I will give thee ___ of stone" (Ex. 24:12)

50 Also on 23 Down
51 Tree noted for fall colors
53 Cyprus is one
55 Recipe measure (abbr.)
58 "As the lad ___" (1 Sam. 20:36)
60 Samuel to Saul: "Ye shall ___ with me to day" (1 Sam. 9:19)
61 Joppa to Jerusalem (dir.)
62 Saul's uncle (1 Sam. 14:50)

ANGELS AND SHEPHERDS

by Tonya Vilhauer

ACROSS

1 "For as in __ all die. . .in Christ shall all be made alive" (1 Cor. 15:22)
5 Harry Truman's Mrs., to friends
9 Ice sheet
13 Article in Berlin
14 What Demetrius caused, concerning 2 Down (Acts 19:23–24)
15 **Word of praise to 32 Across (Luke 2:14)**
16 Droops
17 Not pretty
18 Currency in Mumbai
19 **"__ peace. . ." (Luke 2:14) (2 words)**
21 **Some 49 Down**
23 Buddy
24 "Seek not ye what ye shall __" (Luke 12:29)
25 Employ again
29 "We know that __ things

work together for good. . ." (Rom. 8:28)
30 "I will not __ for forty's sake" (Gen. 18:29, 2 words)
32 **Subject of 15 Across**
33 Like a bump in the night
36 Ancient Scots
37 Kind of nut
38 "Ye clothe you, but there is none __" (Hag. 1:6)
39 "A thing of beauty" poet
40 "There is __ other commandment greater than these" (Mark 12:31)
41 Mimic
42 Personal objectives
43 ". . .the __, and the vails" (Isa. 3:23)
44 A-Team, Rocky III actor
45 "Many of them also which used curious __ brought their books together" (Acts 19:19)

46 Put on
47 South Dakota's capital
49 Mariner's distress signal
50 Beverage
53 **". . .were gone __ from them into heaven" (Luke 2:15)**
55 Kitchen helpers (2 words)
57 __ Gras
60 Rocked an exam
62 Help with a crime
63 "The sucklings __ in the streets of the city" (Lam. 2:11)
64 "They __ to and fro" (Ps. 107:27)
65 "When he sowed, __ seeds fell by the way side" (Matt. 13:4)
66 High schooler
67 "Uh-uh"
68 "They will __ on wings like eagles" (Isa. 40:31 NIV)

DOWN

1 Greek tale teller
2 Subject of 14 Across
3 **Member of 43 Down**
4 Plateau
5 Barbarous
6 Caesar's VIII
7 Martian day
8 Eye infection
9 Redden, as with embarrassment
10 __-eared rabbit
11 Miner's goal

12 "Keep me as the apple of the __" (Ps. 17:8)
15 Welcomes
20 "Because thou didst __ on the LORD. . ." (2 Chron. 16:8)
22 Authoritative documents
26 Ice house
27 "Glory of the Lord shone __ about them" (Luke 2:9)
28 ". . .the sharp sword with two __" (Rev. 2:12)
29 "He hath shewed strength with his __" (Luke 1:51)

30 Uses a rotary phone
31 Fall mos.
33 The Everglades, e.g.
34 Bay of Naples island
35 Craggy mountain ridge
36 Bog grower
39 East Asian nation
40 Parisian's negative
42 American physicist Richard
43 **". . .a multitude of the heavenly __ praising" (Luke 2:13)**

46 Draw absentmindedly

48 Radioactive gas

49 What the shepherds were watching

50 No-no

51 Disease of Luke 14:2, perhaps

52 Daisy cousin

54 ". . .merchants received the linen __ at a price" (1 Kings 10:28)

56 "And it came to __ in those days. . ." (Luke 2:1)

57 Denver winter hr.

58 Shepherd's reaction to 43 Down

59 "My beloved is like a __ . . ." (Song 2:9)

61 Corner office occupier, for short

A BABY IN A MANGER

by Tonya Vilhauer

ACROSS

1 Military band pipe
5 OT prophet, for short
8 Airport security (abbr.)
11 Lesson section
12 Go quickly
13 Chew the fat
14 "God planted a garden eastward in __" (Gen. 2:8)
15 "He hath shewed strength with his __" (Luke 1:51)
16 Computer memory measure
17 Fragrant shrub
19 **"Unto you is __ this day. . ." (Luke 2:11)**
21 "He was __ at that saying, and went away grieved" (Mark 10:22)
22 Remove
24 Fish feature
27 Cozy
28 Nile capital
30 **"...which is __ the Lord" (Luke 2:11)**
33 **"Ye shall find the babe. . . lying in a __" (Luke 2:12)**
34 It might be a grand
35 "__ bulls have compassed me" (Ps. 22:12)
36 "__ to your faith virtue; and to virtue knowledge" (2 Peter 1:5)
37 Scarlett's love
39 Russian fighter
42 Not ashore
43 Frown angrily
45 Anointing fluids
48 "Why make ye this __, and weep?" (Mark 5:39)
50 Margarine
51 "Who smote the firstborn. . . __ of man and beast (Ps. 135:8)
52 Spatial meas.
53 KJV hind
54 Mandolin cousin
55 "...save one little __ lamb" (2 Sam. 12:3)
56 "The Lord sent me. . .to __ out the land" (Josh. 14:7)

DOWN

1 Power producers
2 Eastern reach of Ahasuerus's realm (Esth. 1:1)
3 **"...shepherds abiding in the __" (Luke 2:8)**
4 Sicilian volcano
5 __ Na Na
6 Auto safety built-in
7 Office messages
8 KJV pronoun
9 "People which __ in darkness saw great light" (Matt. 4:16)
10 "I __ no pleasant bread" (Dan. 10:3)
13 Evangelical TV network
18 Expurgators
20 Renounces, as one's faith
23 Track
24 "When thou wast under the __ tree, I saw thee" (John 1:48)
25 Anger
26 "Neither do they reap, __ gather into barns" (Matt. 6:26)
27 "Lamb of God, which taketh away the __ of the world" (John 1:29)
29 "If __ man have ears to hear, let him hear" (Mark 7:16)
30 Tax-time professional, for short
31 "Adam and his wife __ themselves" (Gen. 3:8)
32 Totally out there, in slang
33 "Get up, take your __ and go home" (Luke 5:24 NIV)
35 "Seven well favoured kine. . . fed in a __" (Gen. 41:2)
38 "Ye shall offer up an __ offering" (Num. 15:19)
39 "Cast his idols. . .to the __ and to the bats" (Isa. 2:20)
40 "__; mine eye. . .runneth down with water" (Lam. 1:16) (2 words)
41 **"The __ of the Lord shone round about them" (Luke 2:9)**

42 Cinder
44 Cryptic script
45 Seller's note (abbr.)
46 Debtor's note (abbr.)
47 Company name ender, often
49 College football's __ Miss
   Rebels

90
BETHLEHEM
by Tonya Vilhauer

ACROSS

1 Fictional company favored by Wile E. Coyote
5 "Sound an __ in my holy mountain" (Joel 2:1)
10 Unsightly
14 Essence of an issue
15 Ten Commandments mount
16 "The Lord is the __ God" (Jer. 10:10)
17 "O my strength, haste thee to __ me" (Ps. 22:19)
18 "Do not be fainthearted. . .do not __" (Deut. 20:3 NIV)
19 Noble title
20 "Has thou __ of the tree. . .?" (Gen. 3:11)
22 Pass along, as a message
24 Vigor
25 Ore shafts
27 The Red Sea has one

29 Navigate
32 He was born in Bethlehem, ca. 1000 BC
35 Orchestra instrument
38 For
39 "Set ye Uriah in the forefront. . . and __ ye from him" (2 Sam. 11:15)
40 Rainbow's shape
41 Injurious
43 Paris negative
44 She was buried in Bethlehem
46 Conger
47 Some restrooms
48 "As a __ which melteth" (Ps. 58:8)
49 Like Eglon, king of Moab (Judg. 3:17)
51 Project details, for short

54 "He made narrowed __ round about" (1 Kings 6:6)
57 Luau dish
59 Desert wanderer, as in Jer. 35:7
62 Bible's sackcloth companion
64 Burial ointment ingredient, as in John 19:39
66 Mother of Jesus, in Mexico
68 Hawkeye State
69 Liturgical season
70 "I was __, now I see" (John 9:25)
71 On the ocean
72 Gains "I counted __ for Christ" (Phil. 3:7)
73 Shutter features
74 Man in Munich

DOWN

1 "Even in laughter the heart may __" (Prov. 14:13 NIV)
2 Cat's delight
3 Variegated
4 The Good Samaritan spared none in Luke 10:35
5 Cleopatra's biter
6 "Who is a __ but he that denieth that Jesus is the Christ?" (1 John 2:22)
7 Traditional grandmother of Jesus
8 Tracks
9 He foretold Jesus' birth
10 Native American tribe

11 Common Holy Land plant
12 Entice
13 Dog sound
21 "Cast the __ on the right side of the ship" (John 21:6)
23 Alpine sound
26 Calyx part
28 Judas, in modern terms
30 "Do they not __ that devise evil?" (Prov. 14:22)
31 Romantic fellow
33 It sharpens in Proverbs 27:17
34 Lions' homes
35 Zebedee and sons' needs (Matt. 4:21)

36 Certain muffin
37 "He findeth __ against me" (Job 33:10)
39 One who would come out of Bethlehem in Micah 5:2
41 She launched a thousand ships
42 Lover's mo.
45 Jacob's sore spot in Gen. 32:25
47 He would come out of Bethlehem in Micah 5:2
50 __ of Galilee
52 Tidies tresses
53 Like Bethlehem in Micah 5:2

55 "It came to pass in __ days. . ." (Luke 2:1)
56 Dressmaker
57 Funeral cover
58 Tub spread
60 Opera solo
61 Strenuous effort

63 Moselle tributary
65 UFO riders, for short
67 Radio spots

91 ninety one

THE FULLNESS OF TIME

by Tonya Vilhauer

ACROSS

1 "...they would have repented long __ in sackcloth and..." (Matt. 11:21)
4 Last word of 1 Across
9 __ Four, '60s sobriquet
12 Neaten
14 Gush, as water
15 Quote
16 Woodwind
17 George Burns prop
18 Slightly open
19 Sweat
21 Broadcasting
23 Three to Caesar
24 "Out of the spoils __ in battles..." (1 Chron. 26:27)
25 Beat
28 "Fear not to take unto thee Mary __ wife" (Matt. 1:20)
31 Loch __ monster
34 Idled
36 "Take, __: this is my body" (1 Cor. 11:24)
38 April worker, for short
40 Discharge
41 "They sat down in __, by hundreds, and by fifties" (Mark 6:40)
43 "...an __ of God through Christ" (Gal. 4:7)
44 "I saw Absalom hanged in an __" (2 Sam. 18:10)
45 "All unrighteousness is __" (1 John 5:17)
46 Part of the "host of heaven" (2 Kings 23:5)
48 Use a microwave
51 "Images of your mice that __ the land" (1 Sam. 6:5)
53 "I will lift up mine __ unto the hills" (Ps. 121:1)
54 Viper
56 LAX abbr.
58 61 Down meaning
61 "That we might receive the __ of sons" (Gal. 4:5)
66 First murder victim
67 Plant
69 "For __ you is born this day..." (Luke 2:11)
70 Roman emperor who may have ordered Paul's execution
71 Notched
72 Dorothy's dog
73 Road map abbr.
74 Like some soil
75 Negative prefix

DOWN

1 Perched, as on a roof
2 Insulting remark
3 Smell
4 Electronic character set (abbr.)
5 "God hath sent forth the __ of his Son" (Gal. 4:6)
6 "Were not the Ethiopians and the Lubims a __ host...?" (2 Chron. 16:8)
7 Time period
8 Manger fill
9 South Pacific archipelago
10 "The Son of man cometh __ hour when ye think not" (Luke 12:40) (2 words)
11 Floating ice
13 KJV's "yea"
15 Chili con __
20 Bible instrument, as in 1 Samuel 10:5
22 Charged particle
25 "...made of a __, made under the law" (Gal. 4:4)
26 Seventeen-syllable poem
27 "How __ shall my brother sin against me...?" (Matt. 18:21)
29 Reddish dye
30 Chatter
32 Manger __, a Christmas display
33 Those Rahab hid in Joshua 2
34 Name chosen by 13 popes
35 Medical professionals (abbr.)
37 Cook's meas.
39 "Bethlehem... __ not the least among the princes of Juda" (Matt. 2:6)
42 Goal
43 "Little Lord Jesus, asleep on the __"

47 "Then shall the lame man __ as an hart" (Isa. 35:6)
49 Painter Frida
50 Joppa to Jericho dir.
52 **"To __ them that were under the law" (Gal. 4:5)**
55 Hair care brand
57 Palm sap
58 9 Across followers
59 Aid partner, often
60 Cul-de-sac designation, often (abbr.)

61 **". . .into your hearts, crying, __" (Gal. 4:6)**
62 Ancient Egyptian king, for short
63 "Thine enemies shall. . .keep thee __ every side" (Luke 19:43) (2 words)
64 Boy's palindromic name
65 "I will cause the sun to go down at __" (Amos 8:9)
68 Dairy sound

HOW JESUS WAS BORN IN BETHLEHEM

by Tonya Vilhauer

ACROSS

1 Reformation Day mo.
4 Pungent
9 "...being great with __" (Luke 2:5)
14 Montgomery is its cap.
15 Honshu Island city
16 Shinto rite
17 Mend
18 "The __ of them which have reaped..." (James 5:4)
19 "My son was dead, and is __ again" (Luke 15:24)
20 Lilies "toil not, they __ not" (Luke 12:27)
22 Adhesive brand
24 "When ye fast, be not...of a __ countenance" (Matt. 6:16)
25 Poetic contraction
27 CIA predecessor
29 Riyadh natives

32 Winter weather need
35 "The __ of violence is in their hands" (Isa. 59:6)
36 Toyota sports model
38 Certain woodwinds, for short
40 "Casting all your __ upon him" (1 Peter 5:7)
42 "...sift the nations with the __ of vanity" (Isa. 30:28)
44 La __, weather changer
45 Put on a happy face
47 Peron woman
49 "Make bare the __, uncover the thigh" (Isa. 47:2)
50 "When my glory __ by" (Ex. 33:22 NIV)
52 "There went out a __ from Caesar Augustus" (Luke 2:1)
54 Guess (abbr.)
55 Classic car

56 "They are __ with the showers of the mountains" (Job 24:8)
59 Moses "was powerful in speech and __" (Acts 7:22 NIV)
63 "...with __ his espoused wife" (Luke 2:5)
67 "The Philistines put themselves in __ against Israel" (1 Sam. 4:2)
69 Confess
71 Sleep cycle, for short
72 "Whosoever shall __ thee on thy right cheek" (Matt. 5:39)
73 It might be clean
74 Computer choice
75 "...to be __ with" 63 Across (Luke 2:5)
76 Nairobi's locale
77 Pampering place

DOWN

1 Bumbling ones
2 __ clop
3 Ride on the runway
4 Dog's award giver (abbr.)
5 "...when __ was governor of Syria" (Luke 2:2)
6 Churn
7 Detail
8 Medicine measure
9 Automobile frame
10 Evil computer of 2001: A Space Odyssey
11 Eye part

12 Molten rock
13 "If thou hadst been here, my brother had not __" (John 11:21)
21 Not used in Munich
23 KJV deer
26 Ms. reviewers
28 Look over
29 Rascal
30 Open entryways
31 Caleb and others (Num. 13)
32 "...into Judaea, unto the city of __" (Luke 2:4)

33 Daniel in the book of Daniel, e.g.
34 Actor Zellweger
35 Cancer research org.
37 Sermonizer, for short
39 Droop
41 "I am the Lord, and there is none __" (Isa. 45:5)
43 "One that inhabiteth __, whose name is Holy" (Isa. 57:15)
46 Wrote
48 Hole in one

51 List ender (abbr.)

53 NT book (abbr.)

56 "Who told thee that thou __ naked?" (Gen. 3:11)

57 Humorist Bombeck

58 Cereal name

60 "Wherefore have ye not fulfilled your __ in making brick. . . ?" (Ex. 5:14)

61 "An __ soul shall suffer hunger" (Prov. 19:15)

62 Muscat locale

64 "She. . .strengtheneth her __" (Prov. 31:17)

65 "They that sow in tears shall __ in joy" (Ps. 126:5)

66 Village People song

68 "I __ no pleasant bread" (Dan. 10:3)

70 Beverage

JESUS' GENEALOGY, PART 1

by Tonya Vilhauer

ACROSS

1 Word for David's look at Bathsheba (2 Sam. 11:2)
5 Narratives, such as Israelites' escape from Egypt
10 Former flyer
13 Latin lions
14 Paul suffered "a __ in the flesh" (2 Cor. 12:7)
15 Overfeed
16 Gospel singer James
17 Broadcast receiver
18 Log-in name
19 Single in Cozumel
21 **Patriarch ancestor of Jesus (Matt. 1:2)**
23 "How __ did they provoke him" (Ps. 78:40)
26 **Moabite's son, an ancestor of Jesus (Matt. 1:5)**

29 Some face shapes
30 Waltz style
32 "__ the voice of the Lord your God" (Jer. 26:13)
33 __ Bator, Mongolian capital
34 Buffalo hockey player
36 Internet image
37 **Ancestor of Jesus who had 12 sons (Matt. 1:2)**
38 Trolley car
42 Town bigwig
43 One shone over Bethlehem, perhaps
44 Small fruit
46 Baseball pitcher's dream (2 words)
49 **Ancestor who prefigured Jesus' sacrifice (Gen. 22:1–2)**

51 Moses' "hand was leprous as __" (Ex. 4:6)
52 "Unto thee will I __, O Lord" (Ps. 28:1)
53 Tusked Arctic porpoise
56 "Will a man __ God?" (Mal. 3:8)
58 Smile
59 **Crowned ancestor of Jesus (Matt. 1:6)**
62 **Ancestor of Jesus, and mom of 26 Across**
66 Horse food
67 Old, doddering
68 Sandwich cookie
69 "Thou shalt love the Lord __ God" (Matt. 22:37)
70 Rods and __
71 Garment closure

DOWN

1 Madrid stadium yell
2 "__ wisdom" (Prov. 4:5)
3 Nephew of 21 Across (Gen. 11:31)
4 Sibling of 37 Across
5 Flash intermittently
6 Repeated, a derisive phrase (Ps. 35:21, e.g.)
7 Identity of Jesus
8 Opera number
9 Elitist
10 Glide
11 "Thou shalt not __" (Ex. 20:15)

12 Contract info
15 Debonair
20 Negative in Lyon
22 "And they. . .put on him a scarlet __" (Matt. 27:28)
23 Reproductive cell
24 "They had a __ for the mattocks" (1 Sam. 13:21)
25 Group
27 Samuel Johnson composition
28 "Let the __ be the husbands of one wife" (1 Tim. 3:12)
31 Joppa to Damascus dir.
32 Scepter topper

35 5 on the periodic table
37 What forbidden fruit can get you in?
38 Explosive letters
39 Academic military prog.
40 Assert
41 Mother of Jesus
42 ". . .heard for their __ speaking" (Matt. 6:7)
44 Equivalence
45 Yards
47 Flies flew in them (Ex. 8:21)
48 __ Jima

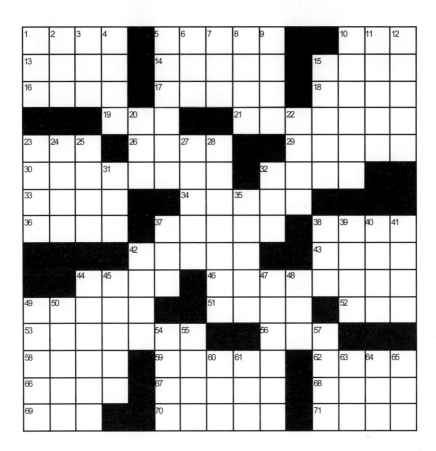

49 Paradise paver, perhaps
   (Rev. 21:21)

**50 Ancestor of Jesus, and wife
   of 21 Across**

54 OT month (Ezra 6:15, e.g.)

55 Type of avenue in Jesus'
   parable (Luke 14:21)

57 Reuben and Levi, e.g., for
   short

60 Compete

61 "Love worketh no __ to his
   neighbor" (Rom. 13:10)

63 64 Down server, maybe

64 Beverage

65 Move like a rabbit

ninety four

JESUS' GENEALOGY, PART 2

by Tonya Vilhauer

ACROSS

1 **Jesus' ancestor and 25 Across' son (Matt. 1:7)**
5 NCAA Div. Bruins' campus
9 Elliptical
13 Widow's offering (Mark 12:42)
14 "__ will I teach transgressors thy ways" (Ps. 51:13)
15 Sarcastically
16 "For this __ is mount Sinai in Arabia" (Gal. 4:25)
17 Baseball glove
18 "I will __ him up at the last day" (John 6:40)
19 **Jesus' ancestor and 42 Across' son (Matt. 1:6)**
21 Baal, e.g.
23 Where the Prodigal Son ended up working (Luke 15:15)
24 Ship's letters
25 **Jesus' ancestor and 1 Across' father (Matt. 1:7)**
29 Denver hours

30 Dice
32 Pharisees' tithed herb (Luke 11:42)
33 **Jesus' ancestor and tribe of Israel (Micah 5:2)**
36 Estimate
37 God said to Adam, "Where __ thou?" (Gen. 3:9)
38 Oklahoma city
39 Apple elements
40 Nativity shiner
41 Speedy transport
42 **Jesus' ancestor and 33 Downs' son (Matt. 1:6)**
43 White poplar
44 Part of a min.
45 Coupe
46 "__ to prepare a place for you" (John 14:2) (2 words)
47 Principles
49 Guard's title, for short
50 Legume

53 "...come forth a rod out of the __ of Jesse" 33 Down (Isa. 11:1)
55 "Do everything without grumbling or __" (Phil. 2:14 NIV)
57 Composition
60 Meat oversight org.
62 Tropical root
63 Gets millions of views, with "goes"
64 Jesus gave his disciples power to "__ diseases" (Luke 9:1)
65 "Heareth the word, and __ with joy receiveth it" (Matt. 13:20)
66 Samson's story, e.g.
67 "...thou shalt bruise his __" (Gen. 3:15)
68 "She was found with child of the __ Ghost" (Matt. 1:18)

DOWN

1 Collect
2 Prejudiced one
3 "They of __ salute you" (Heb. 13:24)
4 Plane prefix
5 "She came from the __ parts of the earth to hear" 19 Across (Luke 11:31)
6 Facial features
7 "__ your light so shine..." (Matt. 5:16)

8 Opposed to
9 Dental brand
10 Caesar's seven
11 Politician Gore and others
12 Caustic solution
15 Wilts
20 Hot cereal
22 "Take away the __ from the silver" (Prov. 25:4)
26 What Paul did on Mars' Hill (Acts 17:22)

27 Hearing-related
28 English measure
29 Grass-eating Nebuchadnezzar's condition (Dan. 4:33)
30 Small cabinet type
31 "Take __, as unto a light that shineth" (2 Peter 1:19)
33 **Jesus' ancestor and 19 Across' granddad (Matt. 1:6)**
34 Not yet hardened, as cement

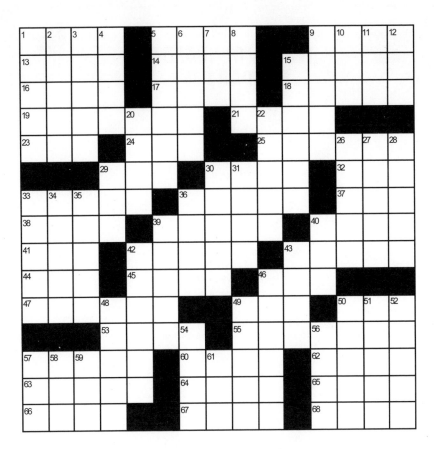

35 "He. . .is fallen into the ___
   which he made" (Ps. 7:15)

36 Ruling org.

39 "For this ___ came I unto this
   hour" (John 12:27)

40 Intestinal disorder (abbr.)

42 Poetic foot

43 Eager

46 Jesus' ancestor's God-given
   name and 33 Across' father
   (Matt. 1:2)

48 Jesus' ancestor and
   Abraham's son (Matt. 1:2)

49 Core group

50 Keyboard instrument

51 Sign up

52 "Being in an ___ he prayed
   more earnestly"
   (Luke 22:44)

54 "Her sins. . .are forgiven; for
   she loved ___" (Luke 7:47)

56 Beehive State

57 Christmastime

58 Drink daintily

59 ___ Lanka

61 "And if any man ___ thee
   at law" (Matt. 5:40)

95 ninety-five
JESUS' GENEALOGY, PART 3

by Tonya Vilhauer

ACROSS

1 "Blessed shall be thy basket and thy __" (Deut. 28:5)
6 Universe descriptor
10 Bad (prefix)
13 Christmas songs
15 Linear measure
16 Winglike
17 Blood disorder
18 Oceano fill
19 Caleb, e.g. (Num. 14:6)
20 7 Down glow, perhaps
22 **Jesus' ancestor and son of 23 Down (Matt. 1:13)**
24 "At thy right __ there are pleasures for evermore" (Ps. 16:11)
26 "Hear me when I __, O God" (Ps. 4:1)
28 Good (Italian)
29 Centers
30 "Give us __ day our daily bread" (Matt. 6:11)
31 Alarm
32 Clerical garment
33 Injure seriously
34 Vowel sequence
35 Soldiers' attitude toward Jesus at His trial
37 Learned environment
41 __ of the covenant
42 Tints
43 "Thou shalt neither __ a stranger, nor oppress him" (Ex. 22:21)
44 How Jonah felt when Ninevites repented (Jon. 4:2–4)
47 "...wrought iron and brass to __ the house of the Lord" (2 Chron. 24:12)
48 Kid
49 "Rich and poor __ together" (Prov. 22:2)
50 Joppa or Caesarea, e.g.
51 John and James vis-à-vis Zebedee (Matt. 4:21)
52 Boarded wall
54 Pampering places
56 "How long will it be __ ye make an end of words?" (Job 18:2)
57 Dueling sword
59 Brainstorm
63 Preacher, for short
64 This Old House host Bob
65 Cap
66 Babylonian Captivity was one
67 If all else fails, read them (abbr.)
68 "Be of good __: it is I" (Mark 6:50)

DOWN

1 Weather warning for boaters (abbr.)
2 Sunbather's hope
3 Miner's quest
4 Sixth New Testament book
5 **Jesus' ancestor and Eleazar's dad (Matt. 1:15)**
6 __ Dolorosa, Jerusalem
7 Nativity narrative's heavenly host (Luke 2:13)
8 Use oars
9 Bangkok native
10 One in disguise
11 Mountain descriptor
12 Church attenders
14 Riyadh currency (abbr.)
21 **Jesus' ancestor and 5 Down's father (Matt. 1:14)**
23 **Jesus' ancestor and 22 Across' dad (Matt. 1:13)**
24 Luau dance
25 Shorten, for short
27 Target, with "for"
29 "Whereas thou __ been forsaken and hated" (Isa. 60:15)
30 "...your bricks of your daily __" (Ex. 5:19)
31 "I did __ I was commanded" (Ezek. 12:7) (2 words)
33 **Jesus' mother**
34 Chilled

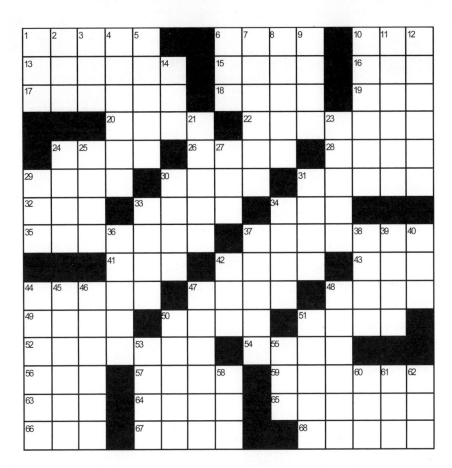

36 À la ___, ordering option

37 Some relatives

38 "___ the winds and the sea obey him!" (Matt. 8:27)

39 "Benjamin's ___ was five times so much. . ." (Gen. 43:34)

40 Bus. card info

42 ". . .brought forth ___ firstborn son" (Luke 2:7)

44 Current unit

45 "Now is our salvation ___ than when we believed" (Rom. 13:11)

46 Swiss city

47 Runway walkers

48 Jesus' foster father

50 Son of Charlemagne

51 Ancestor of Jesus and 21 Down's dad (Matt. 1:14)

53 Priestly tribe

55 "He brought me up also out of an horrible ___" (Ps. 40:2)

58 "Take, ___; this is my body" (Matt. 26:26)

60 One of Solomon's exotic animals (1 Kings 10:22)

61 Greens pin

62 "The proud. . .do ___ from thy commandments" (Ps. 119:21)

ninety six

PROPHECIES OF JESUS

by Tonya Vilhauer

ACROSS

1 Cartoon segment
4 High tea treat
9 Kindness to an enemy __ "coals of fire on his head" (Rom. 12:20)
14 Animal Solomon's ships brought from Tarshish (2 Chron. 9:21)
15 Moons: Lat.
16 Gives off
17 Descriptor for Noah's ark, maybe
18 "Whoever __ his command will come to no harm" (Eccl. 8:5 NIV)
19 Flamboyance
20 Having a sharp point
22 She in Paris
24 Prophecy: Jesus, the Passover __ (Ex. 12:3)

25 Nevada city
27 Lessens
31 Brews
32 __ Provence, France (2 words)
33 Medieval verse form
34 Prophecy: Jesus, Lord of heaven and __ (Isa. 66:22)
36 "He maketh the __ a calm" (Ps. 107:29)
38 Prophecy: Jesus, the __ (3 words) (Isa. 9:6)
42 Lace table decoration
43 Push back
44 Jesus died for __ (John 3:16)
45 Entertained lavishly
47 Garment for Pontius Pilate
51 "Thy mercy, O Lord, __ me up" (Ps. 94:18)

53 God told Moses to make one in Numbers 1
54 Sins
55 Border
57 Prophecy: Jesus "shall redeem __ from all his iniquities" (Ps. 130:8)
59 Type of offering to God (Ex. 29:28)
62 "They came with __, and found Mary" (Luke 2:16)
65 Glasgow negative
66 Circle
67 Organic compound
68 Racing car inits.
69 Lots
70 Versifier's tool
71 The woman at Endor's skill, for short (1 Sam. 28:7)

DOWN

1 Secret writings
2 Heroic narrative description
3 Green bean, e.g.
4 Put into position
5 Ice shape
6 Prophecy: Jesus is He that "I have exalted __ chosen" (Ps. 89:19)
7 "And he said, __; but thou didst laugh" (Gen. 18:15)
8 Dead Sea Scroll writer, most probably

9 Prophecy: About Jesus: "thou shalt bruise his __" (Gen. 3:15)
10 Meeting host, for short
11 Fall ill
12 School grp.
13 Former London–Paris flyer, for short
21 Rappel
23 Pioneering actor Chaney
25 Church ritual
26 What a sermon does
28 Alliance

29 "And Hagar __ Abram a son" (Gen. 16:15)
30 Cell phone card
32 Rainbow descriptor
35 Prophecy: Jesus' "visage... marred more than __ man" (Isa. 52:14)
36 Min. seg.
37 Shred
38 What held Moses' brass serpent (Num. 21:9)
39 Stream
40 Jesus washed them (John 13:14)

41 Cat's paw feature

42 Morse Code element

45 What you might get a shot for

46 "Turn __ to the right hand or to the left" (Num. 22:26)

48 Citrus

49 Heroes

50 Jesus during a tempest once (Matt. 8:24)

52 Prophecy: Jesus, Son of __ (Matt. 1:1)

56 Stakes

57 Detail

58 Like the bones in Ezek. 37:4

59 Today in Madrid

60 Victorian was one

61 Shortened, as a novel (abbr.)

63 "He planteth an __, and the rain doth nourish it" (Isa. 44:14)

64 Pig's place

ninety seven

A VIRGIN BIRTH

by Tonya Vilhauer

ACROSS

1 "...the mother of my __ should come to me?" (Luke 1:43)
5 With 72 Across, Jesus' term for Himself in Revelation
10 "In him was __" (John 1:4)
14 Bread spread
15 Potter's materials
16 Tel __, Israel city
17 Put on a liturgical garment
18 Artist's need
19 "Singin' in the Rain" Kelly
20 Colorado park
22 "The Son of __ shall come in the glory of his Father" (Matt. 16:27)
23 Defeated one
24 Ten (prefix)
26 Tekoa prophet
28 Initials on tires

31 Commercials
32 "...which taketh away the __ of the world" (John 1:29)
33 Scepter feature, often
36 "The __ thereof said unto them, Why loose ye the colt?" (Luke 19:33)
38 "It is. . . __ than hell" (Job 11:8)
40 Mary became one
41 "I will __ to give thanks unto thee" (Ps. 119:62)
42 Mystery
45 One of the Muses
47 Reigning king's title
48 Pie __ mode (2 words)
50 Hydrocarbon suffix
51 72 Across definition
52 High school class, for short
53 "...followers of God, as __ children" (Eph. 5:1)

55 "Do not be surprised. . .if the world __ you" (1 John 3:13 NIV)
58 Bus. name ender, sometimes
60 Picture puzzle
64 Arab chieftain
65 Eagle's nest
67 "His __ pierceth through snares" (Job 40:24)
68 Pixies
69 Cause apprehension
70 "Or __ believe me for the very works' sake" (John 14:11)
71 "I am the __ of Sharon" (Song 2:1)
72 See 5 Across
73 "The __ was made flesh" (John 1:14)

DOWN

1 What God showed to us through Jesus' birth
2 Madrid stadium cheers
3 "Come. . .I will give you __" (Matt. 11:28)
4 Pampered, with "on"
5 Combat pilot honor
6 Camel cousins
7 "Que __?"
8 "Laughing" carnivores
9 Handy communication (abbr.)
10 Nigerian city
11 Burl __, screen star

12 "...clothed in purple and __ linen" (Luke 16:19)
13 "He shall reign. . .for __" (Luke 1:33)
21 Scorch
23 Isolated
25 Bank investments, for short
27 Center position
28 "The __ of the Highest shall overshadow thee" (Luke 1:35)
29 Prodigal Son's charges (Luke 15:15)
30 Implant
33 Speak up

34 Tree product
35 "I am the __ of life" (John 6:35)
37 Brain-wave test (abbr.)
39 Time period
43 Hill in Athens where Paul spoke (Acts 17:22)
44 __ Baba
45 Maine-based educational institution
46 "Wilt thou __ it up in three days?" (John 2:20)
49 Shining, like the Nativity star
50 Finding the sum
52 Succinct

54 "___ a right spirit within me" (Ps. 51:10)

55 "...then an ___ of God through Christ" (Gal. 4:7)

56 For David, it was a stone in a slingshot, for short

57 Slants

59 "That was the ___ Light" (John 1:9)

61 Knife

62 Former country inits.

63 "Christ cometh of the ___ of David" (John 7:42)

65 "Much ___ about Nothing"

66 LAX abbr.

WISE MEN FOLLOW A STAR

by Tonya Vilhauer

ACROSS

1 Kind of curve
4 Frankincense property
9 "Their wine is. . .the cruel __ of asps" (Deut. 32:33)
14 Repeated, word of mockery, as in Psalm 35:21
15 Lone Star stater
16 *Aida* is one
17 Costa del __, Spain
18 Kick out
19 Vertical lines on a graph (2 words)
20 Pop band that sang "Africa"
22 Native New Yorker
24 Little one
25 Caesar's seven
27 "Eeew!"
29 RV brand
32 Some girders (2 words)
35 Rock genre
36 **The king the Wise Men heard (Matt. 2:9)**
38 **". . .it came and __ over where the young child was" (Matt. 2:7–9)**
40 Put to flight
42 Clock faces
44 **"When they saw the __ . . ." (Matt. 2:9-10)**
45 Parents brought Jesus to Jerusalem "__ the custom of the law" (Luke 2:27)
47 Ragouts
49 "__ the spirits whether they are of God" (1 John 4:1)
50 Calico, e.g.
52 "I agree"
54 John in London
55 Harsh cleanser
56 "To this __ was I born" (John 18:37)
59 Gardener's scoop
63 Seth's dad (Luke 3:38)
67 San __, CA
69 "Whose soever sins ye __ . . ." (John 20:23)
71 Josaphat's dad (Matt. 1:8)
72 French province
73 Pickle juice
74 Russian jet fighter
75 "Neither desire thou his dainty __" (Prov. 23:6)
76 Worsted cloth
77 Pressure meas.

DOWN

1 **". . .which they saw in the __" (Matt. 2:9)**
2 "Scram!"
3 "Ye are the __ of the earth" (Matt. 5:13)
4 "I took the little book. . .and __ it up" (Rev. 10:10)
5 **". . .they __ with exceeding great joy" (Matt. 2:10)**
6 "All sheep and __, yea, and the beasts of the field" (Ps. 8:7)
7 Spiked club
8 Against (prefix)
9 Apostle Paul took many of them
10 Pollution org.
11 "Let us go into the __ towns" (Mark 1:38)
12 Popular cookie
13 ". . .he that lieth upon the top of a __" (Prov. 23:34)
21 Reproductive cells
23 Give a nickname to
26 More or less (suffix)
28 ". . .bound in their coats, their hosen, and their __" (Dan. 3:21)
29 "Outta here!" (2 words)
30 All in France
31 "__, shine; for thy light is come" (Isa. 60:1)
32 Wasted time
33 Something to live by
34 What an eagle does
35 Period
37 Horse's tidbit
39 "O ye __ bones, hear the word of the Lord" (Ezek. 37:4)
41 "Go, __ It on the Mountain"
43 Guzzling

46 Prodigal Son "wasted his substance with __ living" (Luke 15:13)

48 Where the Prodigal Son ended up working (Luke 15:15)

51 "Provide neither gold, __ silver" (Matt. 10:9)

53 It could be iced

56 Dutch wheel

57 "Doth he not leave the ninety and __ ..." (Matt. 18:12)

58 __ vu

60 Spheres

61 "When they __ come into the house" (Matt. 2:11)

62 Arab ruler

64 Moist

65 "Eat so much __ sufficient for thee" (Prov. 25:16) (2 words)

66 Wise Men

68 "Take the girdle that thou hast __" (Jer. 13:4)

70 Ball holder

ninety-99-nine

WISE MEN GIVE GIFTS TO JESUS

by Tonya Vilhauer

ACROSS

1 And so forth (abbr.)
4 Moscow was its cap.
8 Thighbone
13 Eatery, for short
15 13 Across condiment, for short
16 Express oneself
17 "Tubalcain, an instructor. . .in brass and __" (Gen. 4:22)
18 Witty word plays
19 Performed
20 **Second treasure in Matthew 2:11**
23 Long-haired ox
24 Victorian is one
25 Things
28 Before (prefix)

29 Great tennis serve
30 "Given to hospitality, __ to teach" (1 Tim. 3:2)
32 Eva or Zsa Zsa
35 ". . .neither __ nor sown" (Deut. 21:4)
37 Caesar's three
38 Oklahoma tribe
39 As easy as __
40 Jesus' grandmother, traditionally
41 Actor Chaney
42 **Third treasure in Matthew 2:11**
44 Express contempt
45 Chalkboard warning (abbr.)
46 Conger

47 ". . .Andrew his brother, casting a __ into the sea" (Matt. 4:18)
48 KJV's dropsy
50 Break beverage
51 Streets (abbr.)
54 Chicago university
58 ___ Matisse, artist
61 KJV tare
62 Water (Sp.)
63 Pergola
64 Gemstone
65 Stoat coat
66 Blue-greens
67 "He that loseth his life for my __ shall find it" (Matt. 10:39)
68 KJV firmament

DOWN

1 "Comfort yourselves. . .and __ one another (1 Thess. 5:11)
2 __ cotta, earthenware
3 ". . .let him have thy __ also" (Matt. 5:40)
4 Referee
5 Steam bath
6 In __, agreed
7 "I am the __ of Sharon" (Song 2:1)
8 "His sons went and __ in their houses. . ." (Job 1:4)
9 51 Down, at times
10 Bon __, witty remark
11 Great Basin tribe

12 "To him which divided the __ sea into parts" (Ps. 136:13)
14 ". . .there was no room for them in the __" (Luke 2:7)
21 "Quo Vadis?" actress Deborah
22 Sweet
26 Acadia National Park locale
27 Vertebral column
28 "The Raven" poet
29 Via Dolorosa sight
31 Level
32 **First treasure in Matthew 2:11**
33 "Sin offering to __ for all Israel" (2 Chron. 29:24 NIV)
34 Fish may be served this way

35 Peer
36 Audiologist's test (abbr.)
40 "Go to the __, thou sluggard" (Prov. 6:6)
42 Autobiographies
43 "His parents went to Jerusalem every __" (Luke 2:41)
44 "Which stilleth the noise of the __" (Ps. 65:7)
47 ". . .easier for a camel to go through the eye of a __" (Matt. 19:24)
49 Register
50 Slight fix
51 TV personality Philbin

52 "Be not __ with wine" (Eph. 5:18)

53 Winding

55 Pairs

56 Filter, as for a vacuum cleaner (abbr.)

57 Edinburgh cap

58 You might pull a rabbit out of one

59 "Come down __ my child die" (John 4:49)

60 Athletic org.

ANSWER KEY

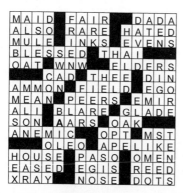

PUZZLE 1

PUZZLE 2

PUZZLE 3

PUZZLE 4

PUZZLE 5

PUZZLE 6

PUZZLE 7

```
PLUS  EDOM  FETA
EAST STAVE IRAN
EVER CAMEL SIFT
PERISH PROPHET
   POOR SNOW
ARC ROAR SWIFT
DOE ELVES FIRE
ADDER ERE TEXAS
MEAL NURSE ESP
OREOS NICK SHY
  PUPA FOOT
ACHIEVE WARDER
ARIA NEPAL ERMA
SCAN DRESS SEMI
SHOT STEP SWAN
```

PUZZLE 8

```
HONG MAMBA SIR
ALONE CREEP ARE
JESUS CANTO RAN
JOE KNOB SLATE
  TINY MATTHEW
VOLUME CALLA
IMAGO LUKE BRA
CARS SCALY NOEL
END PTAS READS
  CROSS TATTOO
CORRUPT JOBS
LLOYD LAMB RPM
ADM ISLAM IVORY
SEE SKATE SIMON
PRO HIDES MESA
```

PUZZLE 9

```
AMAM IDIOT LOP
HOLY SURGE COMA
AMEN ROILS HUES
ALA SETTINGS
DAY EEL ALGAE
ANABOLIC DUDE
LOCO TRAIT
INKY GHOST AHIO
LEECH CALF
VIOl KERCHIEF
SHIRR ROW RSS
MARKDOWN BOP
ANTE DIEGO AMOS
LOUD ONSET IOUS
LIE RESTS ROTS
```

PUZZLE 10

```
TLC HARTS ELBOW
EEL APART PARSE
AVE MONEY IDOLS
LIFE STEELS SOT
  GMT ITS
SHOULD RELIEF
CIA DERBE ELVES
SLIP SAUCE OATH
TAKES ISAAC DIE
SULTAN PRAYED
FAS PRE
JAB CHURCH SAUL
ACOCK SOLON FCA
VALUE ARENA ALI
ADDED FOGEY RAD
```

PUZZLE 11

```
SAWS EBON WAGER
NERO ARIA ABOVE
USAF TILT LOVED
COTTA BEHOLD
KPH SCARAB FRAS
GLIB NIL ODE
EVIL ALI AMMON
LOSES EWE YEARS
IDLER ONE ANNE
AKA III SMUT
MAMA OSMIUM COB
NEURAL PROVE
ALIGN ARAB OPUS
WIRED EDGE OSLO
LEERS LIED FEET
```

PUZZLE 12

```
SOS PASTA SECTS
CUP ALOOF EMAIL
ATE RULER MERCY
RACISM AKIN
EGIS OBIE DIMS
SEER GAUDY DIE
  AMITY MOOSE
CLEANS SHELLS
GUILLT UPEND
ARD ESSAY MASS
LESS MIEN ACCT
  PAUL RANCOR
SPAIN VATIC ERE
ARCED EDICT DEW
MESSY ROPES ERN
```

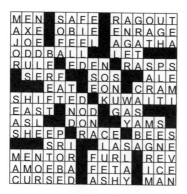

PUZZLE 13

```
MEN SAFE RAGOUT
AXE OBIE ENRAGE
JOE FEEL AGATHA
ODDBALL    JET
RULE EDEN RASPS
 SERF SOS  ALE
 EAT FON CRAM
SHIFTED KUWAITI
EAST NOD  GAS
ASI  DON  YAMS
SHEEP RACE BEES
  SRI  LASAGNE
MENTOR FURL REV
AMOEBA FETA ICE
CURSED ASHY MAN
```

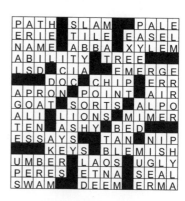

PUZZLE 14

```
PATH SLAM  PALE
ERIE TILE EASEL
NAME ABBA XYLEM
ABILITY  TREE
ISD CIA  EMERGE
   DOC CHIP ERR
APRON POINT AIR
GOAT SORTS ALPO
ALI LIONS MIMER
TEN ASHY  BED
ESSAYS  TAN NIP
  KEYS BLEMISH
UMBER LAOS UGLY
PERES ETNA SEAL
SWAM DEEM  ERMA
```

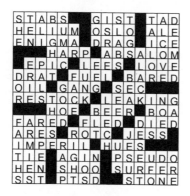

PUZZLE 15

```
STABS GIST  TAD
HELIUM OSLO ALE
ENIGMA DRAG ICE
 HARP ABSALOM
EPIC LEES LOVE
DRAT FUEL BARED
OIL GANG  SEC
RESTOCK LEAKING
 HOE BEER  BOA
FARED FLED DIED
ARES ROTC JESS
IMPERIL  HUES
TIE AGIN PSEUDO
HEN SHOO SURFER
SST PTSD  STONE
```

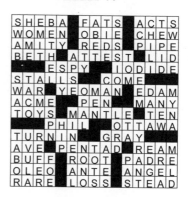

PUZZLE 16

```
SHEBA FATS ACTS
WOMEN OBIE CHEW
AMITY REDS PIPE
BETH ATTEST LID
  ESPY IODIDE
STALLS   COME
WAR YEOMAN EDAM
ACME PEN  MANY
TOYS MANTLE TEN
  PHIL OTTAWA
TURNIN  GRAY
AVE PENTAD REAM
BUFF ROOT PADRE
OLEO ANTE ANGEL
RARE LOSS STEAD
```

PUZZLE 17

```
EMUS  ASSOC DNA
MACAW REACH AIL
MULTI MANTA UNO
ALA DYES MONTH
  ROAD TABITHA
MOHAWK BAGEL
IRONS EMIR TLC
SALT ALIEN HEAL
SLY BRAG FARTO
 ALIVE DONNED
AGGRADE LORD
COATS SICK VIA
HUB TENET EMEND
EGO EPOCH DITCH
DEN DANTE LOAD
```

PUZZLE 18

```
WOLF CLAW  MAPS
ABEL GUAVA ONTO
ROSE ADMIX DEAD
MESSRS BADNEWS
  HOPI NIBS
ASH BEST MATCH
CWO IDAHO LAOS
LINEN ARC SYRUP
UPON COTTA PSI
 ERECT BEAM SET
  RUED TUBA
CAVEMAN TAWDRY
SODA PROSE AREA
SLAT LETIN SAAR
TAME EDEN  HYMN
```

PUZZLE 19

```
E L I S H A   H A D   D A D A
R O D E O S   O D E   A L A N
A S L E E P   R E M   D O N G
S T E M   G E N E   O N C E
    A H A B       E E L
C O O   P A L   D U C T
D A M S O N   S E N I O R S
S T I L L S M A L L V O I C E
  S T A L E S T   O I L J A R
    B O L T   W A C   A T E
S P A       E N D S
C U R B   S H A W   L A S S
A R I A   L E T   A P I C A L
M E S A   A R E   H E A R M E
P E E L   Y E N   A G R E E D
```

PUZZLE 20

```
D E N   S H R U B   S P U R T
E V E   H O U S E   E R R O R
V E T   A N G S T   M O N E Y
O N T I M E     T W I X
I L L S   T R E E   Y M C A
D Y E R   A W A R D   E O N
    A E S O P   E S S A Y
S H E L L S   A C T U A L
C H A L K   A U R A L
I O N   L O R R Y   T R A P
A D D S   I D E A   R A G E
    E P E E   P S Y C H E
A L E V E   S H E E P   H A L
L E P E R   S U G A R   E S E
B E A N O   A N G R Y   L T D
```

PUZZLE 21

```
L A D E N   E B B S   P I N T
A G O R A   L O L L   A R E A
T O P A Z   I N T O   L A W S
E N E   A C A D   G D A N S K
    P R O S   A K C
S C A R E D   D A N G E R S
P L A I T   F O G S   E P A
A A R G H   E R E   A S A I L
T W O   P A I D   V O D K A
  S N I P E R S   S A W Y E R
    S O N   S A I S
B A R R E N   P H I L   E L M
A P I A   A S E A   I N D I A
I S L E   N E A R   N I G E R
T E L L   T A L K   G L E N S
```

PUZZLE 22

```
T I F F   A T T I C   E L L E
A I D E   F A U N A   B I O S
B I R T H R I G H T   O B O E
    C O O       A T O N E
S I G H T   F A L L S   R E D
I O N   R E D E E M   I R E
S U P P L I E D   I S A A C
    R O O D   T R U E
H A N O I   A R O M A T I C
I C E   T R I P O D   A B R
D E W   E A S E D   B A R M Y
  S E R V O     S I R
A L M S   A M P H I B I A N S
L E A P   G E T A T   S H O O
B O N Y   E R A S E   E A T S
```

PUZZLE 23

```
S S T   L O O   S S W
C L U B   O A R   F A I R
A U N T S   A H A   W R I T E
B E A U T I F U L M A I D E N
      A D S   U R
I L L   N I   O R P H A N
D O O   Z O R I L   U S E
S U C H A T I M E A S T H I S
  S H E   S P O R E   E G O
  E S T A T E   E T   S H Y
      P A   A N T
O N H I S O W N G A L L O W S
P E A C E   A I L   E E R I E
E R I E   N N E   G E N E
N O R   E A T   O E D
```

PUZZLE 24

```
B A T S   C A R O B   N O T
A B H O R   I D E A L   A P R
B L A M E   G A F F E   D I E
Y E N   C L A M   S K I N S
    L I A R   D E S I R E S
E N M I T Y   S I D E D
V O I C E   I C E D   M O D
I D L E   V I X E N   B I K E
L E D   R I O T   W O M A N
    D E A T H   H O N E Y S
T E Q U I L A   P I K E
B L U E S   T I D E   A R K
O L E   S P I R E   U R B A N
N E E   U T T E R   P I E C E
E N N   E A S E S   B L E W
```

PUZZLE 25

```
B O P   A M O N G     M A R
A R I A   F E M U R   H O M E
L E N D   F A E N A   A D E N
M O T O R I N N   C L I E N T
    A X E     F A T
  K I N G   R A D   W I S P
B O R N E O   N A P     P O I
R A K E   L I G H T   B U R R
A L E   E L L   A Z O R E S
A D A R   L O B   E A T S
    D I V     E B B
S C R I B E   B E A U T I F Y
O H I O   R I O T S   A C L U
P U P S   S T O L E   M E A L
S B E     A S K E D   D Y E
```

PUZZLE 26

```
S C R A M   C D S     V A
N A A C P   L E E   H O B O S
U R G E   A G E   A A R G H
B L E S S E D A R T T H O U
      P A S S   R E U S E
M A S T I C   N U
I S W I T H T H E E   B O N
R E A R   W A C   I R O N
  A T E   S I L K S C R E E N
    I N   P A R O L E
  A M O N G   A V I S
  T A K I N G P I C T U R E S
A S I A N   L A X   N O D E
K E N Y A   A C E   S T A G E
C A     D E N   W O M E N
```

PUZZLE 27

```
E B B S   R I G I D     M S T
S A R I   I R O N Y   F E T A
C R A G   P E A C E   U S E R
  N A P   T H R E S H E R
T S P   D E N     N E E D Y
R A I N D R O P   O D D S
A U T O     L U C A S
P L A T   B A R A K   F A L A
  M I N I M     E V I L
  Z E E B   M E S H W O R K
S N I P S   L I E   W A Y
W I T H H E L D   S R I
E C H O   M O O S E   R U T H
D E E D   M O W E R   A S I A
E R R     A P N E A   N A P S
```

PUZZLE 28

```
O M A H A   H E A R   W R A P
P A R A N   E D G E   H A L E
A N E N T   A G E S   O B O E
L E A D   P R Y   I S R A E L
    M A I D   A D U L T S
S T R A I T   F L U B
T H E I R   A R I E S   S R I
A A N D W   D I E   I S A A C
B I D   A V I A N   S L A V E
  V E E R   S T O R E D
M A S E R U   M U S T
C U R T S Y   T E N   H I T S
A R I A   B A I T   A F O R E
L A S T   I D L E   T U T O R
F L E E   G O L D   E L A T E
```

PUZZLE 29

```
N E T S   C H U B   P E A L
E M I T   G R A T A   A L M A
W I N E   L I N E N   C L E W
T R E E S E E D   Q U E E N S
    P E A S   H U R L
C A R E E N   R E E N A C T
A D A R   S P E N T   P A R E
I I I I     R A N     R U N
N O S E   N O M A D   F L E D
S E A S O N S   E R R O R S
    G A T E   S H O E
T E B E T H   E P O W E R E D
H A I R   I D L E R   D O D O
U S F L   N I S A N   O M I T
D E F Y   G E E K   M E T E
```

PUZZLE 30

```
S W A P S   A R E A   S W B W
A I D E S   D E A D   M A L E
I N A N E   O A T H   I R A N
D E M I   I B M   E A T E S T
    N A T O   P R I E S T
P R I N T S   B E E R
R U R A L   F L E S H   W E T
A L O H A   E A R   E P H A H
Y E N   N E E D S   A R O S E
    T A L F   I D E A T E
  B E F I T S   R O S E
S E N E C A   Y I N   N A S A
T I D E   B O W S   B I S O N
A G E D   L A C K   O N I O N
B E D S   E R A S   A G A T E
```

PUZZLE 31

```
FISC   CPS   WARS
ANTI  BAITS  AXES
SCAT  REGAL  SLEW
 ABATIS  RACHEL
  DREAM   PRO
FUSEE  RAM  YUCCA
ASHLEY LAB  THIS
SUE  SATANIC  ASK
TRAM  PAR  BODICE
SPRIG III  HEROD
  ROE  ANGEL
 CRAVAT  CANALS
ERIC  SHEEP  YALE
GALL  TENSE  EMIT
OGLE   YET   RAMA
```

PUZZLE 32

```
BALM  EBBS  HONG
OBIE  SNORE EVEN
SEER  MESON ZEBU
STUCCO  CISTERN
  YOKE  LEEK
FCA  HEAL  SAINT
URN  EDGES  AERO
REIGN LAP  SHEIK
YELL  ENOCH  DKR
 PEARL  STAY  YEA
 DOUR  STEM
PINESOL  CRYPTS
TARE  ABASH  NEAT
ALAS  KINKY  ARMY
DENS  ANDY  HOPE
```

PUZZLE 33

```
LIMBO  ADAR  FLUE
ISAAC  COME  LISP
FLIRT  HOOF  UTAH
TELL  WORSEN  EGO
 EMIR  REARED
LIBYAN   BETH
ERA  PEOPLE  ADAM
NOAH   WOO   ZITI
ONLY  LETTER  EON
  MAID  LOAMMI
SIENNA   OMEN
CNS  TIGRIS  GALA
UNTO  SAUL  COMIC
FEEL  OGLE  DRONE
FRED  NEED  SAKES
```

PUZZLE 34

```
CEDAR  CHIC  ABUT
ALONE  LOCO  NONO
BLOOD  AMEN  JAIN
SEMI  AWE  GHOSTS
  NESS  BEAUTY
FLITCH  NEAR
EASEL  FOALS  ARK
TILDE  ABR  HAGUE
ERE  CHILD  ETUDE
  TUNE  ISRAEL
 CHRIST  UNTO
PREACH  LPN  COAL
RANG  IRIS  LIMBO
ONCE  NAME  ATILT
FEED  GNAT  BYTES
```

PUZZLE 35

```
NASA  ALSO  FIFE
AMOS  UNITS  IDOL
DENS  STRAP  SEAL
ANGOLA  ABRAHAM
 COBB   SEPT
MPH  FLED  YEAST
YEA  TERRA   ITEM
NESTS  EAR  SLOPE
ALTO  DICTA  PET
 SEEST  NEED  SEE
 SOIL  DELI
GHOSTED  NYMPHS
BOAR  HAYES  AREA
ANNE  EVERY  GARY
REDS  SERE  EYES
```

PUZZLE 36

```
UTAH  SOL  CLEF
MIRE  SQUIB  HEEL
PLEA  TUTEE  ONLY
 LATVIA  SMARTS
  HERTZ  ADD
WAFER  SAD  SALAD
ORANGE  PAS  LEVI
ORE  ESTONIA  TAN
DONE  EAT  PURINA
SWANK  REF  TENTH
 TIM  CAROB
 ISRAEL  JOSEPH
FREE  LICIT  KEEP
LAMA  TENTS  ASIA
UNIT  USA  HORN
```

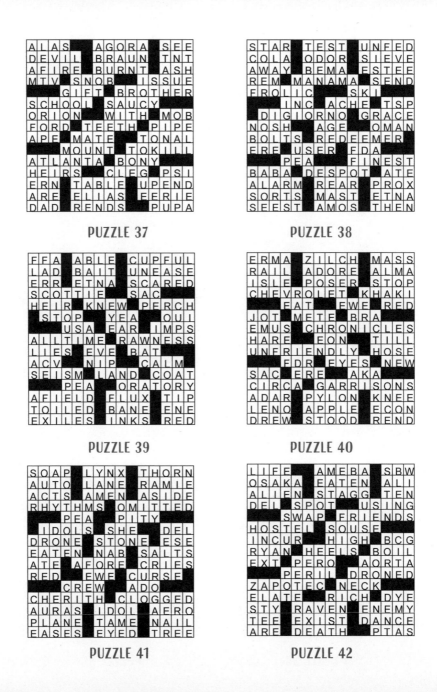

PUZZLE 37

PUZZLE 38

PUZZLE 39

PUZZLE 40

PUZZLE 41

PUZZLE 42

PUZZLE 43

```
OFFAL  ESPY  SPIT
GOOSY  ALOE  LENO
ROUSE  TOIL  IRAN
ELLE  JEW  LACING
   SOON  SICKLE
LASSIE  PANT
EXTOL  MANGO  AHA
SEERS  ONE  FAVOR
TSP  TRUER  GRIMM
   OURS  HORSES
  TANNIN  FADE
BALEEN  FIG  STUB
ABLE  ISLE  STARE
ROAD  NOEL  SERGE
BOYS  GLAD  TREES
```

PUZZLE 44

```
SYNC   PST   NOAH
SEAR  SLEET  ANNE
TAME  HATCH  ICON
 REASON  HEAVEN
   SHEAF  ESE
UPPER  ROE  PLASM
TEARUP  ORB  YMCA
TEN  GUMDROP  EAT
EVEN  PAW  WOBBLE
RESIN  LEO  LEADS
   PEN  BROIL
 SEPTIC  PROOFS
FADE  LATHE  VIOL
EVER  ELIAS  ERMA
DENS   MEN   DEAD
```

PUZZLE 45

```
SBE  WRITE   SPA
LACY  HEROD  HEAL
OBOE  APING  OMIT
GENTILES  ELNINO
   BEN   SSE
 GOBI  TAD  DYER
CHRIST  DAY  RED
PAID  ALONE  ROAR
UNO  BIB  SHODDY
ANNE  ZOO  OBEY
   ASP  DOL
SIESTA  RETYPING
COAT  TRASH  ASEA
AWRY  HORSE  SLAT
TAN  SWEAR   ERE
```

PUZZLE 46

```
ERAS  AARON   FFA
MACAW  SAUDI  LEG
MIAMI  PREEN  OUR
ADD  SHIP  ETUDE
  CHIC  OBVERSE
 ASLEEP  QUEEN
SPEND  UTAH  FCA
EAST  BEAST  BROW
ANT  BODY  PROVE
  FOLDS  SEEMED
 APLENTY  WIND
GRIEF  WORM  DAH
LEE  IDAHO  ARISE
EGG  RIGID  NADIR
TOE  ENEMY  GOAD
```

PUZZLE 47

```
SPATE  SLAB  ELSE
AARON  WERE  MOAN
UNITS  OAKS  BAND
LTD  NERD  PRANKS
   LAND   EAR
ADHERE  BLANKET
CRANE  BEAK  RIM
NESTS  RAM  AWARE
EAT  NOSE  RESET
 MEANEST  IMPEDE
   REP   SCAT
WARMTH  WHET  VIM
ASIA  EMIR  UNITE
REND  WADE  RISES
SAGA  SLEW  EXAMS
```

PUZZLE 48

```
ACED  ABBA  ADZE
FAVE  ACORN  LOIN
AGIN  BESOT  LOPE
RELISH  COLOURS
   MOON  MEND
SAP  PREP  REIGN
OBI  PSALM  NOON
MONEY  TEE  AGATE
EDEN  HATED  DEW
 ESTER  SOLD  SST
   IRON  OMAN
 BARROOM  EXERTS
KINE  FREER  COAT
IDOL  ESTES  KILO
DENY  REEL   SLEW
```

PUZZLE 49

```
JAVA   SWARD  ELF
ODORS  HAGUE  POE
EVITA  IRONS  OWE
LTD  BORN  TAXED
   WIFE  MARTYRS
SPLINT  CANOE
AROSE   ARTY  HIS
VISE  ARISE  EAST
EXT  FEAR   CALLA
   BURIN  FASTER
PARASOL  FLEE
EMITS   DIMS  HAG
SIP  IDIOT  ARENA
ONE  NEWEL  RUINS
SON  GLORY   TRAP
```

PUZZLE 50

```
PASS  DUST   NOSE
ELLE  EPEE  TOAST
ATOP  FEAR  UNTIE
CAPTAIN   MALE
ERE  LED   CATTLE
   GOD  BAHN  YAM
ISSUE  DIXIE  SRI
MITT  LETIN  FORT
PEA  MOSES  TONYS
EGG  INKS   HUR
LEGUME   NUN  ACT
   LORD  ELEAZAR
TENTS  EBAL  RULE
AGORA  LUTE  ISEE
NOVA   IGOR  DABS
```

PUZZLE 51

```
LEVI  RHODA   AJAR
OMEN  PANIC   REDO
PERT  MEATH   CRAM
ENDED  SNEAK  UMP
  DINAH   SNOBS
   SHAME  BEAMS
LATE  LAG  GAELIC
ERE  LONGGUN  ERA
ANANAS  OUI  AMEN
DEMOB   NYLON
   STAFF  TWIST
HAT  NAILS  ESTES
IDEA  DROLL  EARL
FERN  ESSEN  ELSE
INST  STEWS  DEED
```

PUZZLE 52

```
SEAN   ARK   BAWL
TAROS  VII  SUSHI
ISITI  EOS  ASSET
RES  EAR  SST  OLE
  LEIGH   NAACP
   BEEN   BAND
SWIM  MIXUP  ONTO
IAN   FIR    FED
MYNA  STING  GLAD
   SLAY   TUNA
   ASSAI  TILDE
OPT  CDT  ASH  ETC
SHOCK  ASP  IAMHE
LIONS  DOS  LLOYD
ODDS   APE   ISLE
```

PUZZLE 53

```
BLOW  AFAR   SLAW
AERO  LORE  CHIVE
MAIN  LUKE  OOZED
BROTHER   FAST
INN  UGH   MISSED
   ICE  GRIN  HER
SPEAK  HOUSE  ARE
HELM  FEATS  APIA
ETA  DEATH  AKEEM
EAT  EARS   NBA
PLEATS   SEE  SIT
   BETS  ELLIPSE
ASTIR  ERRS  BOAT
GILDS  NOVO  ROAR
ONCE   TEEN  INCA
```

PUZZLE 54

```
CAPT   STY   DUCE
ALOHA  IWO  JESUS
VOWEL  COG  ACURE
ENE  IRK  ASP  AIL
GRAVE     TABLE
   WEPT   MINI
SOUL  SUGAR  BACA
ABS   LAX    LTD
CIAO  ALGID  ALUM
   COME   MEAL
METRO     ALATE
NIX  ESE  ADO  OAT
IDAHO  ADD  FORTH
NAMES  CIA  TUTEE
ASSN   HER   TERM
```

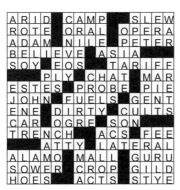

PUZZLE 55

A	C	H	E		S	P	A	R		C	A	M	E	L
P	E	A	R		U	R	S	A		I	N	U	R	E
H	A	R	M		N	E	T	S		A	G	G	R	O
I	S	A	A	C		T	I	P	T	O	E			
D	E	N		E	N	T	R	E	E		R	E	I	N
			G	O	B	I		D	A	N		G	N	U
W	I	S	E		C	E	L		R	A	G	E	R	
A	G	L	E	Y		R	A	P		O	D	O	R	S
S	L	A	K	E		W	A	R		A	N	T	E	
P	O	I		S	A	D		P	I	E	R			
S	O	N	S		S	E	L	E	C	T		F	D	A
			P	A	I	L	O	R		C	A	R	O	B
L	A	B	A	N		E	Y	E	S		X	I	I	I
S	P	E	E	N		T	A	R	E		L	E	N	D
D	E	N	S	E		E	L	S	E		E	D	G	E

PUZZLE 56

	P	U	T		B	A	D		T	B	N			
G	E	N	O	A		A	R	E		O	R	E	O	S
A	S	C	O	T		C	A	A		W	Y	E	T	H
B	T	U		I	R	K		D	A	N		F	R	Y
	S	T	O	L	E			M	E	U	S	E		
		U	T	A	H		G	O	D	S				
L	E	F	T		D	A	M	E	S		A	N	E	R
A	G	O			S	A	N				I	O	U	
W	O	R	D		S	T	R	U	T		E	L	S	E
			I	S	L	E		S	O	M	A			
	M	A	N	T	O			F	I	R	S	T		
C	O	W		U	P	S		S	U	N		H	E	W
D	W	A	R	F		A	S	H		S	P	A	R	E
S	E	R	I	F		V	I	E		K	A	R	A	T
	R	E	D		E	N	D		M	P	H			

PUZZLE 57

A	R	I	D		C	A	M	P		S	L	E	W	
R	O	T	E		O	R	A	L		O	P	E	R	A
A	D	A	M		N	I	L	E		P	E	T	E	R
B	E	L	I	E	V	E		A	S	I	A			
S	O	Y		E	O	S		T	A	R	I	F	F	
			P	L	Y		C	H	A	T		M	A	R
E	S	T	E	S		P	R	O	B	E		P	I	E
J	O	H	N		F	U	E	L	S		G	E	N	T
E	N	E		D	I	R	T	Y		C	U	L	T	S
C	A	R		O	G	R	E		S	O	N			
T	R	E	N	C	H		A	C	S		F	E	E	
			A	T	T	Y		L	A	T	E	R	A	L
A	L	A	M	O		M	A	L	L		G	U	R	U
S	O	W	E	R		C	R	O	P		G	I	L	D
H	O	E	S		A	C	T	S		S	T	Y	E	

PUZZLE 58

C	R	I	B	S		S	H	E	D		B	A	G	
P	A	R	L	E	Y		S	A	R	I		E	V	E
U	N	S	U	R	E		T	R	U	E		H	E	Y
			F	I	S	H		A	C	T	I	O	N	S
G	A	F	F		O	U	S	T		S	L	U	E	
C	U	B	S		R	U	G	S		A	L	D	E	R
O	R	B		D	A	S	H		D	I	E			
S	U	R	F	A	C	E		G	O	D	S	S	O	N
			L	I	E		H	O	M	E		E	L	F
D	A	R	E	S		D	O	G	E		N	A	I	L
E	P	E	E		C	A	P	E		P	A	S	O	
V	I	C	T	O	R	Y		T	E	L	L			
I	C	E		V	E	T	O		R	U	L	E	R	S
L	E	D		A	T	O	P		A	M	E	L	I	A
S	S	E		L	E	N	T		P	Y	L	O	N	

PUZZLE 59

S	T	A	R		S	P	E	D		H	E	L	P	
A	B	L	E		T	R	O	Y		P	O	L	I	O
G	O	O	D		R	I	S	E		I	R	K	E	D
A	N	N	O	Y	E	D		D	I	E	D			
S	E	E		W	E	E		O	R	E	I	D	A	
			A	C	T		Z	I	N	C		N	O	N
S	C	U	B	A		C	U	R	I	E		T	U	G
T	A	L	E		S	O	N	I	C		M	E	S	S
A	N	T		D	O	R	I	S		B	E	R	E	T
M	A	R		A	L	P	S		H	O	T			
P	L	A	S	M	A		S	O	D		P	S	T	
			C	A	R	E		T	O	Y	W	I	T	H
A	S	S	E	S		A	T	O	P		H	A	I	R
S	T	I	N	K		T	O	O	L		O	N	C	E
K	Y	T	E		S	O	D	A		P	O	K	E	

PUZZLE 60

U	G	H		A	H	E	A	D		T	E	M	P	T
T	A	I	L		L	A	D	L	E		U	N	A	R	Y
A	L	I		A	N	G	E	L		R	E	C	A	P
H	E	L	M		D	E	S	I	G	N		E	Y	E
			I	A	M				O	R	B			
	C	O	G	N	A	C		I	D	E	A	L	S	
B	O	P		T	I	L	E	D		D	R	E	A	M
O	U	R	S		D	U	V	E	T		D	A	T	A
W	R	A	C	K		B	E	A	R	D		S	A	D
	T	H	A	N	K	S		L	O	O	S	E	N	
			B	E	G		U	N	O					
S	E	C		A	B	S	O	R	B		N	A	B	S
L	U	R	E	D		O	V	A	L	S		N	U	T
A	R	O	S	E		R	A	G	E	S		N	N	E
P	O	W	E	R		E	L	U	D	E		A	S	P

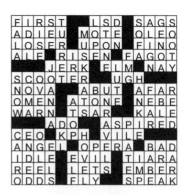

PUZZLE 61

C	H	A	S	M		S	A	N	G		A	S	S	N
A	O	R	T	A		O	R	E	O		T	H	E	E
S	P	E	A	R		L	O	R	D		F	E	L	S
H	E	A	R	T	S		S	O	L	D		B	L	T
			C	H	I	M	E		I	O	T	A	S	
B	E	T	H	A	N	Y			K	E	Y			
A	P	R			G	R	A	V	E		P	A	C	T
L	E	A	F			R	Y	E			O	D	O	R
D	E	M	O		T	H	E	I	R			E	M	U
			U	G	H			N	O	M	I	N	E	E
	F	U	R	O	R		A	S	P	E	N			
A	I	M		D	I	C	T		E	S	C	O	R	T
L	O	B	E		V	A	S	E		C	U	R	I	O
A	N	E	W		E	V	E	N		A	B	B	O	T
R	A	R	E		D	E	A	D		L	I	S	T	S

PUZZLE 62

F	I	R	S	T		L	S	D		S	A	G	S	
A	D	I	E	U		M	O	T	E		O	L	E	O
L	O	S	E	R		U	P	O	N		F	I	N	O
A	L	E		R	I	S	E	N		F	A	G	O	T
			J	E	R	K		E	L	M		N	A	Y
S	C	O	O	T	E	R			U	G	H			
N	O	V	A			A	B	U	T		A	F	A	R
O	M	E	N		A	T	O	N	E		N	E	B	E
W	A	R	N		T	S	A	R		K	A	L	E	
			A	D	O		A	S	P	I	R	E	D	
C	E	O		K	P	H		V	I	L	E			
A	N	G	E	L		O	P	E	R	A		B	A	D
I	D	L	E		E	V	I	L		T	I	A	R	A
R	E	E	L		L	E	T	S		E	M	B	E	R
O	D	D	S		F	L	Y		S	P	E	A	K	

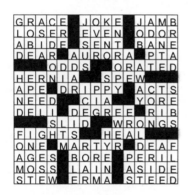

PUZZLE 63

G	R	A	C	E		J	O	K	E		J	A	M	B
L	O	S	E	R		E	V	E	N		O	D	O	R
A	B	I	D	E		S	E	N	T		B	A	N	E
D	E	A	R		A	U	R	O	R	A		P	T	A
			O	D	D	S			O	R	A	T	E	D
H	E	R	N	I	A			S	P	E	W			
A	P	E		D	R	I	P	P	Y		A	C	T	S
N	E	E	D			C	I	A			Y	O	R	E
D	E	L	I		D	E	G	R	E	E		R	I	B
			S	L	I	D		W	R	O	N	G	S	
F	I	G	H	T	S			H	E	A	L			
O	N	E		M	A	R	T	Y	R		D	E	A	F
A	G	E	S		B	O	R	E		P	E	R	I	L
M	O	S	S		L	A	I	N		A	S	I	D	E
S	T	E	W		E	R	M	A		S	T	E	E	D

PUZZLE 64

A	R	E	A		H	E	A	R			F	A	L	L
P	U	N	S		Y	A	L	E		M	A	F	I	A
A	L	E	S		E	R	A	S		A	R	C	E	D
R	E	M	N	A	N	T		T	E	R	M			
T	R	Y		D	A	H		M	I	S	S	U	S	
			G	A	S		M	E	A	N		P	R	E
A	R	M	O	R		E	E	R	I	E		A	G	E
G	O	O	D		A	V	A	I	L		E	W	E	R
A	B	S		T	R	I	T	E		H	A	N	D	S
T	E	E		O	I	L	Y		N	E	T			
E	S	S	A	Y	S		O	I	L		P	T	A	
			T	O	E	D		L	E	P	R	O	U	S
H	E	L	O	T		E	R	I	C		O	W	L	S
A	R	E	N	A		L	O	V	E		M	E	S	A
G	A	T	E			L	E	E	S		P	R	A	Y

PUZZLE 65

T	A	B		S	A	N	G		S	C	A	R	A	B
E	P	A		A	G	U	E		C	H	O	I	C	E
R	P	M		R	A	R	E		A	I	R	M	E	N
R	A	B	B	I	T	S			B	L	T			
A	L	O	E		E	E	L	S		D	A	C	H	A
L	O	R	D			E	O	S			R	E	D	
			T	I	M		O	W	N		C	O	R	E
G	O	D	H	E	A	D		N	O	T	O	P	E	N
U	S	E	S		R	A	D		W	I	N			
A	L	A			Y	I	N			P	T	S	D	
M	O	D	E	M		S	A	G	A		A	C	R	E
			T	O	M		L	A	O	C	O	O	N	
A	C	C	U	S	E		D	A	R	N		T	W	O
S	P	A	D	E	S		I	D	O	L		I	N	C
K	A	D	E	S	H		D	E	N	Y		A	S	H

PUZZLE 66

S	A	D		F	L	E	W		R	A	I	S	E	S
A	P	E		A	I	R	S		E	L	N	I	N	O
B	L	T		S	N	O	W		P	A	D	R	E	S
R	O	A	S	T	E	D			S	R	I			
E	M	I	T		N	E	X	T		M	A	N	E	S
			B	L	U	E		I	R	K		A	V	E
	P	S	I			I	I	I		E	M	I	R	
S	P	L	O	T	C	H		O	N	E	S	E	L	F
Y	O	U	R		E	E	L		G	O	T			
N	O	T		D	A	Y			S	H	E	D		
C	R	E	P	E		R	E	N	T		E	Y	E	S
			L	S	D		A	R	M	R	E	S	T	
I	D	E	A	T	E		A	S	I	A		L	I	E
T	A	S	S	E	L		W	A	L	K		E	R	R
S	H	I	M	E	I		E	L	L	E		T	E	N

PUZZLE 67

```
P E A C E   C H O S E   G M T
A T L A S   L E A S T   R O E
S N I P E   E A R T H   I N N
T A F T   E A R   A G L E T
    A E O N   S A N E L Y
L I M I T S   L E P E R
A B A N A   F I V E   M O O D
V I I   L A T E X   U N O
A D D S   O M E N   D I S C O
    P I P E R   L E T T E R
    H O R S E S   P I N E
S A T Y R   R U E   R A G E
U G H   A D M I T   C A N O E
C U E   E N A C T   A T O L L
H E R   L A N K Y   L E N D S
```

PUZZLE 68

```
B E S T S   E W E   S H O P
U N T R U E   G E M   T O I L
G R O U N D   G N P   M U L E
L O R E   E M O T E D   S E A
F I L M   O M A N   R A R E R
      F L A N   Y O R E
C H I L D   A A R D W O L F
P I T Y   A R K   A U T O
A S S E M B L E   G R I M E
    R E A L   A C A D
  A S S E T   E Y E S   S A M
I B M   K I L L E D   D I V E
L O O N   S A D   A S I D E S
L U T E   T I E   R I V E R S
S T E W   E R R   N A S T Y
```

PUZZLE 69

```
J E S S   C H I E F   A P T
O R E O S   H A I T I   T A R
H I N D U   A L I A S   I R E
N E T   N A M E   H A L S A
      S H I P   S K I R T E D
G R A H A M   F L I N T
L I M I T   L U N G   D K L
O P E N   S T A G G   N O N O
B E N   D O W N   P A L E R
    B R O O K   J E T T E D
R E M A I N S   F I R E
A D O R N   R I B S   S P A
D I S   K A B U L   O T H E R
I C E   E L I T E   N O O S E
I T S   R I G H T   P E T S
```

PUZZLE 70

```
A C T S   L O A N   D A C H A
S H E A   E R M A   A L L O W
S I N G   T E E M   H O U S E
O N O   A T O N E D   N E E D
C A R A F E   N B E
    B A R   F E A R   W S W
T H I R S T E D   A S A P H
G O O D   A T E   C L A Y
M U L E S   K I N G B O L T
T R Y   A G E D   H O W
    A D O   O O L O N G
A B B R   D A M A S K   B O A
L L O Y D   L E N T   D E B T
M O R A Y   P A N E   I S L E
S C E N E   S H E D   S E E S
```

PUZZLE 71

```
P T S D   F A N G   M E S A
R I C E   O L E O   S Y N O D
E D A M   R O W S   P R E Y S
G A L I L E E   H E I R
O L D   U S S   S C H I S M
    A R T   L A T E   S P A
G A F F E   G I B E S   L E D
E P I C   L A G E R   R E A L
E R R   N I G H T   R I S K Y
S O S   I N S T   G O D
E N T I C E   A H A   R A D
    S E N T   F E R R U L E
A M A S S   O M I T   E L A N
K A P U T   T A R T   N E T S
A N T E   O R E O   T R E E
```

PUZZLE 72

```
A D M A N   U R G E   G A F F
C A I R O   N O U N   U C L A
A L T A R   D A Y S   M O O N
D E E R   P U R S U E   R O T
      A B L E   R W A N D A
T I P T O E   W E E K
E N E   W A T E R S   I L L S
A C E D   A K A   N E A T
S A K I   C R E P E S   V I A
      E Y E S   V I K I N G
T R A D E R   C I T E
H A I L   T E A S E L   A L P S
E M I T   A R E A   S T O A T
F I V E   L I E S   S O F I A
T E E N   S A N E   E N T R Y
```

PUZZLE 73

PUZZLE 74

PUZZLE 75

PUZZLE 76

PUZZLE 77

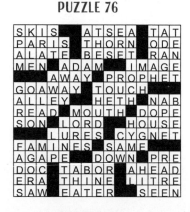

PUZZLE 78

PUZZLE 79

```
A C T G ■ F L O R A ■ D E W
C A R O B ■ J A C O B ■ E R A
C R E D O ■ O U T E R ■ C A T
T E E ■ D A R D ■ A R O S E
■ F I N D ■ A D H E R E R
A M U L E T ■ C H E A P ■
J E S U S ■ R O A M ■ N B A
A R A B ■ L L O Y D ■ F E E S
R E F ■ S E A S ■ T E X T S
■ H A N D S ■ B H U T A N
A T T A B O Y ■ G O O D ■
T H U M B ■ B E A R ■ F B I
A R T ■ A R S O N ■ N Y L O N
L E E ■ T I T L E ■ S E E R S
E W E ■ H O M E S ■ S E N T
```

PUZZLE 80

```
L A B A N ■ F R I ■ A T O P
A D A G E ■ R A M ■ E D E M A
T H R E W ■ U M P ■ L O N E R
H E R S ■ D I A L E D ■ T N T
E R E ■ S A T ■ A S E A
■ E N V O Y ■ N A R R A T E
■ A D S ■ B T U ■ M I E N
T A L U S ■ B U S ■ B A R E D
U P O N ■ Y E T ■ B O D
G R O T T O S ■ A R A B S ■
■ S E G O ■ E R N ■ R A N
P T A ■ L I T T L E ■ L I V E
A R G A L ■ T A I ■ S O D A S
S O U L S ■ E X T ■ A V A N T
S T A B ■ D I E ■ M E L T S
```

PUZZLE 81

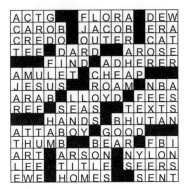

```
O D O R ■ A L E S ■ U S E D
P A P A ■ B L A N C ■ N O D E
E D E N ■ L I N D A ■ P A G E
C O N C L A V E ■ R E A P E D
■ H I D E ■ B L O C
R E C E D E ■ D O E S K I N
A V E R ■ S T R U T ■ S T E P
M I D ■ O I L ■ E P A
S C A B ■ S K E E T ■ O M A N
T R E A T E D ■ H A S S L E
■ E L A N ■ P R I M
A R C T I C ■ F A E R O E S E
C O O L ■ K O A L A ■ S L A Y
M A R E ■ E R R E D ■ I S L E
E N D S ■ D E E R ■ S E E D
```

PUZZLE 82

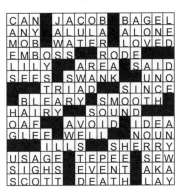

```
C A N ■ J A C O B ■ B A G E L
A N Y ■ A L U L A ■ A L O N E
M O B ■ W A T E R ■ L O V E D
E M B O S S ■ R O D E ■
L I L Y ■ A R E A ■ S A I D
S E E S ■ S W A N K ■ U N O
■ T R I A D ■ S I N C E
■ B L E A R Y ■ S M O O T H
H A I R Y ■ S O U N D ■
O A F ■ A V O I D ■ I D E A
G L E E ■ W E L L ■ N O U N
■ I L L S ■ S H E R R Y
U S A G E ■ T E P E E ■ S E W
S I G H S ■ E V E N T ■ A K A
S C O T T ■ D E A T H ■ L A Y
```

PUZZLE 83

```
D R A M A ■ S C A B ■ A D E N
I O T A S ■ E L L E ■ K I N E
M O T H S ■ T I P S ■ C E D E
S T Y L E D ■ M O P E ■ G O D
■ O R A L B ■ E L B O W
C O U N T R Y ■ A K A ■
A B R ■ D R U N K ■ L E A F
S E G O ■ I R E ■ M A M A
E D E N ■ A C N E D ■ S O S
■ T E N ■ D E A R E S T
■ A M O N G ■ U S A G E ■
B U Y ■ D E E R ■ D A M S E L
E R R S ■ R U B E ■ S A U D I
T A R O ■ E R A S ■ S I N G S
A S H Y ■ D O N E ■ I N S E T
```

PUZZLE 84

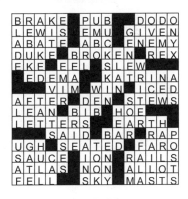

```
B R A K E ■ P U B ■ D O D O
L E W I S ■ E M U ■ G I V E N
A B A T E ■ A B C ■ E N E M Y
D U K E ■ B R O K E N ■ R E X
E K E ■ E E L ■ S L E W
■ E D E M A ■ K A T R I N A
■ V I M ■ W I N ■ I C E D
A F T E R ■ D E N ■ S T E W S
L E A N ■ B I B ■ H O E
L E T T E R S ■ E A R T H
■ S A I D ■ B A R ■ R A P
U G H ■ S E A T E D ■ F A R O
S A U C E ■ I O N ■ R A I L S
A T L A S ■ N O N ■ A L L O T
F E L L ■ S K Y ■ M A S T S
```

PUZZLE 85

PUZZLE 86

PUZZLE 87

PUZZLE 88

PUZZLE 89

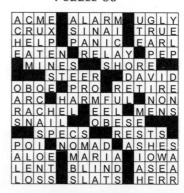

PUZZLE 90

PUZZLE 91

```
AGO   ASHES  FAB
TIDY SPURT CITE
OBOE CIGAR AJAR
PERSPIRE AIRING
  III  WON
WHOP THY NESS
LOAFED EAT  CPA
EMIT RANKS HEIR
OAK  SIN PLANET
NUKE MAR EYES
  ASP  ETA
FATHER ADOPTION
ABEL EMBED UNTO
NERO LOBED TOTO
STR  LOAMY NON
```

PUZZLE 92

```
OCT ACRID CHILD
ALA KYOTO HARAI
FIX CRIES ALIVE
SPIN ELMERS SAD
   EEN  OSS
SAUDIS DEICER
ACT SUPRA SAXES
CARE SIEVE NINA
SMILE EVITA LEG
PASSES DECREE
   EST  REO
WET ACTION MARY
ARRAY ADMIT REM
SMITE SLATE MAC
TAXED KENYA SPA
```

PUZZLE 93

```
OGLE SAGAS  SST
LEOS THORN SATE
ETTA RADIO USER
  UNO  ABRAHAM
OFT OBED  OVALS
VIENNESE OBEY
ULAN  SABRE
MEME JACOB TRAM
  MAYOR  NOVA
  PLUM NOHITTER
ISAAC  SNOW CRY
NARWHAL  ROB
GRIN DAVID RUTH
OATS ANILE OREO
THY  REELS SNAP
```

PUZZLE 94

```
ABIA UCLA  OVAL
MITE THEN DRILY
AGAR MITT RAISE
SOLOMON IDOL
STY USS ROBOAM
  MST CHOP RUE
JUDAH GUESS ART
ENID CORES STAR
SST DAVID ABELE
SEC AUTO IGO
ETHICS CSO PEA
  STEM ARGUING
ESSAY USDA TARO
VIRAL CURE ANON
EPIC  HEEL HOLY
```

PUZZLE 95

```
STORE  VAST  MAL
CAROLS INCH ALA
ANEMIA AGUA SPY
  AURA ELIAKIM
HAND CALL BENE
HUBS THIS SIREN
ALB MAIM IOU
SARCASM ACADEME
ARK HUES VEX
ANGRY MEND JEST
MEET PORT SONS
PANELED SPAS
ERE EPEE IDEATE
REV VILA TOPPER
ERA INST CHEER
```

PUZZLE 96

```
CEL SCONE HEAPS
APE LUNAS EMITS
BIG OBEYS ECLAT
ACUATE ELLIE
LAMB RENO EBBS
ALES AIXEN LAI
  EARTH STORM
PRINCEOFPEACE
DOILY REACT
ALL FETED TOGA
HELD LIST ERRS
  ABUT ISRAEL
HEAVE HASTE NAE
ORBIT ESTER GTE
YARDS RHYME ESP
```

PUZZLE 97

PUZZLE 98

PUZZLE 99

Looking for More Fun?

COZY BIBLE WORD SEARCHES

Like to get cozy with a good word search? Love the Bible?
Here is the perfect book for you!
Bible puzzles are a great way to pass time while learning scripture—and here's a collection
of 99 word searches sure to satisfy. With search words drawn from the breadth
of scripture, these themed puzzles will challenge your sleuthing
skills and expand your knowledge of the Good Book.

Inside, you'll find

- traditional word list puzzles
- Bible passages with search words underlined
- "secret message" puzzles, in which the leftover
  letters spell out a related trivia question

Based entirely on the King James Version of scripture, this book features dozens
of fun, challenging word searches—including twelve that celebrate Christmas.
If you enjoy Bible word searches (and who doesn't?), you'll love *Cozy Bible Word Searches*!

Paperback / 978-1-64352-151-0/ $12.99